Women in Parliament

This book has been researched, written and produced with support from the Women's National Commission and the Fawcett Society.

Women in Parliament

THE NEW SUFFRAGETTES

Boni Sones

with Margaret Moran and Joni Lovenduski

POLITICO'S

First published in 2005

Politico's Publishing, an imprint of
Methuen Publishing Limited
11–12 Buckingham Gate
London
SW1E 6LB

10 9 8 7 6 5 4 3 2 1

Typeset by SX Composing DTP, Rayleigh, Essex
Printed and bound in Great Britain by St Edmundsbury Press, Bury St Edmunds, Suffolk

Methuen Publishing Limited Reg. No. 3543167

A CIP catalogue record for this book is available from the British Library

ISBN 1 84275 140 9

This book is dedicated to our sons and daughters and to mine in particular: Tanya, Jenna and Guy Barnard.

Boni Sones

AUTHOR'S NOTE

There are many people who have helped in putting this book together over the last four years. For additional interviewers and professional support I would like to thank Linda Fairbrother, Angela Lawrence, Deborah McGurran and Eva Simmons.

For transcribing the interviews thanks go to: Freya Lodge, Gytha Lodge, Carole Loynes and Hannah Poole.

For proofreading their text I would like to thank Frances Hughes and Hannah Postgate.

For their expert advice I would like to thank Natalya Cernecka for her help with the manuscripts; Chris Pond at the House of Commons Library; Martha Stevens for her analysis and Janet Veitch at the Women's National Commission.

For general help and encouragement I must thank Stephanie and Colin Barnes, Diana Brittan, Alison Cook, Barbara Gorna, Rosie and Tim Phillips, Alison Sargent and Peta Sones.

FOREWORD

This book is a must for serious students of politics, of feminist history and of sociology. It is also a must for people who enjoy a good informative read. Boni Sones and her colleagues have used their vast interviewing experience to draw from women MPs a mass of fascinating anecdotes which illuminate attitudes and change in society at the turn of the twentieth century. She has also coaxed from these women an account of their first impressions of Parliament, often a deeply unflattering one, their juggling of private and political life, their approach to the greasy pole.

The book leads the reader along the path trodden by the MPs as they get accustomed to dealing with prejudice, extraordinary parliamentary customs, the onslaught of the media, and sexism at work. Some readers will be left asking themselves why these women bothered. The book tells them and, cheeringly, outlines the changes achieved by women MPs in the House of Commons. It also lists what they themselves see as their own most outstanding political achievements. It is an impressive list.

Throughout, the women's optimism, public spiritedness, dedication and self-irony shine through. What they think individually about their own foray into politics, what they say, and which is documented so vividly in this book, is summed by Boni Sones at the end, 'The enthusiasm, optimism, and spirit with which they convey their "do come here", "Do it too" message is a sign of how much they . . . enjoy the job of being an MP and making a difference to the lives of others. Their words are an inspiration to other would-be MPs in the making.'

Rt Hon. the Baroness Shephard of Northwold J.P., D.L.

PREFACE

This book is long overdue. The testimonies of the 83 women interviewed will form an important historical record for many years to come. It is a tribute to the authors not only that so many women spoke so frankly, but also a sign of how women are making their voices heard in Parliament and driving change on many levels. It is about time that the achievements of women MPs across all parties are talked about. Women MPs have made a unique and individual contribution to British political life but their achievements have not always been acknowledged. This book sets the record straight by telling their story, in their own words.

When I entered Parliament in April 1992 as the MP for Dulwich (now Dulwich and West Norwood) I was one of 163 women MPs ever to take up their seat in Westminster. It wasn't until the Labour Party used all-women shortlists in the May 1997 general election that this number exceeded 200 and rose to 239. Following the 2005 general election the number now stands at 290, but we have still not reached a 'critical mass'. We need more women in Westminster and I hope this book will help encourage them to come. The women's movement has brought tremendous positive changes to society, and the growing number of women in Parliament is a living legacy to how far we've come, of which I am proud to be a part.

Rt Hon. Tessa Jowell MP

CONTENTS

Introduction

The participation of women in Parliament may be traced back to 1919, when Lady Astor took up her seat in Westminster, soon after women got the vote. Countess Constance Markievicz was the first woman to be elected, in December 1918, but, as an Irish Republican, she refused to take the oath of allegiance to Britain and was not allowed to sit in Parliament. By 1940, only 37 women had ever been elected to Westminster; and by 1960, that number had risen to 75, Margaret Thatcher being the 75th woman MP when she was elected in October 1959. It is only in the past decade that we have seen women arriving to take up parliamentary seats in any great numbers.

The Representation of People Act was the first Act to give votes to women in February 1918, after the suffragettes had been jailed many times for resorting to violent protest. Under this Act, women over 30 were allowed to vote if they were householders, the wives of householders, paying an annual rent of over £5, graduates of British universities, or women who were qualified but not graduates. Remarkably even then, those under 30 were still thought too 'flighty' to have the vote.

About 8.5 million women were able to vote in the 1918 election. The war had helped to establish women in the workplace, where they had proved themselves, and women were eligible to stand as MPs too. Several suffrage campaigners stood for Parliament in the 1918 election but none were successful (only Markievicz was elected again in Dublin). Lady Astor, a Conservative, gained her seat a year later when her husband stood down.

Lady Astor soon made her mark on Parliament when, in her maiden speech, she spoke in favour of the Temperance Society, and in 1923 she introduced a Private Member's Bill that raised to eighteen the age qualification for the purchase of alcoholic drinks. Over the next few years, Astor campaigned for women's suffrage at 21 and equal rights in the Civil Service. She paved the way for other women MPs, and regularly used her sharp wit to stand up for herself.

Many women MPs have since won the hearts of the British people – Margaret Bondfield (the first woman to be a British Cabinet minister), Jennie Lee, Bessie Braddock, Barbara Castle, Shirley Williams, Margaret Thatcher, Mo Mowlam, Edwina Currie and Betty Boothroyd, among others. All have adopted different styles as politicians and all have won the approval and disapproval of the British media during their parliamentary careers. All have proved that women as MPs, ministers, secretaries of state and even as prime minister are a very real match for the men. They have become a legend in their own times; and in Liverpool they still sing songs to the memory of Bessie Braddock.

All these women have encountered prejudice in their parliamentary careers and have not only had to prove themselves as one of the men, but also better than the men. Even Margaret Thatcher, who was hostile to any thoughts of furthering a feminist agenda, and openly spoke of her role models being men, writes of how difficult the selection procedures were for women, and how there was an attitude that the House of Commons was not really the right place for a woman anyway.

Once in Westminster, women have not always found it easy to make their voices heard in a debating chamber that favours loud voices and adversarial debate, and some have not liked the 'clubby' atmosphere. Others like Mo Mowlam have loved it and talk of how they 'just shout back', and some have worked hard to adapt – even Margaret Thatcher resorted to voice training early in her parliamentary career.

But the number of women MPs is increasing. The Labour Party's victory in the 1997 general election, when 101 Labour women were elected to Westminster, brought the number of women ever elected to Parliament to 239. Since 1997, the proportion of women, their high visibility, their energy and campaigning instincts have transformed the Commons beyond recognition and have given a new direction to policy-making. In May 2005, 38 new women were elected to Westminster, bringing the total of women in the House to a record 128. There were 26 new Labour women, six new

Conservatives and six new Liberal Democrats. Even so, there is still not a 'critical mass' of women in Parliament and it is likely to take many years to achieve this.

The 1997 election, when Labour used all-women shortlists for the first time, was a turning point in women's representation. A leisurely lunchtime walk round the National Portrait Gallery in Trafalgar Square will remind one of what the Commons used to look like in a different age – Victorian and Edwardian men in long coats and tall hats clustered together and waving their order papers at the male speaker. Not a woman in sight. What a difference that 1997 general election made, suddenly taking Parliament out of the 'male club' era, as women as a group became highly visible politicians for the first time. It was a truly historic election.

Now if one switches on the television news on a Wednesday evening, one will see each party leader appropriately or opportunistically flanked by a woman on one side or both during Prime Minister's Questions. Tired of jaded media coverage of these women's achievements, I set out to interview all women across all parties in Westminster since 1997, including those who had left. From the famous, Baroness Boothroyd, Mo Mowlam, Ann Widdecombe, and also the younger Oona King and Sarah Teather, to the not-so-well-known, my research team managed to conduct interviews with the majority of them. Out of a possible 135 MPs, we managed to speak to 83, between May and October 2004. Edited extracts of these interviews form the basis of this book, allowing the interviewees to speak for themselves. Their contributions have been arranged by theme, to create a strong narrative and clear impressions of the problems, pressures and hard work that has been necessary for them to succeed.

In Chapter 1, it is surprising to find that recently elected women MPs share similar introductory experiences to those elected 20 years earlier. The atmosphere of the Commons being a 'boys' public school' and an institution is what most women MPs who are new to the Commons comment on. Transforming the traditions of the House to become a more acceptable working environment has been a slow process. Change, we are told, is incremental.

In Chapter 2, we learn that while some women respond well to the adversarial nature of the Chamber, others do not. They find the procedural rules confusing and those rules often lead to embarrassment in the Chamber when they make mistakes. Many now prefer speaking in the smaller Westminster Hall. They want Parliament to look and sound more relevant to the constituents they represent.

In Chapter 3, we see that women MPs, particularly those from the 1997 intake, believe that they have developed a new way of doing politics. They believe they are translating the concerns and experiences of their constituents into better policy-making.

In Chapter 4, women MPs tell shocking stories of the sexism that existed in the Chamber when they got up to speak. This sexism appears to have got worse in 1997 because the sheer number of women MPs was perceived as a threat to many of the older male MPs. The attitudes they encountered belonged to a bygone age, and there is evidence that some new male MPs of 1997 found the behaviour shocking too.

In Chapter 5, we find that women MPs have adapted their family lives to life in Westminster. A few of them are now employing their husbands as their assistants. Some husbands have given up their jobs to become the carers of their children, so-called 'househusbands'. Women MPs have proved themselves adaptable.

In Chapter 6, it is fascinating to observe that the views on party loyalty across all parties are far more complex than is commonly reported by the media. Women MPs talk of sleepless nights and the 'trauma' of voting against your own party. Others say they see 'loyalty' to be a good word, even though it can be used as a criticism against them.

In Chapter 7, it is clear that women MPs feel the media trivialises their contribution to British political life. That ridicule may have begun with the 'Blair's Babes' picture, but the Labour women now feel that their achievements speak for themselves and that things are improving. There is a feeling, however, that the Labour Party should have been more prepared for the attention their 101 newly-elected women MPs would get, and that more could have been done to project a positive image from the outset.

In Chapter 8, it is heartening to learn that women MPs enjoy their jobs greatly. All the women interviewed talked of their great pride in their constituency achievements; however, very few spelt out a clear career path for themselves or felt free enough to talk about their personal ambitions.

4

In Chapter 9, we see that women have 'humanised' the House. They have challenged the established working practices to make Westminster a more efficient and professional working environment. Some believe that this process began before 1997, but that the increased number of women MPs gave new impetus to the reform agenda. The decision in January 2005 to revert back to late-night sittings on a Tuesday disappointed many. Some would support an even wider reform.

In Chapter 10, women MPs spell out their achievements. Across all parties it is clear that they have not only developed and succeeded at taking and converting constituency issues into new legislative changes but that they have also achieved significant policy shifts in areas such as child protection, domestic violence, the work/home-life balance and in helping women to achieve greater financial independence.

In Chapter 11, women MPs talk of how women can achieve a greater representation in Westminster. All-women shortlists are universally unpopular with the Conservatives, reluctantly favoured by sitting Liberal Democrat women, and surprisingly remain controversial among Labour women. However, across all parties women do believe that more work needs to be done in the parties themselves to get more women elected to Westminster sooner. It will still be a long time before there are equal numbers of women to men in Westminster, and the legislation that makes all-women shortlists legal may well have been rescinded before this is achieved.

We came away feeling privileged to have conducted and been part of these 'fireside' conversations with highly intelligent and capable women. Not only did we learn a lot more about politics, but we also learnt a great deal more about ourselves as women in our own workplaces. The engaging, witty and tenacious stories are our stories too. I hope that this portrait in words will help you to picture the women MPs more clearly, who they are and what they have achieved. I hope this book will encourage more women to become MPs too; there are still far too few of them.

Boni Sones

ONE

Moving in

Whose secretary are you?

The 2005 general election resulted in a record number of women being elected to Parliament. There are now 128 women in Westminster representing six parties, Labour, Conservatives, Liberal Democrats, Ulster Unionists, Democratic Unionists and Sinn Fein. This is an increase of 10 on the 2001 general election, when all-women shortlists were disallowed and just 118 women were elected – a disappointing decrease from 1997 when a record 120 women were elected. The story of women's march in significant numbers into Westminster began with the 1997 general election when Labour first used positive discrimination through all-women shortlists.

In May 1997 the Labour Party's landslide victory was not only a shock for the many defeated Conservative candidates from 'safe' seats, but it also heralded a sea change in the representation of women in British politics. Many of Labour's 101 women were surprised to find the swing to Labour was in double figures and that there they were standing on rostrums in town and city halls up and down the country being enthusiastically applauded as they made their acceptance speeches. The election that became associated with the defeat of some of the most loathed Tories and the now famous election-night question, 'Were you up for Portillo?' also became synonymous with a victory that included women on a scale not seen in British government before. Not only was the Palace of Westminster not ready for them, but the women MPs of 1997 were also totally unprepared for the attention they would receive because, even 79 years after women first voted in the election of 1918, their numbers and physical presence was still a novelty. They had to make their home and come to terms with an institution that still boasted a shooting range but no crèche.

In just one election the number of women in Westminster doubled to 18 per cent, a record number, but far from a representational 50 per cent. In total the 1997 Parliament had 120 women MPs, including 101 Labour, 13 Conservative, 3 Liberal Democrats, 2 SNP and the Speaker, Baroness Boothroyd. The overriding impression of the intake of 1997 was that it was still difficult for many to come to terms with women as MPs. In the main, it was a case of mistaken identity, and that identity was usually the role of support staff such as secretaries or simply the wives of male members. This book is designed to give them a voice, to let them tell their historic story in their own words.

It was the intake of Scottish women MPs in 1997 who found their identity was mistaken even before they got to the Palace of Westminster. Anne McGuire tells the story on behalf of her colleagues: 'The first time we got into a taxi coming here, just after we were elected; there was myself . . . I think Linda Clark, Rosemary McKenna and Sandra Osborne in a taxi and we said we wanted to go to the House of Commons, and the taxi driver said, "Oh, the PoW", which is apparently what the London taxis call it, and we said, "What?" and he said, "The Palace of Westminster", and we said "Yup, that's where we're going" and he said, "are you the wives of the new MPs?" and we said, "No, we are the new MPs".'

It was not a wife but a secretary that Charlotte Atkins recalls being mistaken for: 'We were leaving about one in the morning and we were fairly jolly, you know, I think by this stage we may have had a drink or two; but we were sort of, "Oh we've done it now, fantastic", you know we were tired. And I remember one of the doorkeepers saying, "Oh, who are you, are you secretaries?" And I remember saying, "No, we're Members". It's frightening isn't it? But, you know, we won.'

Yvette Cooper had a similar experience: 'I had one conversation with an ever so nice doorman, and I was trying to work our where those steps were that you can see on the telly. You could never work out where they were unless you'd been around the chamber and around the lobbies, and how you got in through the back, so I was asking him. We were talking at completely cross-purposes because he thought I was somebody's secretary and wasn't allowed there at all, and I was trying to work out where the steps were. And he finally said to me, "No, no, no dear, who do you work for?" And I said, "I don't work for anybody, I'm an MP," and he was so shocked and so apologetic, he's been terribly nice to me ever since.'

In 1992 Estelle Morris, a former MP who is now in the Lords, found similar confusion over her status; she says of one male MP: 'He says to me "Oh, how lovely to see you Estelle, are you working here, are you a researcher or a secretary?" I said "No, I'm a Member of Parliament," and he froze, absolutely froze. He was absolutely horrified. But it goes to show how deep the psyche goes.'

Bridget Prentice was also from the 1992 intake: 'I remember people stopping us, as women using areas of the building that are for Members only because they had just not been used to there being women members. I remember one old Conservative Member stopped me going in the Members' lift for a vote. I'm afraid he got one of my terrible looks, at which point he said, "Oh, I'm sorry, are you a Member?"'

Something similar also happened to Harriet Harman when she was first elected fifteen years earlier: 'It was rather odd when I first arrived because there was no system of House of Commons passes in those days, you had a system whereby the officers of the House were supposed to know who every Member of Parliament was, so there was no question of showing your pass, and basically, if they would see me walking down a Members-only corridor, they would always think that I was a secretary who had strayed off the path and needed to be got rid of, out of, the Members-only area.'

Dawn Primarolo, who was elected in 1987, recalls how there was an attitude that all women looked the same, whatever their ethnic background. She says: 'Diane Abbott might tell this as a funny story, in that we walked in together one day and I was greeted by – this was before '97 – by one of the security people as "Hello, Miss Abbott, how are you?" and Diane and I walked away chuckling and saying "The problem is all these women look alike, don't they?" And I think there was under fifty of us at that point and they couldn't remember what each one of us looked like.'

The Prime Minister, Tony Blair had his own way of remembering who was who. Judy Mallaber explains: 'There was a point at which Tony Blair wandered past, and he said, "At least when I say hello to people, if it's a woman, I tend to sort of say hello and assume that she's one of the one's that's just got elected!"'

Friends and colleagues

The scale of Labour's victory had surprised many, not least the winning candidates. Claire Curtis–Thomas notched up a majority of 8,353 over her Conservative rival. Her swing of just over 18 per cent was the third largest in the country. She was more unprepared than most. Pregnant with her second child she readily admits she never expected to be elected: 'I wasn't supposed to come here, so it was pretty shocking when I arrived. I was eight weeks pregnant and nobody knew apart from my husband and I. I had the most appalling morning sickness, and my preoccupation was with, "where are the toilets",', she recalls. Not only did her morning sickness 'take the gloss off my victory' but when she stepped into Westminster itself she found their victory had not been anticipated. 'The arrangements and reception were totally chaotic. There were hundreds of new people, and there was clearly no sense that this had been anticipated: you didn't know how to get a room, you didn't know how to get anything. It was a perfectly beastly, awful place to come.'

Like other new Labour women MPs she was mystified by the red ribbons on the coat hangers, and thought they were there to celebrate National AIDS week. It never occurred to her that they were there to hang your sword on until she mentioned it to colleagues later on: 'Months later, in the tearoom, there was this sort of conversation, and it went, "This place is absolutely crap, it's stuck in the Dark Ages," and I went, "Of course it's not stuck in the Dark Ages." And they all looked, the conversation stopped and they just turned and said, "Well, what do you mean?" and I said, "Take, for example, our AIDS ribbon on the coat hangers in the Members' cloakroom," and there was this absolute thunderous silence, and then somebody turned to me and said, "Claire, that's for your sword, everybody's got one of those, when you bring your sword in you drop it into the ribbon, it's to secure your sword."'

In 1992 Glenda Jackson also found the red ribbons objectionable: 'I mean, in the twenty-first century to afford space for Members to hang their swords on a plastic coat-hanger . . . is ludicrous. And one Christmas, I did think I'd buy wooden swords and hang them on every one, but there were too many MPs. It was too expensive . . . To actually afford to honourable Members the potential that they would come to physical blows, is to me outrageous . . . You shouldn't be affording MPs the opportunity to bring a bloody sword in.'

The red ribbons and the swords became a joke amongst the 1997 intake of women. It came to signify the sweeping-out of one power structure as harbingers of change arrived on tiptoe. They also began to utter a new number aloud – 239! Their victory was historic and the women who were already there reminded them of it. Only 239 women had ever been elected to Westminster. The number was a potent reminder that they were about to share power with the men.

Oona King, who lost her seat in 2005, recounts: 'I remember Harriet Harman very early on in the first week or so saying to me, "Congratulations on being one of the 239," and I was like, "The 239 what?" "The 239 women ever to be elected to the British Parliament, in the whole of its history," she said. And I was like, "Oh wow, that's amazing." And then it was like, why am I here at 3:30 a.m. voting on whether you can have ice cream vans outside royal parks? You know, there was just this disjuncture between the perception of the momentous surroundings, and the banality, and frankly, the appallingly poor practice of the reality.'

Of those 101 Labour women, 66 were new. Most had fought for their seats under Labour's controversial all-women shortlists policy and some of their male colleagues in the party were still coming to terms with a woman winning the party's nomination, rather than a 'favoured son' stepping automatically into the seat. In some areas the battles had been bitterly fought.

Labour's Welsh all-women shortlist candidate Jackie Lawrence, who stood down in 2005, sums up how deep those antagonisms were at first: 'What happened with my experience, and what I hear from so many other people is, where the all-women shortlist took place, Members were saying, "Gosh, we've had some pretty good-quality candidates," as if they're almost surprised that women should be such good-quality candidates. I mean, why should they be surprised?'

Labour's all-women shortlist candidates drew strength from one another. In the months leading up to their election victory they had got to know one another, attending various courses and events, and those friendships were to prove extraordinarily useful.

Hazel Blears explains: 'We'd been on training courses together, some of us had been candidates several times previously, so we knew some of the women who came in. But there was a solidarity between us, and it persists to this day. I think one of the most valuable things that's helped me in my political career is knowing that, at every turn, I can go to the Lady Members' Room and find a sympathetic ear and a bit of personal support as well as political support.'

Anne Begg, who is disabled, says the training and one-off weekends together in the prelude to the 1997 election had broken the ice between her and her colleagues: 'It was great. It was like being in the first year of university. That's what it was like. It was a quite exciting time, as you can imagine, and we did help one another a lot, and we did have a lot of fun together.' They even met up each year for a 'Class of '97' reunion.

One of Anne's colleagues, Sandra Osborne, agrees: 'There was a great camaraderie among the women MPs to begin with because we had this historic number of women, especially within the Labour Party, being elected. But I think in general there was such an excitement in the party because after being out of government for so long we had won and we had won so overwhelmingly. And so to begin with I think really across the parliamentary Labour Party there was a tremendous atmosphere, a tremendous excitement and a tremendous optimism and that very much helped us to settle in.'

Others looked for support from their families. Husbands, fathers and even sisters who had been or were MPs themselves helped. Maria Eagle looked to her sister Angela for support and as a qualified solicitor, to the law books too: 'My twin sister, who'd been an MP from '92, was the first port of call, but I'm also a lawyer, so you get the standing orders out, you get *Erskine May* out – I actually bought myself a copy of *Erskine May* – and you look in the Law Book.' She, like others, also felt the sense of Labour's historic victory: 'There were an awful lot of new boys and girls in 1997 and so it was almost like a new school had opened and we all felt like we were doing it together, and actually in the parliamentary Labour Party we were celebrating just winning for months.'

A driving force behind the rule changes that allowed all-women shortlist candidates into the Labour Party, Angela Eagle, was impressed by many of the candidates, including her sister: 'I thought the calibre of the women-only shortlist was massively higher than most other people, actually. Not just because my sister was one of them, but I actually think constituencies were very surprised at the standard of women candidates that came through on a women-only shortlist. I was heavily involved in getting those rule changes.'

Even some of the Conservative women were excited by the victory for women Labour had engineered. Gillian Shephard, who was first elected in June 1987 and stood down in 2005 to be given a seat in the Lords, says: 'I thought it was great. I wish they'd been Conservatives, but they weren't, and I thought that it was splendid that we'd had such a sea change.' Later she felt some disappointment with their performance: 'I don't think that the changes we perhaps expected to flow from that have occurred actually. We've got a less satisfactory set of working hours for the House of Commons. I don't really perceive very much difference in policy approaches, and some of the women allowed themselves to be trivialised by having make-overs and I don't know what else. There was a sort of collective giggle when they got in, which I don't think did the women's cause much good.'

New Conservative MP Eleanor Laing felt a sense of awe at her surroundings and her new responsibilities as an MP representing a constituency of nearly 73,000 people: 'I actually had to find someone I knew and ask him if I could go into the chamber with him and sit beside him. Can you believe it? After all that time! It was like my first day at school when I was five, and I was quite overwhelmed by the chamber itself, especially when it was absolutely full of people for the election of the Speaker that day. I'll never forget it, it felt quite, quite different actually to be in there as an MP, as opposed to just being in the building as a person working there, and I think the difference is the sense of responsibility.'

While some did not feel at home in the House, others felt immediately welcome, even though they represented not just women but also a new generation of younger MPs under 40 years old and still in a minority even today. Julia Drown was 35 years old when she was elected and she stood down in 2005: 'I did feel welcome. I remember the staff of the House of Commons, all the Sergeant at Arms staff, who wear the funny uniforms, largely they were really pleased to see new faces, fresh faces, something different, and I remember one of them saying, "You know, how different you are, you're not like the rest, all those old stuffy people, all those old stuffy geezers." And that was really nice that they found it refreshing too.'

Anne McGuire has similar memories of being made to feel welcome: 'My abiding memory was being in the lift one day with a couple of women MPs, and one of the women members of staff giving us a big hug, saying, "We've waited for years for you to arrive." Now I don't know whether or not she meant it was women she was waiting for or whether it was a Labour government, and we didn't ask her. We were just very pleased to accept the hugs that she gave us.'

The building and the working environment

Despite the warmth and friendliness showed by some of the staff, the buildings that make up the Palace of Westminster may be historic but they certainly are not seen by some to be welcoming. Angela Eagle calls it 'Gormenghast': I always thought that as soon as I came in. I'm sure there is a little person somewhere and a little tunnel that nobody's discovered yet, hobbling along on crutches.' While the 1997 Liberal Democrat, Jenny Tonge, who stood down in 2005 and is now in the Lords, says: 'I can remember very early on doing some sort of programme about new women in Parliament with Virginia Bottomley . . . and she was saying, "I just love this place, I adore every bit of it, I just love it, love it, love it." And I remember thinking, "You must be mad, this awful fusty old place, Dracula's Castle." I still call it Dracula's Castle, but sort of fondly now.'

In 1997 the more modern and expensive £234 million office block of Portcullis House was still an architect's dream and MPs who found themselves the furthest away in offices down the road at 7 Millbank would have to embark on a seven-minute sprint and cross a busy road to get to the Lobby in time to vote. All the time the division bells would be ringing in their ears.

The public entrance of this eight-acre site is through St Stephen's Hall. Westminster Hall branches off to the left, while straight on is the Central Lobby, or Octagon Hall, which is the centrepiece of the building. This is where MPs usually arrange to meet their guests, after security guards have frisked them and waved them and their bags through the security checks. Sitting on the green leather benches in Central Lobby facing the entrance, you can see the Commons chamber to your right and the Lords chamber to the left. The Royal Gallery and the Victoria Tower lead off the Lords chamber. Facing the river at the front of the Palace is the Lords library, the dining rooms, the Commons library and the terrace, where in the summer MPs entertain their guests. There is a huge chance of getting lost in this labyrinth of corridors.

Claire Curtis-Thomas found the building mystifying, and she was not alone: 'I remember once saying to a police officer, "Could you tell me where I am?" and his response was magnificent, he said, "If you don't know where you are, you shouldn't be here" . . . The lack of any written instructions didn't help . . . It's all pretty basic stuff, but I think it's all done to undermine your confidence; you become completely reliant on the administration to guide you around. It's about impotence management, people who have been here a long time are less impotent than those who have been here no time at all, who, of course, are totally impotent.'

Finding office space proved more difficult for the 1997 intake, but plenty of other women from previous parliaments had experienced similar problems. Former MP and Speaker of the House, Baroness Boothroyd was elected in 1974. She remembers: 'I had no place to work, because in those days – sounds like we were in sedan chairs – but in those days, we didn't have a place to work. You sat in a corridor or anywhere else you could find to put your bottom, and nobody really helped you to find a desk, you just had to push your way through things.'

Margaret Beckett took her seat in 1983 and proved to be more fortunate: 'I did have an office quite early actually, because of course there were so few women, we got special treatment. Ann Taylor and I had the most awful, grotty office. You know, a really kind of defunct Victorian lavatory type in one of the old parliamentary buildings, but the advantage of having been given that office was that when that building was closed, which was within about six months, we then got an offer of the new offices, so we did very nicely out of that, thanks to the Deputy Chief Whip.'

In 1992 when Tessa Jowell came in she found herself opening her post on a bench: 'I remember the early days being a dizzy non-stop round of meeting people, trying to sort out the simple logistics of where your post came to, opening it, being absolutely appalled. On about the fourth day I was a Member of Parliament, when I went to the Members' post office and said, "Could I have my post," I was presented with a pile that was about three feet high, which I then had to stagger with to a bench so that I could sit and start opening it because I didn't have an office.'

Even in 1997, Hazel Blears thought her working environment resembled a museum: 'There was a real sense of the physical environment of the place, which I found quite disappointing in that it felt like a museum. It was full of wood panelling, flock wallpaper, patterned carpets, tiled floors and it had all the hallmarks of what I imagined to be a kind of public school, populated by messengers in archaic tailcoats and lots of large men around the place; a real institution. And I think in my first six months in Parliament, I suggested to the Speaker that we should perhaps turn the House of Commons into a museum and we should build a purpose-built new democratic headquarters, and I didn't get called to speak again for quite some time after that.'

Not only did some find the working environment in 1997 hostile and difficult, but they also perceived it to be unwelcoming to women and families. Betty Williams sums up the feelings of many: 'It was a male-dominated society, and had been allowed to be like that for such a long time, and my first impression was that I couldn't see many high chairs in the cafeteria, things like this. As if mothers with babies wouldn't be coming here at all. And we've changed all that. There are high chairs and babies here now. It didn't make sense. You could have a shooting range in this place, but not simple facilities like a chair for the baby.'

Melanie Johnson, who lost her seat in 2005, also found it hostile, but like many others found warmth and friendship in the Lady Members' Room: 'The only really good thing, which I must say they've tried to take away from us several times, was the fact that there were some Lady Members' Rooms, which were dedicated, obviously, to the needs of women Members when they were a real minority in the House, no doubt a place you could segregate yourself away from a predominantly male environment. And what was really good about that was that we could actually go and just sit there and chat with each other, and it was a place where you could be quiet.'

The discontent was not confined to the Labour women. Conservative MP

Virginia Bottomley, who stood down in 2005 and is now in the Lords, had similar difficulties when she was elected in 1984. She found herself in the wrong Lady Members' Room for the wrong party: 'Finally, I found this wonderful room called the 'Lady Members' Room', which had an ironing board, a sofa, a bath, a notice on the board saying "please do not steal the *Guardian*, it's very selfish to steal the *Guardian*." And I used to sit there from time to time, feel rather lonely and people like Harriet Harman came in and gave me funny looks, and I think then a colleague . . . said "We never see you in the Lady Members' Room, Virginia," and I said, "well, I'm often in there, I haven't taken the *Guardian*." "No, no," she said, "that's the Labour Lady Members' Room; you should be in the Conservative Lady Members' Room," but nobody, nobody had told me.'

Even having a husband who was an MP did not help Virginia settle in as much as she thought it would: 'I found it much more difficult to settle in than I had anticipated. My husband had been an MP already for ten years, so I thought I knew about it. I didn't. I didn't know all about routes and passages, and when women were then still an endangered species, Mrs Thatcher was prime minister, so people thought, Well, we've done women, but actually, there were only 23 women. There'd never been another woman in Surrey, my whip never had another woman in his team, and just small things, like he showed me where to go and what to do, but he never showed me where the ladies' room was, and if you went to something called a Members' Room, that was always a gents.'

But not all found the working environment hostile, some loved the building; Ann Cryer is one: 'I just love this building; and when people come down to see it, it's a great pleasure to show them round and explain who Pugin was, and who Charles Barry was, and the little stories that go with each part, and the history of each part of the building.'

Julia Drown liked the building as well: 'I love it, I just think, I've always liked working in old buildings and I just think, Well, if you're going to get lost in a corridor, you might as well get lost in a corridor that's got a nice picture in it.'

Some actually enjoyed the walking all that corridor space afforded. Conservative Jacqui Lait recalls: 'Its geography's very difficult. You have to remember all the time. I always explain to visitors, it's a series of hollow squares. So you can't go anywhere quickly. It's very good for getting some walking in.' Fellow Conservative and newcomer in 1997, Julie Kirkbride does not mind either: 'It's a fantastically beautiful place to work and it does involve miles of corridor, but that's great for the waistline, so I don't mind that.'

Mo Mowlam also found the Commons fun when she entered in 1987, even though she broke the rules on the first day: 'I was very excited and I thought it would be great fun. In fact, I was told off on my first day because I entered the House through the gate where the cars enter and I walked the little wall eating an ice cream, and I was told by one of the police that this wasn't "parliamentary behaviour".'

In May 2000, Liberal Democrat Sandra Gidley still found the Commons confusing and she thinks it is deliberately so: 'It's very confusing and the thought that I had was that it was designed to be like that to keep you in the dark for as long as possible. The place doesn't actually thrive on people knowing what they're doing; you are far too much trouble, so the longer – I'm not saying this is a party thing – but the longer they can keep you in the dark, the easier it is.'

Very little had changed by the time her colleague Sarah Teather was elected in 2003: 'Everybody says, "It was like that in my day," but nobody actually helps you and it's a very odd, odd place. It's easy to fall foul of rules before you've realised it. Lots of people say it's like an old boys club. To me it feels rather more like a teenage public school.'

In early 2000 breastfeeding in the chamber became an issue when Julia Drown tried to breastfeed her second child on returning to the Commons, only to find herself locked in combat with the Speaker Baroness Boothroyd: 'The rule, at that time, as I was told by the Sergeant at Arms, was that in a committee you could breastfeed your child, providing you got the agreement of the chair, and so when I went to my first committee, I got the agreement of the chair, sat down with my Labour colleagues, who all said that would be fine, just carry on; but really, really unfortunately that committee finished so quickly that I didn't need to breastfeed my child. Somebody went to ask for advice, saying, "Oh, I don't know if there should be different rules for each committee, I don't want to have to rule on whether she should breastfeed or not, so shouldn't we get the Speaker to rule overrule?" and the rest is history. The Speaker banned it and the next Speaker banned it again, against the advice of every single professional organisation in maternity services, against the majority of MPs saying that breastfeeding should be allowed; and it's just the most ridiculous thing I've ever come across.'

Baroness Boothroyd was opposed to breastfeeding: 'I don't know why they should do that in the Commons. They have the facilities to feed their babies elsewhere in the Commons. There are all the facilities here; they have the Lady Members' Rooms, they have their own offices. They don't breastfeed babies on the floor of Harrods, there's a room provided. There's a room they can take their babies.'

Men too have found the environment unwelcoming to children. Meg Munn was elected for Labour in 2001. She was shocked by the reaction Commons staff had to a male colleague's children: 'I said, "Do you want me to go and look after your kids while you go and vote?" and he said, "Yes, that would be great," so we went into the Members' Lobby and he left the kids with me, who of course, weren't terribly happy about being left with a strange woman while he went off to vote. The doormen who were there started going mad, saying, "Strangers in here, strangers, you can't be in here with these strangers" . . . and these were two small children under five who were already a bit scared – people running around and bells ringing and everything – wanting to get them out of the area.'

However, one of the new 1997 intake was impressed by how the Commons staff went out of their way to accommodate her and her wheelchair. Ann Begg: 'Within six months I'd worked out what I needed . . . I needed to have someone with me all of the time. When you're disabled and you're travelling on your own, nobody will do anything unless you give them 24 hours' notice. But I don't know where I am 24 hours from now, things change constantly. So that was just trial and error and the House, once I'd worked out what it was I needed, they were actually very good at allowing me to have it.'

As an institution, the Commons does not take to change easily. Two women MPs among earlier intakes had found smoking objectionable and tried to do something about it. Joan Ruddock came into Westminster in 1987: 'I think there were 21 women Labour MPs at that time, so it was a very different world from the most recent one . . . I was daft enough to ask in the first meeting, which was some open meeting about how we acquired our desk and the rest of it, to be told – 'You new lot, you'll be the last,' and I said, "Is it possible to express a preference for non-smoking?" You can imagine, hoots of laughter, and "You'll be lucky enough to get a desk at all," from the male whips. That was the atmosphere, really. It was very, very aggressive, very, very male and it struck me straight away. Really, this was a cross between a gentlemen's club and a boys' public school.'

Years later, Anne Campbell, another of the 1992 intake who lost her seat in 2005, complained about the smoke-filled environment: 'I really got myself into hot water, because a couple of the whips were smoking in the voting lobby, and I thought, "This is just the end, expecting us to go into the voting lobby and vote and then filling it with cigarette smoke when you get there," and so I complained, I think to the Chief Whip at the time, and so it was raised at a whips' meeting and there were a couple of whips who were really furious that I had dared to raise it.'

Barbara Follett wrote about her first impressions of 1997: 'I wrote an article saying it was like Alice in Wonderland, falling through the rabbit hole. And you found all these people with crowns on (that was the opening of Parliament) and all these people with silly rules. You felt sometimes one inch tall or at times six foot tall. I still, I have to say, don't like this place. I don't enjoy it. I love being an MP in my constituency; I love it when I'm doing good work in committee, or having an interesting debate on the floor of the House. But the floor of the House is not often very interesting. It's a medieval joust, a theatre, and the outcome is already decided, and most of what people are going to say, you've heard a hundred times.'

In June 2001, Liberal Democrat Patsy Calton, who died of breast cancer in May 2005, just after her swearing-in, found Westminster detached from reality: 'I always think of it as a little ship moored by the Thames. Completely separate from everything around it and you could go for days, actually, and have no contact with the outside world at all. I think that's actually quite dangerous in many ways; that we don't feel very involved in what's going on outside of our own little life. It's called the Westminster Village, and I think it is a village and there's quite a few worrying things about that.'

Michael Portillo, who recently stood down after 20 years as an MP, writes: 'I have never been at ease speaking in the House. As a minister, knowing my brief and having a loud, deep voice, I was good enough to prevent the wolves from tasting blood, but I never mastered the easy style or particular brand of humour that turns a competent Commons performance into a memorable one.

'Nor have I settled into the Commons as a club. In the tearoom or over dinner, I have scarcely ever had a memorable conversation with fellow members. Serious discussion seems to be taboo and the small talk is banal . . .'[1]

The approach to political debate in the chamber and in Cabinet can also make women feel like outsiders rather than members of the 'Westminster Club'. Mo Mowlam: 'Being in Cabinet I found reasonably boring, because you didn't do very much. You turned up and felt important for turning up; you waited outside the Cabinet door, chatting to everybody before they went in. More often than not, the women weren't chatted to, they had to chat to each other.'

Patricia Hewitt felt the way men conducted politics was childish: 'People never say anything to your face – it's one of the ways in which the culture of government and politics is childish in many respects. And it doesn't function as well as it should, because so often, people bitch and gossip and beef behind your back, instead of addressing the issue openly, which is what you want in a grown-up, modern culture.'

Theresa May would also like to see a culture that is more professional and more business-like: 'I think there is a slight element of entrenched red tape, but I think the more difficult issue is the sort of culture of the House and the approach to what an MP's job is . . . It's right that there are limits on budget and so forth, but it's getting more restrictive in terms of the way you can employ people and the sorts of levels of salary and so forth. But it's not just that, I think there is just an attitude that the job of being an MP is different to what it has actually become these days.'

Fiona Mactaggart says: 'In Britain, we have the word "clubbable", which is a very male word; it's not applied to women, and I think gendered words are very interesting. "Hysteria" is another example, usually applied only to women. Westminster is, like other legislatures, a bit of a club, and it has about it some of the qualities of clubbability, which are very male, and are often connected with having a bit of a drink, being a bit laddish sometimes, and so on, which I think are potentially excluding for women.'

Women politicians of the past have reacted in different ways to that 'club'.

Barbara Castle also disliked the 'male clubbiness of Westminster, not because it was male – she loved male environments – but because it was clubby.'[2] Jennie Lee was 'never seduced by Westminster, was not a good Commons Speaker, and was not "clubbable".'[3] She was not interested in women's issues either.[4] In 1919 the first woman MP to take up her seat in the Commons was the Conservative Lady Astor. She found herself having to use her sharp wit to stand up for herself. She once exchanged jibes with Winston Churchill and told him that if she were his wife she would put poison in his coffee. He said, 'If you were my wife, I'd take it.'[5]

However, reactions to the 'club' amongst the female politicians vary enormously, and some do fit in and like it. Ann Widdecombe is one who feels at home, even in the smoke room: 'It's a place for grown-ups.'

The need for a modern workplace

It was on 7 May 1997 that the new MPs and their colleagues from previous Parliaments arrived in Westminster for the first day's work of a new Parliament. It was a Wednesday. The biographies and memoirs of their predecessors might have prepared for the haphazard way they would be allocated their office and equipment. Plenty of women before them had found themselves working in corridors, cubbyholes, and desperate to find a ladies' loo. Many of the women MPs of 1997 came from local government or professional backgrounds such as the law, teaching, social work, universities, banking and business. They were used to modern workplaces with email and computers. The shock of finding themselves in an environment that was not wired up, in which email was viewed with suspicion, and where there were not enough desks and offices, was real. Years earlier a MORI poll of MPs in 1990 found that 58 per cent considered the House to be a very or fairly poor place in which to work.

Labour's Melanie Johnson was not impressed: 'It wasn't a modern organisation; the things you'd expect a modern professional business to do, any reasonable business to do, were not being done here. I think the state of some of the older practices and some of the history of the House of Commons – which I support maintaining that, understanding it, knowing about it, cherishing it – the question is whether you want to operate within it, and whether you want it to spill outside the chamber into the everyday operation of the House of Commons and the physical environment.'

Conservative Theresa May had a similar experience: 'For several weeks I didn't have a secretary or an office, so I was walking around with vast armfuls of paper, finding somewhere to "hot-desk", but without a computer at the time, so it was really quite difficult.'

Her colleague Jacqui Lait would like to see a better system introduced: 'What you're having to do is set up a completely new office from scratch, which happens whenever you have a general election, it's not like a business that continues from day to day; every four or five years, there's a huge changeover. So there's a tremendous delay while you get your office allocated. If you are lucky you have a secretary, but you may not; you then have to get headed paper printed; you then have to set up systems, filing systems, and buy your computer kit, and all the rest of it.'

The problems of fitting out the office were also there in 1992. Bridget Prentice: 'The big problem that everybody complains about when they first arrive is office space, even getting an office and the length of time it takes. Actually we do it much more efficiently than we did twelve years ago. We spent months in the committee room, a group of us on one phone between us . . . We didn't have fax machines and such things, and even now we're not supposed to have more than two phones. There's some bizarre rule about what kind of phone you can have. So we're moving towards the twentieth century, but haven't quite reached the twenty-first yet.'

MPs effectively run their own offices much as any small business would. Each political party chooses who should stand in a particular constituency but once an MP is elected their salary and allowance come from the taxpayer's purse. They are paid centrally by the House administration, and are employed on contracts. A body called the House of Commons Commission is the supervisory body of the administration. It is responsible for the House's finances and it is the employer of almost all its 1,500 staff. Chaired by the Speaker, it meets monthly.

Previous generations of MPs are used to the way the House is run. Thirty years earlier Gwyneth Dunwoody felt she had no reason to complain about the facilities although she admits it was not always plain sailing, arguments and disputes did arise: 'We were all delighted to be here, and thrilled with the work, and very anxious to find out all the different facilities that were available. I was amazed, for example, at having an advantage like the library, which is really, in my view, one of the best libraries, not just in the United Kingdom, but in the world . . . I had an enormous pitched battle with a very large Conservative lady called Dame Irene Ward, who had taken over one of the ladies' rooms, and terrified everybody. So she and I had a very amusing set-to, after which stumps were drawn, and we decided we'd have to live together.'

As an 'old girl', Ann Clwyd, who was elected in 1984, has spent many years campaigning for change. First it was for a hairdresser for women, and secondly she tried to change the menus in the Commons restaurants and tearooms: 'There was a men's barber here, but no unisex hairdresser, and I remember being told that the barber did women's hair as well, and I remember ringing him up and he said, "Oh yes, I can do women's hair." I went along and it was a traditional barber's shop, with cut-throat razors and ivory-topped hairbrushes. My hair was washed, and then instead of the blow-dry you'd normally expect, lifting your hair up over a brush, the man just held the drier at the side of my head. I said, "Have you got one of those brushes?" and he really didn't know what I was talking about.'

Ann lists one of her many achievements as getting grapefruit in the tearoom: 'In terms of food, it seemed to be very traditional, sort of school-menu type stuff, and I tried to get things like that changed. But I always said my biggest achievement was to get grapefruit in the Members' tearoom. Because it takes a long time to change things, and anybody who thinks you can change things overnight here is making a big mistake.'

However, by 1997 Jenny Tonge found the staff helpful and responsive to her 'little' requests: 'The doorkeepers, the permanent staff and the library staff, the people in the cafés and the restaurants, the Members' tearooms are like mummies to everybody. They are so lovely . . . I remember wanting a footstool and I asked very tentatively downstairs of the housekeeper, would it be possible, because it's lovely to put your feet up, because there are late evening sittings. The next morning it arrived.'

Labour women, in particular, feel the system does not help them serve their constituents well, particularly when they are representing some of the most deprived constituencies in Britain. Harriet Harman: 'I think that there's things like not having a desk or a room to work in, not having enough money for your constituency office to do a good job for your constituents on individual case work issues; all of those things were very bad when I arrived, and they are much better now, and so they should be, because we want to do a proper, professional job for our constituents. It's all right for a lot of the Conservative Members of Parliament, most of whose constituents probably don't have a huge number of problems that require their interfacing with government agencies like the local authority for their housing, like benefits for their social security. It's in Labour constituencies for the most part where those things are really big issues, and therefore for us, the lack of good properly financed constituency offices was a huge problem.'

Oona King agrees: 'In my particular case, I feel the House of Commons isn't set up to administer a system that allows me to deal with the amount of work that is coming in. I'm only allowed to have three members of staff, I get over 500 letters a week, often about very complex issues, many of them immigration cases. I need a full-time immigration case worker, the House of Commons won't pay for that; I need interpretation staff because perhaps the majority of the people who come to speak to me don't speak English, and the House of Commons won't deal with that; I need IT support, like many MPs I have two offices, the House of Commons can't create an area network so that I can network my stuff . . . I spend a lot of my time dealing with issues like IT, trying to get the computers to work in both offices, trying to have a case-load manager system that can deal with the 33,000 cases that I have in the constituency office.'

Getting onto committees and achieving acceptance in them was also hard for some. It was in the Defence Select Committee, with two new Labour MPs of 1997 Dari Taylor and Laura Moffatt, that the impact of women was felt most.

Dari Taylor recalls: 'There had never been a woman on the Defence Select since its inception, so the first shock to the whole lot of them was that two women were coming on, and they tutted and they gently joked. But one Conservative . . . spoke in the House on one occasion and he said, "I want to say to you, Mr Deputy Speaker, as I end: the two women who have joined the Defence Select Committee have been a very important, powerful force. They have changed . . . the context of the debate, they have changed the focus of the debate and I must say, I was very wary when they were put on the Defence Select. I have to say, it was a good move by the government, and they've proved they were very constructive."'

But the women do enjoy the environment. Oona King has taken to showing strangers round the House of Commons if she thinks they would like to come. She says: 'I love being able to bring people actually physically into Westminster. Sometimes I just pick up random strangers on the tube, honestly, because I just love people when I hear them talking they go, "oh, we're at Westminster", and I'm like, "Have you ever been?", and they're like, "No." "Well do you want to come?", and they're like, "Okay." You know, just ordinary British people, getting them in, physically inside the building, I quite like. I like being able to change things where I can, and the thing I like the most, is when people write to me and say, "You've changed my life for the better."'

Induction

In the early days there were no induction courses but by 1997 Anne Campbell had helped to organise some: 'We did have an induction process by 1997, which was run by the Party – by the Labour Party – and I got involved in that and did a few lectures and talks to people, because I knew I'd felt very lost when I arrived, and I wanted to make sure other people settled down more quickly than I did.'

Harriet Harman explains: 'I became an MP in 1982, I think that they got a rudimentary induction process at general election time, but I came in a by-election, so therefore I just kind of arrived, and there was no induction process at all, and in those days, the House authorities weren't very user-friendly. Now they have quite good brochures and booklets on how to use the library, on claiming for your costs on covering your office, they have standard contracts for your research and constituency employees . . . They had none of those, so literally, you leapt into the deep end.'

Margaret Beckett was also plunged in at the deep end when she arrived a year later in 1983: 'We certainly didn't have an induction course or anything like that. People just kind of did the best they could as they went along. I was on quite friendly terms with quite a number of MPs, and there were so few women, we were kind of driven to be good friends almost straight away. There was one of the sitting rooms that was usually used by Tory women and one that was usually used by Labour women, and there was a great camaraderie, so you kind of picked things up, but there wasn't anything at all formal.'

In 1987, Joan Walley recalls those colleagues who ended up sitting in the chamber with the wrong party: 'I remember going in with a woman colleague and we knew that the entrance to the chamber was at the end of that corridor, and what we hadn't realised was that there were two entrances, and I remember this particular woman colleague ending up sitting on the government benches because she hadn't realised that she'd gone in through a different entrance, she knew she had to go in and turn right, but in fact she'd gone in through the other entrance and turned right, and she ended up sitting in the same position on the government benches, and then realised her mistake.'

Barbara Follett did not think subsequent changes went far enough: 'In 1997, there wasn't much help, although there were the beginnings of some help, to be fair to the House authorities. They did try. But who helped me? Other MPs. Other women who'd been here longer than I, but sometimes they tried to give it more mystique than it had. What hindered you were all the unspoken rules, and people generally don't tell you about them until you transgress them. It works here on an embarrassment factor.'

Ruth Kelly thinks a mentoring system would have helped more: 'One of the single most important things, probably, would be to have someone assigned to you – a mentor to guide you through the initial stages, to tell you what works, what doesn't work, who you should go and see.'

However, even in 2000 Sandra Gidley found she was left to fend for herself: 'I came in on a by-election, and there's absolutely no help for by-election winners whatsoever. I had an hour with the Chief Whip, who helpfully went through the whip for the week, and told me what was a one-line Whip, what was a two, what was a three, what they meant; advised me to carry my diary around for the week on one piece of paper, and that was about it.'

Again, three years later, her colleague Sarah Teather found herself in the same boat: 'My party is obviously the smallest party, and everybody was very willing, but there is a tendency for everybody to plough their own furrow, and work their own constituency. I think everybody thought that somebody else was looking after me, so I was not terribly well looked after at all by my colleagues. It wasn't until around Christmas that I said, "Hey, look, guys, I haven't got a clue what's going on," and then everybody suddenly panicked and realised that nobody had shown me even the most basic things.'

Most eventually learn how to fend for themselves. Gwyneth Dunwoody used her voice to get noticed in that famous battle with Dame Irene. She recalls: 'This is my favourite story. She [Irene Ward] was in the ladies' room on the telephone, having a very abrasive conversation with a bank manager about assets. And he was obviously getting the worst of the thing. And I said, "Good morning, Dame Irene," and she ignored me. Now I thought, perhaps, poor old dear, she didn't hear me. So I said, "Good morning, Dame Irene," later on, and she still ignored me. So I thought, Right, and at that time, it was full of sort of metal filing cabinets. So I started singing at the top of my voice, and first of all I went into the bathroom, turned on all the taps as loudly as I could, and then I went to every one of those filing cabinet drawers, opening and closing with an enormous clang, still singing, and when I'd been doing this for about five minutes, she suddenly said to me, "Um, um, aren't you Mrs Dunwoody?" I said, "Yes," and asked, "Who are you?" And then we never really had any difficulty after that, there was no problem.'

Nudging this conservative institution towards change has been a slow process. The new women MPs of 1997 came to the House to do a professional job but their attempts to be professional were often thwarted by the environment in which they were working. History had been made, but as those women who had entered Parliament before them had learnt, reforming it would take far longer. The men in tights are still there.

TWO

The House

Professionalisation of the House

Members of Parliament were first paid in 1911. MPs' salaries are decided by an outside organisation called the Senior Salaries Review Board (SSRB). The SSRB reviews MPs' pay every three years. It may make recommendations but it is, controversially, up to MPs themselves to vote for or against those recommendations. Since 2003, MPs are paid £55,118 a year. The Prime Minister gets an additional £116,436; a Cabinet minister £69,861; a minister of state £36,240 and a junior minister £27,506.

MPs can employ up to three staff. Some base them in Westminster itself, others prefer them to be based in their constituency. The staff of MPs are paid centrally by the House administration and are hired on standard contracts. There is no standard way of doing the job of an MP and subsequently it is left up to the individual MP to decide how to apportion their staffing costs and allowances; in 2005 these totalled between £61,980 and £72,310 a year.

They also receive £18,234 a year for 'incidental expenses' and £19,722 a year to cover the costs of staying away from home while in Westminster. They have free travel throughout the UK if on parliamentary business, and a motoring allowance. An MP is also entitled to three visits a year to EU institutions or the national parliaments of EU member states or candidate countries. The House also provides MPs' IT equipment, three PCs, a laptop and two printers, for parliamentary business. Increasingly, constituency computers are networked, allowing email to flow between the Westminster and constituency offices.

If you tot up all the allowances an MP receives, they total about £90,000 a year, this is less than their colleagues in Europe, but more than members of the Scottish Parliament or Welsh Assembly. Some MPs agree with Oona King, that the current pay and allowances do not allow them to do a good enough job for their constituents. However, MPs are often accused by the media of being overpaid or even downright dishonest with their various parliamentary allowances. Once inside Westminster, MPs therefore had to come to terms with how archaic their working conditions are.

Teresa Gorman had been a businesswoman before becoming an MP in 1987. She found the lack of professionalism and the entrenched old-fashioned ways of doing things in the House difficult to adjust to: 'Everything is done in that hierarchical structure. I think it must be a little like the military, because a lot of the men in Parliament have been in the military, or they have in the Tory Party. Or they come from those families, like the Churchills, or the whatsit family. You know, this snobbish hierarchical thing. You could be the biggest oaf on earth, but if you come from the right family background, you're bound to get on the front benches. I could name one or two right now . . .'

It is usual for an MP to have a secretary or personal assistant and a researcher or an intern. These interns are often not paid. They work for MPs in order to gain valuable experience of politics. Parliamentary staff often go on to stand for Parliament themselves. For example, Baroness Boothroyd used to work as a secretary for Barbara Castle, among others.

How much does Parliament cost? In the fifth edition of *How Parliament Works*, by Robert Rogers and Rhodri Walters, the authors write: 'In 2002 to 2003 the House of Commons cost £280 million, almost exactly half of which went on MPs' pay and allowances. The whole of the House administration cost £140.8 million. To put these figures in context, public expenditure as a whole was £466 billion of which the Commons – responsible for calling government to account for the effectiveness of its spending – cost 0.6 percent. Expenditure on the House of Lords on administration and works was £57.5 million. As a whole, Parliament thus costs about 0.07 percent of what the government spends.'[6]

Writing in the fifth edition of *Political Issues in Britain Today*, Philip Norton says: 'The resources available to MPs to carry out their jobs have improved enormously. In the early 1960s, few MPs had offices. Most had to content themselves with school-style lockers. They had no separate allowance to hire staff. They were poorly paid. Support facilities were limited. Many had difficulties coping. The situation has improved dramatically in recent decades: all MPs now have an office. Every MP has an office cost allowance, enabling each one to hire two or more staff. Resources, including library and technological resources, have expanded. Since the 1960s, there have been a number of increases in pay, on occasion voted for by MPs against the advice of government.'[7]

They also have better IT equipment and they are now told what the business of the House will be two weeks ahead of time, instead of the Thursday the week before, allowing them to plan their timetables better. However, in 1997 not all these changes had taken place. It was up to the new generation of MPs and subsequent ones to fight for them. Once they had been allocated their desks, computers and found their secretaries a desk too, the women MPs began to suggest that changes were needed.

Theresa May had difficulties knowing just where her secretary would be sitting: 'At one point – when I was trying to move offices – I was told that I couldn't move into a particular office with my secretary next door because the next-door office was designated an MP's office, and so a secretary couldn't be in it, but that my secretary could have a very nice desk in a room with some other secretaries in an entirely separate building. I said, "How do I run an efficient office if my secretary is in a different building?" And I was told that she would be with some very nice people. I didn't think that this was actually conducive to running an efficient office.'

Although MPs purchase their own equipment, with an allowance made by the House, their pagers are supplied by their political party. However, as 'self-employed' people they have no boss to turn to when they need help, support or even praise! Virginia Bottomley found this situation difficult: 'The other bizarre thing about the House of Commons is you don't have a boss. It is completely a place of sole operators, and when you've made a speech, nobody comes up and says "You could have improved it," or "You could have done better." or 'That was very good" – people congratulate each other in a matey sort of way – but it is extraordinary the degree to which you have no feedback, no management, no supervision.'

Estelle Morris has become tired with the traditions: 'It's totally inefficient, and I think what my own view, as time has gone by, is that I think I've always understood the balance of tradition and respect for these things and modernisation. In the last few years, I've become far more impatient of the quaintness of some of the procedures.'

Phyllis Starkey got into a position where she could begin to change things. Many of her parliamentary colleagues thought that change was long overdue: 'I was on the modernisation committee at the beginning, the only representative of the 1997 intake. It was quite a hard struggle, I have to say, because the more long-serving MPs, particularly, though not exclusively, the Conservative ones, had become so used to procedures that they couldn't understand that there was anything wrong with them at all, and also, many of them had not had the extensive experience outside politics that many of the 1997 intake had. They had no experience of working in organisations that are properly organised and professionally organised, and so there was a huge resistance to the notion the Parliament should be made more efficient and more effective.'

Attitudes to the chamber

The chamber of the House of Commons is to the right of the Central Lobby. The Speaker sits on high, presiding over debates at the far end of the chamber, looking down upon rows of green leather benches, surrounded by wood panelling, where the Honourable Members sit. In the middle of the chamber is a table and either side of that table, the opposing parties sit facing one another. The layout is old fashioned and adversarial but small and cosy by comparison with some others – just 68 feet by 46 feet. Whilst much of the work of MPs takes place elsewhere in committees, in constituencies, in their offices, in party meetings and conferences and increasingly dealing with the media, the chamber has long been the symbolic heart of their careers and it is here that reputations are made. The European Parliament, the Scottish Parliament and the Welsh Assembly all now have the friendlier horseshoe formats, which are thought to be more conducive to civilised debates.

In that chamber some, but not by any means all, women have often felt uncomfortable with the aggressive jibes and exchanges at the dispatch box. The obscure procedures and arcane language does not immediately appeal to all and usually finds most favour with those who have learnt their debating skills at public schools or elite universities like Oxford and Cambridge, where similar debating formats are used. It can make others feel downright uncomfortable, particularly when those jibes and exchanges are peppered with farmyard noises, sexist remarks, taunts and finger stabbing. Before the reforms of the hours of the chamber, debates took place late at night, after the Honourable Members had been out to dinner or to their clubs and had a drink or two, so the chamber was often not just loud but cacophonous.

Women politicians have often complained about how difficult it is for women's higher-pitched voices to carry across the chamber. The Labour politician Anthony Crosland noted how difficult it was for Barbara Castle to speak in debates: 'If you have a high-pitched woman's voice and if you are trying to still the postprandial, alcoholic clouds of noise, you are at a terrible disadvantage.'[8] Margaret Thatcher says of her first speech as Leader of the Conservative Party, 'I reflected that as a new Leader of a shaken and still badly split party, and as a woman striving for dominance in the noisy, boisterous, masculine world, I could expect difficulties ahead. And so it proved.'[9] She famously resorted to voice training to increase her authority.

Some women do love the battles at the dispatch box, the raised voices, the finger stabbing and the quick retorts, but many others do not. Tessa Jowell thinks women can adjust: 'It is a very masculine environment, but I think that there are ways in which we as women play into that as well; just as I believe, because I'm an optimist, that most men have a feminine side, so too I think that women have a masculine side, and that the House of Commons brings that out. I think that as women, we fight it, but the fact is, you score well in the House of Commons if you do well in the chamber; and the chamber is adversarial, confrontational, and very masculine. It's also a difficult forum for women to command by virtue of size, tone and pitch of voice, all those sorts of practical things.'

The former Speaker, Baroness Boothroyd is definitely in the 'love it' rather than 'loathe it' camp: 'I love the adversarial chamber that we have. It is small in design, which gives it a theatrical appearance when there is high tension and an extremely good quality of debate. At the same time, in the early hours of the morning and late at night, when you're on the adjournment debate, and there's only yourself as a backbencher and the Minister on the frontbench . . . it's still quite cosy, but it's not overwhelming. I think the chamber is very well designed in that respect. It's cosy when it's comfortably full, and it's not bad at all when it's relatively empty and you've got something to say.'

Some new MPs are not only intimidated by the chamber itself but by parliamentary procedure and those who implement it. For the first six months the new 1997 MPs were not pulled up for every mistake they made but others did feel their treatment was harsh. Charlotte Atkins: 'To start off with [I was] petrified. But I was determined to throw myself into it on the basis that if you don't do it early on, you don't learn. Even under the then speaker, Betty Boothroyd, if you made mistakes in the early stages, you'd get away with it. But after that, of course, you're expected to know what you're doing.'

Barbara Follett felt the Speaker Baroness Boothroyd embarrassed her publicly the most: 'Betty Boothroyd, in particular, enjoyed shaming women when they got it wrong. The contrast between her and Michael Martin was interesting. She would say things like, "You ought to know better" in front of everyone else. I remember I made the mistake of crossing between her line of vision and that of an MP who was standing up to give the Adjournment Debate when hundreds of us were leaving the chamber, and she picked on me, and said, "Mrs Follett, I will have you thrown out if you do that again."'

While some of the new women MPs thought Betty had been unduly harsh on them, pulling them up for points of order before they knew the ropes, others felt she was helpful. The Speaker says she tried to be a friend to them: 'I hope I was a friend to them in those early days, because the House can be very intimidating. I couldn't say anything encouraging when I was sitting in the Chair like, "Don't worry, you'll do it well" or anything like that, but I do firmly believe in body language and eye contact. I would sit bolt upright in the Chair, turned towards whoever was making the speech – it didn't matter who it was – and look at them in the eye and sort of will them to go on. I hope I gave them a bit of encouragement with that. It was the best I could do.'

The lack of engagement in the chamber by some MPs led to the establishment of a new debating chamber in Westminster Hall, which was friendlier and smaller in scale to the main chamber. Charlotte Atkins: 'It must have been after two years, but we had the Westminster Hall Chamber, and some MPs, who hadn't got into the habit of going into the chamber and engaging, were then encouraged to get involved much more in the Westminster Hall Chamber, because it's a much more relaxed chamber to get them back into intervening; interrupting people and so on.'

Virginia Bottomley likes the main chamber: 'The House of Commons is something between a sort of church and a marketplace, so it completely changes. It's either crowded, noisy, busy, people interrupting and taking no notice, or it's totally silent. It's actually more difficult when it's totally silent. I think the other first impression of the Commons is I used to think, How on earth do you get in? It's like seeing people playing squash, table tennis and bowls all at the same time: the questions go backwards and forwards, the debates come in, people interrupt, and everybody seems to know what they're doing and why they're doing it, and when they're going to speak, but I couldn't for the life of me work out how you got to a moment when you actually said something.'

Dawn Primarolo took time to get used to it, particularly the sexism she experienced and had to learn to overcome: 'I wouldn't say I liked the adversarial nature, I've just got used to it, and then I have to adjust when we come back after a break, like the summer recess. I do like speaking in the chamber, but I've had some really rough times. It's very easy to become terribly self-conscious, because people will be commenting on what you are wearing, the speed at which you're speaking, the sound of your voice, what your hair might look like, and then that is used to infer somehow a level of competence in your job. The way that the opposition will try to undermine – any opposition tries to undermine a minister at the dispatch box – is to barrack them, and so you get thrown off your stride in terms of what you need to say and need to have on the record as well as answering the debates.'

Even those who are used to performing find the chamber a difficult place to speak in. Former actress Glenda Jackson says: 'I think it is inordinately patronising to the theatre to equate Parliament with it. I'm tired of reading that the chamber is a stage, a theatrical cockpit – it's nothing of the kind. It's under-rehearsed, it's badly lit, the acoustic is even worse – it has nothing whatever to do with the rigours, the disciplines, the sheer professionalism which is employed by every actor everywhere in the world when they first walk onto the stage.'

Others admitted they felt plain terrified. Helen Jackson, who stood down in 2005, says: 'I was terrified of speaking. I was, in a way, quite startled how really nerve-racking it was standing up in the chamber and speaking. It's partly that you're with your peers; you're with your colleagues. It's not so much the feeling that the televisions are on you, but that you're in front of all the people you don't want to make a fool of yourself in front of, you get quite scared; and that is something – that churning feeling, that scary feeling – something which I still have.'

Some feel much the same as Baroness Boothroyd and love the atmosphere and the debate. Margaret Beckett: 'I enjoy the House, I enjoy the sort of cut and thrust. I enjoy the challenge of somebody putting you on the spot and having to cudgel your wits to get yourself out of that and deal with whatever it is that they're throwing at you.' And Angela Eagle: 'I love the chamber, yes. I think it's less important now than it was even when I came in, in 1992. I took a lot of time just to sit there and observe. Some people immediately stuck their name down for Prime Minister's Questions and made – I won't name names – but made pretty silly fools of themselves because they just weren't prepared. That is the pinnacle of being able to perform in the chamber; you have to do it very carefully. So I went in and watched before I put my name down and observed what worked and what didn't.'

Yvette Cooper feels there is a need for adversarial debate in the chamber: 'I like the debate and I like argument. In fact there are huge value differences between members of the House of Commons and between different political parties. I don't think we should be trying to pretend that there is consensus all the time because frankly there isn't. There are very strong political differences, and it's right that those should be aired. It's also true that the chamber can be a strange place and doesn't necessarily air the debate effectively all of the time, but I think it's also right that there is a forum for argument and disagreement too.'

However, others would push for further reforms and even a circular chamber more in the style of Europe. Oona King: 'I think it's true that there is an atmosphere in the Commons that is very Punch and Judy, and I would like to think that that's male in some sense, it's just incredibly immature, and you'd think that women were going to be a little more adult about this, and not act like little boys. But in fact I have to be honest; women get sucked into that very, very quickly because anybody does. You're socialised by a place, you become institutionalised by a place . . . because human beings have that tit-for-tat nature, and that's very much the atmosphere in the House of Commons, although it can become far more violent, really, in its nature than a simple tit-for-tat. I worked in the European Parliament for five years, and there was always a different atmosphere, perhaps because it was in a horseshoe shape, it wasn't just sort of one side against the other. It's a very bipolar world in the House of Commons.'

Tessa Jowell believes that there is a great sense of solidarity in the Commons and points out how supportive Members in the chamber can be when a colleague is in trouble: 'Certainly in the early days, and still now, we used to always organise it so that if one of us was making our maiden speech, you'd have lots of pals going in with you, who'd sit around you, and I remember the very first time that I spoke from the front bench as a newly-appointed member of the opposition front bench. I was aware of the benches filling up behind me as I came to my debate; and as I rose to my feet there was this deafening roar of approval, and it was so touching I could hardly speak. And that sense of solidarity in the House of Commons is something very special and it's a sense of solidarity that is on show when somebody's going through a bad time, when somebody's being hounded by the press, when somebody's done particularly well, or, most recently . . . when Beverley Hughes resigned, when the sense of support, affection, respect, and regret was palpable.'

Women MPs often know they have gained acceptance in the Commons when they speak in debates. They have experienced that human warmth. Fiona Mactaggart recalls being congratulated by Tony Benn, after she broke down and cried when talking about an issue that was difficult for her: 'There was a moment where I took a big risk in the chamber talking about IVF and my infertility, because it was a free vote, and in a free vote, actually how the debate goes, really changes it. I have multiple sclerosis and I'm infertile. I have frozen embryos through a fertility attempt. Those frozen embryos would be able to be used for research into my infertility, about which, at the age of fifty, I don't care any more; they couldn't be used for research into my illness and I spoke about that in the chamber, which was very risky, talking about things like that . . . Ann Winterton intervened . . . in effect saying that infertility was a social disease, you know, implying that it was a consequence of promiscuity, and it just got me, and I very nearly started to weep, and it was a completely terrifying moment, because I weep very easily.'

The rules, procedures and language

The arcane language and procedures used in the chamber mystify many. A great deal of power is given to the Speaker, who can decide who to call for debate when. This helps to create what some perceive to be a 'pecking order' for those who are 'favoured' more than others.

Even when they look to distinguished colleagues for support those colleagues can lead them into trouble. Tessa Jowell remembers making a gaff when Tony Benn lead her into the wrong voting queue: 'We nipped in too quickly, so at the point of which the Chief Whip comes and says "All out", this is in the Tory lobby, Tony Benn and I were still there. The sitting had to be suspended for a few moments, the speaker was very cross and all the rest of it, and you can imagine that as a new MP of about six months' standing, I felt absolutely mortified. I learnt a very important lesson from Tony Benn, which is just keep your shoulders back and stick your chin out.'

Hazel Blears found the procedure strange: 'You've no idea where to stand, where to sit, which lines not to cross, how to address people, and because this is a stage ritual of politics, then learning the rules is so important. Disobeying the rules is fine if you do it deliberately; if you do it accidentally then you're a fool. It is quite important that you do know what you're doing . . . how select committees work, how to move a motion, what an early day motion is, how to get an adjournment debate, all of that.'

The title by which you had to be addressed also angered one. Valerie Davey, who lost her seat in 2005, says: 'There is a very tiny procedure that I think is symptomatic of this place. Soon after I arrived, I was asked how I wanted to be addressed in Hansard and I said, "Valerie Davey," and the immediate response was, "No, that's not possible, it has to be Mrs or Ms or

Miss." I'm a married person, but always in politics I've been Valerie Davey; so I suggested that perhaps if I was a Quaker like my husband, no title would be the norm and I would want it on religious grounds, to which they said, "Oh," and went away.'

Linda Gilroy wishes they would speak in plain English: 'When they see us debating that sort of thing in the House, referring to the "Honourable Member this" and putting it all into the third person; I mean, before I came into Parliament, I've had a life-long passion for plain English, and for good-quality communication, and for getting rid of gobbledy-gook.'

Some however, do see the point of the procedures. Jenny Tonge: 'I can remember thinking it was a terrible fusty place with silly old-fashioned procedures, and particularly the curious way we debated, always addressing the speaker and using "Honourable Member" and things. Now I've got used to it, I can see how valuable it is, and how the way we debate, for instance, diffuses situations. It means that we never attack each other directly, we only attack someone via the Speaker, which makes it a more elegant process.'

Dame Marion Roe, who stood down in 2005, also supports the language: 'You refer to somebody by their constituency name, now I thought that was mad – I knew he was Bert Bloggs, but I could never remember where he represented, just a nightmare. However, I learnt there is a very good reason for that, it is because it removes that very personal attack on people, you are addressing a representative from a constituency and therefore it takes away that very personal attack, that very personal intervention and makes it just that little bit more distant from that personal attack or whatever it is undermining the person.'

Some come to their parliamentary careers prepared for it. Anne McGuire: 'As regards procedures, etc, I grew up in Glasgow University debating, and our debates, every Friday during term-time, were based on House of Commons rules, so the language of the "Honourable Member" was not alien to me when I came here, and in some respects, as a matter of fact, it was almost like going back to my student days in terms of the procedures.'

Some believe the language and procedures can actually hinder debate. Julie Morgan cut her teeth on the devolution debate: 'That was my first experience, the real big Bill that affected me very dramatically because devolution changed the whole nature of MPs from Wales. It was there that I saw how the House operated, in what I considered a very old-fashioned sort of way, and you didn't get a chance to get your points of view across, and most of the new MPs, men and women, felt that. They couldn't get their say.'

Others have been given tips by friends as to what makes a good debate. Baroness Boothroyd: 'I do remember Lena Jaeger, a dear friend of mine, and I said to her something like, "You know I haven't spoken for quite a while. I ought to pick up a Bill and speak on a clause of a new Bill that's coming in." She said, "You only speak in this House, Betty, when you have something that you're burning to say, then you will be listened to. Otherwise, you're over-egging the pudding, because you'll be a rent-a-mouth. You speak when you've something passionate and special to say, that is the way to do it." And she was right.'

Talking about what you really believe in also helps you to stand out. Baroness Golding: 'I just told them how my father had come home, and the effect that it had had on me, and the whole House was still. And when we went in to vote, everybody was talking about the four-minutes speech I'd made. But the most important thing was, up in the balcony, there was somebody who'd been in Auschwitz, and he came to me as I went out into the Central Lobby, and he said, "Llin, I sat listening to you up there, and I cried. The tears streamed down my face. I couldn't stop it." And he said, "I have never shed a tear since I came out of Auschwitz, because I never could. When I listened to you, I did, for the first time." And I thought, That's what politics is about.'

Once upon a time, MPs could make their mark as a politician by notching up their credentials as being a good parliamentarian, a good speaker and debater in the chamber, and some still do, but others do not like the term. Glenda Jackson says: 'I must admit, I don't know what being a parliamentarian means. Well, I think I do, and I would never ever want to be that. I can't imagine a more recondite, useless thing to be. It seems to me to accord to a kind of veneration for the chamber, which has nothing to do with what the real veneration should be about. It's automatically rooted in the past, the past is always presented here as growing in a golden way. If you ever bother to read any of the speeches, because everyone says, "Oh, you know, speeches are nothing, rhetoric is gone, the debates are awful. There was a golden age." No there wasn't.'

How you perform in the Chamber can give a wrong impression of your strengths as a politician. Melanie Johnson: 'I think the truth is it favours a certain sort of style of doing things and a certain sort of delivery and certain sorts of people. It's an environment in which people can look very good or rubbish, and that's not necessarily what they're like in the outside world, as it were, or at other aspects of their job. So it's a very particular part of the role. It's actually not a very major part of the role for most people.'

The TV cameras in the chamber put off some. Julia Drown: 'It has become easier, but I think most people, men and women, are still aware the cameras are on, there is that tension in the chamber, so it is not the easiest place in the world to speak, and I don't actually like it, I don't think it is a helpful ambience; but it's important to do it, so you do it.'

Some are grateful that Hansard, which is the formal written account of what is said in Parliament, is a corrected record of what they say in the chamber. Charlotte Atkins: 'I always used to believe that Hansard was actually what people said, which of course it's not, it's a corrected record of what people have said, and it makes people sound far more articulate than they really are.'

Maiden speeches

Undoubtedly the most nerve-racking experience for many of the new Members of the 1997 intake was their maiden speech. Some decided to get it over with sooner rather than later, while others decided to sit in the chamber and observe the customs and procedures first.

Beverley Hughes points out that from the start, women are disadvantaged by their voices. Beverley says: 'The whole voice thing, that just got parodied very early on. It's part of some of that shouting that took place, in which women's voices, generally, did sound shrill, compared to the general tenor of the House. All of that has completely gone now, because people have got used to a multiplicity of different kinds of voices. But at that time, it was another way in which you – if you even opened your mouth – were made to kind of feel like you didn't fit: it didn't sound right.'

She says her maiden speech was a disappointment: 'There were hundreds of people having to line up to do their maiden speeches, so it took months. And there was a sense of panic generated; people wanted to get it out of the way, you didn't want to be the first, but you didn't want to be the last either, the only person who hadn't done it. And there were such a lot that they had to be kind of slotted in. In each debate, they'd try and make sure four or five people got in with their maiden speech. So actually, it was a bit sad in a sense, because instead of it being a proper maiden speech in which you could say – I mean, you're not supposed to say anything political – something of concern to you or your constituency, you ended up just having to do it in any old debate, whenever you could get in. I think I ended up having to do mine on housing, which is an important issue, but it was not something I'd made my particular area of interest at all.'

Like many others, Hazel Blears remembers the waiting and the crossed legs: 'When we did our maiden speech, I'll never forget, myself and Beverley Hughes, who's a good friend of mine now, we sat in the chamber together from 2.30 p.m., I think, until 9.30 p.m. I got called to make my maiden speech at 9.30 p.m., and neither of us knew that you could – with the permission of the Speaker – go to the loo, so we sat on the bench for seven hours together – it's a good job there were two of us – and we supported each other enormously . . .'

The maiden speech is designed to ease you into the customs and protocols of the chamber in a friendly way. Anne Campbell: 'The House is quite kind to you on your first occasion, on your maiden speech, because the tradition is that nobody interrupts you, nobody comments and everybody says nice things about you. I talked about the divided nature of Cambridge . . . and I didn't get any adverse comments at the time.'

Glenda Jackson recalls her 1992 maiden speech: 'I can remember it very clearly, because it was without doubt the most frightening experience of my life. I knew I had to be in the chamber on the day that there was a possibility I would be called to make my maiden speech, from 3.30 p.m. And I had to wait to see if my name was going to be called. And I also knew the tradition was that maiden speeches are listened to in silence. Nobody heckles you. There is that unwritten code of how MPs treat a new incumbent. So I sat there from 3.30 p.m., and I think I was called at about 8 p.m. The chamber was virtually empty, I was absolutely petrified, because the minute I got to my feet, I suddenly realised that I was responsible for the trust that all those thousands of people of Hampstead and Highgate had placed on my shoulders as their representative in Parliament. And also, that I was representing a constituency where some of the great giants in the use of and expression of the English language had lived. I mean, names like Keats came bursting into my mind. However, I got through it, and that was fine.'

Angela Eagle resorted to writing hers down: 'In terms of my maiden [speech], that's the only speech that I ever really have written beforehand, but I did write it beforehand as a sort of failsafe. And I remember I sat there for seven hours, I think, waiting to try and get my maiden speech in, and in fact I followed Glenda Jackson, who I'd grown up watching as Elizabeth R on the telly, so it was a slightly funny experience to be suddenly sat next to her; and she made her maiden speech just before me. I realised she was incredibly nervous – she was shaking – and I thought, Well, if an actress can be nervous . . .'

Sylvia Hermon made her maiden speech on the hoof: 'So I sat there, relaxed, thinking, Well, these two gentlemen know better than anyone here how these things operate, so I sat there oblivious to the fact that I was going to be called in a very few minutes. So I didn't even have the speech in my hand when the Speaker announced my name, and all I could feel was elbows in both sides of my ribs, to the left and to the right as I was propelled onto my feet by both my party leader and my Chief Whip.'

But Karen Buck came up with the most graphic description of fear and intimidation: 'I still find them complex and baffling. I would say that my maiden speech was worse than childbirth. It was the most terrifying thing . . . and the most painful.'

Talking to ministers

The one thing MPs agree on is that however time-wasting talking in the chamber might be, or however infuriating lining up to vote in the Lobby is, it affords you access to ministers and even the Prime Minster on occasions. 'Collaring' those in positions of power as you go through, to talk about your pet subject, is standard practice for the many MPs who don't hold ministerial rank. As MPs undergo the tedious procedure of being counted in one by one, they regularly have access to the 'ears' of ministers, or they may use other devices to request a meeting.

Christine Russell explains: 'I think it was Margaret Hodge. I said, "Can I just sit and talk to you, Margaret, about this?" I think the ministers are remarkably accessible. Of course there's the odd exception, but with most of them – which I suppose is the argument for retaining the antiquated voting system – it brings you direct and physical contact with the ministers, I just find in nearly every case that if you say, "Look, this is a real issue, I do feel strongly about it, either personally, or my constituents do," they will say, "Well, okay, let's meet in the tearoom and have a coffee," or if you want a formal meeting, "Come down to the office and we'll talk about it."'

Angela Eagle: 'I voted against having electronic voting [because] I think that it's important that ministers are around in person to vote. Otherwise you'd really never see them, and there would be a complete separation from executive and legislature, and if you're going to do that, you should do it as part of a constitutional change and decide you're not going to have MPs as ministers.'

Anne Begg does speak to ministers: 'I'd like to think that in some areas of policy the government has either torn down what it was going to do or has changed the emphasis on what it was going to do, because people like myself, and others, have actually said to ministers, "This is not playing well," or, "You're sending out the wrong message"; but how you actually phrase that when you're selling that policy has to be very careful.'

Worst moments in the chamber

The worst moments Honourable Members often experience in the House are related to embarrassment. They feel embarrassed when they don't get the arcane language and procedures quite right, and when the Speaker or a Member from the opposing party barracks them as a result.

Maria Eagle has analysed those feelings: 'Earning your spurs is a good thing. Embarrassment is a bad thing, believe me, because you can bet your life the sketch writers will all write about the embarrassments and the bad things, and they won't pick up the good things, and so, it is squirming when you make a mistake like that, and I shall try never to do it again. It has taught me some things.'

Sandra Gidley was made to squirm: 'I thought I was beginning to get to know everything, and I was. I'd put in for health questions, came up number one, and I thought, Oh, that's great, and then I realised that I had the first question to a new Speaker. I still wasn't unduly worried about this, but I stood up and about halfway through it, I suddenly got very nervous, and the question just seemed to go to pot really, and the Tories started jeering and being awful because I was trying to say, "It's your first question, it's my first question" – I think it was the first question, yes; and they were going "Oh, she hasn't asked a question before," and all the rest of it, it's this sort of male barracking that the Tories are excellent at.'

Patsy Calton remembers her own mistake leading to a round of applause: 'I got a round of applause from everybody, because they realised what had happened, that I'd just been left completely stranded on something that I wasn't expecting to speak on at all and I guess that was a good moment to have got through without actually dying on the spot.'

However, some women MPs feel that this is not just hostility towards new members with poor knowledge of procedure, but a more worrying misogyny. Glenda Jackson: 'They will accept women as their inferior but they find it virtually impossible to accept [them] as an equal. I mean, I can remember one of my colleagues when I first came in, said to me, "Why did you want to come here? You're already famous." I find that deeply, deeply shocking. Where's democracy? Where's politics? Is that why people want to come in here? To be famous?'

Claire Curtis-Thomas had a bad moment when her seven-year-old disabled daughter, who was going through a very bad period of flapping her hands involuntarily, was told by a policeman that she had to remove her daughter from the Lobby just outside the chamber. She remembers: 'That was the worst, it was the very worst. I was too shocked to complain. I just sort of walked away, really, and I felt humiliated, offended, angry; all those reactions that you could expect, not for me but for her, that her obvious disability should be so disregarded, and that no accommodation could be found for it in this place, when this place is supposed to be for all. It was just terrible.'

But sometimes even when you make the most dreadful gaffe, your colleagues from all sides of the benches will come to your aid. Linda Perham, who lost her seat in 2005, says: 'I was sitting next to the Prime Minister's parliamentary private secretary . . . [and] I got up to ask a question. I got halfway through the sentence and I hit the words "reinvigoration of the peace process" and I couldn't speak and I stopped, and at that point, the Tories just howled, including Alan Clark, they were just rocking with laughter. And this wall of derision hit me.' However an opposition MP, Gillian Shephard, came to her rescue with some kind words later. Linda continues: 'Afterwards, Gillian Shepherd, a [former] senior member of the Conservative government, who I'd met the week before at a book launch, wrote me a little note on A5 paper, handwritten, and she'd put, "Nil desperandum. A lot of us have a rough time at our first PMQs [Prime Minister's Questions]. You will live to fight another day. No need to reply to this, don't worry. P.S. I thought you looked wonderful. Men should have their colours done as well." '

The traditions of the chamber inspire some but clearly terrify others. For a significant number of the women of 1997, the arcane rules and language put them off. They were used to speaking on public platforms but they found the chamber of Westminster a turn-off. Why should they be put through the ordeal of embarrassment on procedural rules when those rules were not even written down for them to read or learn? Many now prefer speaking in the smaller Westminster Hall. They want Parliament to look and sound more relevant to the constituents they represent. It seems some former male MPs might agree. Michael Portillo writes: 'Looking at Parliament while I was away from it, I saw it differently. Having been steeped in its rituals, I could recognise how odd it seems to voters. The Commons speaks in a strange language and its priorities are different from the public's.'[10] How refreshing that the once unspeakable can now be spoken.

THREE

How women do politics

Persistence

Some women really take to the adversarial nature of debate in Westminster, while others do not. Since 1997 a significant body of women politicians believe they have developed a more consensual and grassroots approach to developing policy issues. They overwhelmingly enjoy the job of talking to constituents in their Friday surgeries, and being able to champion and campaign on concerns to achieve change for the better. They often find these 'softer', some might say more feminine, skills of talking to constituents on a one-to-one basis more enjoyable than the cut and thrust of being in the chamber; but while this is true for some, it does not hold for all.

Their parliamentary critics might accuse them of having become 'glorified social workers', but over the years the job of an MP has changed and evolved to such an extent that constituents now have high expectations of their MPs and expect to be able to approach them if they have a problem. There was a time when MPs did not even think they needed to visit their constituents, they believed that once elected to Westminster that was where they stayed. They were actively encouraged not to worry too much about constituents' problems. Jennie Lee's biographer Patricia Hollis writes: 'In the late 1940s and 1950s, this was acceptable. Quarterly visits were not uncommon.'[11] No MP, male or female, could get away with that today.

There is by no means agreement among women politicians that women are more consensual in their approach. However, two words do occur again and again in the vocabulary of women MPs – 'persistence' and 'persuasion'. Once they get the bit between their teeth, they don't like to let it go until they have succeeded.

Mo Mowlam remembers driving her civil servants almost to distraction with her persistence: 'I used to drive them mad, because I used to make a list of everything I wanted that day and go in the morning and ask, "Have they done this? Have they done that? If not, it goes on the list the next day." So I did try and manage them in a way that I could make sure that there were things being delivered. To be very clear about what it was you wanted, and then to give it to one or two people to do, and then chase them, meant that you eventually got it done. But you always had to consult first, because if you didn't have the people with you, you weren't in a very strong position.'

Ann Widdecombe finds herself for once agreeing with Labour women: 'I'm afraid the word is persistence. You won't get it the first time, but if you persist, you will . . . It took Wilberforce years and years to abolish slavery. Now, you and I would say, "Abolish slavery? Of course they ought to abolish slavery." But that wasn't the outlook of his time. It took one man – I mean, there were others, but all the same – it took one man really, really pressurising and never going away. And you can imagine the pressure he would have been under in his London clubs: "Oh come on, Wilberforce, you know, not that again. It doesn't matter. It's not important, old boy. There are more things to think about." He would have had that the whole time, and he never gave in to it.'

Persuasion is another skill that women politicians value. Hilary Armstrong says having powers of persuasion are essential when dealing with individuals or groups: 'You've got to know them, you've got to know what motivates them, you've got to know who their peer group are, which of their peer group influences them, but at the end of the day, it comes down to political argument and political debate, and that's why we win some, but we don't win them all. We win the vote, but we don't win everybody's heart and mind. You can't twist arms, because they immediately run out to the media and tell them. You've got to argue, you've got to persuade, you've got to be political.'

Hazel Blears identifies persuasion as a feminine skill: 'I like to think that part of my skill is persuasion, exultation, cajoling people, convincing them that there's a better promised land out there if they only come with me on that journey, a bit of inspiration, being able to paint a picture that life can be better, motivating people or team building. I suppose typically feminine skills, but then a little bit of edge at the end of that so that you can close the deal, because politicians have to know how to close the deal.'

They also use those powers of persuasion at the highest level. Karen Buck: 'On the issue of Iraq, and on the issue of asylum and immigration, which I've also voted against this government on, on a number of occasions, you talk to ministers, you write letters, you make a decision about how much you do it privately and how much you do it publicly. Well, I've done both over the years, but you use every access possible that you've got, if necessary right up to the top, which I've also done on occasions.'

Louise Ellman also takes her concerns to the top: 'It's always a combination, it isn't just one person, it depends what the issue is. I always think, "Who is it who's in charge here? Which minister is responsible? How do I get continued attention for this issue?" and that usually means publicity of some sort in the media. I think that if the minister's being told something I believe is misleading, they need other sources of information too, so they can go back to their officials, if I need somebody else to speak up to produce other facts, and you need persistence, a lot of persistence.'

Barbara Castle was certainly persistent. 'Her political career's most striking, although not its most consistent, feature was her success in identifying issues on which she could make a difference.'[12] When she was Secretary of State for Transport, her Road Safety Bill introduced the breathalyser, extended the 70 mph speed limit trial, and required new cars to be fitted with seat belts. Later she increased the penalty for driving while drunk from a fine to disqualification. Her biographer, Anne Perkins writes: 'What Barbara brought to the Bill was her unremitting determination to get it on the statute book. It provoked a media storm . . . Now her postbag was bulging with angry letters from aggrieved men; but there were also touching letters of gratitude from wives "allowed to go to the pub for the first time" if only so that they could drive their men folk home. And there was even a death threat, which Scotland Yard took seriously enough to provide Barbara with a bodyguard for a fortnight.[13]

Networks and 'sisters'

Women across the parties do offer support to one another to achieve change. This may happen so that they can lobby for change in the chamber or when women ministers work with one another to assess how a certain policy issue will affect women in general. They also network to establish contacts that can help them progress the issues they are concerned about. Whether or not they do this more effectively than men is open to debate. Some think women do not network enough.

Those networks have held them in good stead when they come into the Commons and make their first appearance on the floor of the House. Tessa Jowell recalls: 'I remember the very first time that I came into the House of Commons, and walked into the Members' cloakroom, which I did with Bridget Prentice, we linked arms, we looked at each other, we said "See us", because we're both from Scotland, and "see us" is a very Scottish term, and we stuck our chins up, put our shoulders back and walked into the Members' cloakroom, which is one of the most sacred Members-only parts of the House of Commons, and we felt as proud as could be.'

Phyllis Starkey was another new entrant who used her regional contacts for support: 'There was a regional network. There was also a network essentially between all of the MPs that Labour had selected for what it called its "key seats". So those were the hundred seats that we needed to win to be in government. Those MPs had been meeting for various training sessions in the whole of the election campaign, I mean for two years, so we knew each other very well. Half of those were women, and we supported each other as a group of new MPs.'

Sally Keeble agrees: 'I think quite a lot of us who came from the marginal seats – the archetypal "Blair's Babes" – we came with a particular agenda, we went for the seats for particular reasons, we came into Parliament for a particular purpose; we actually got to know each other quite well in the two years run-up, and quite a few of us had known each other before, in local government and all sorts. I think that it's not very surprising that quite a lot of what we've done has been fairly similar and has been fairly loyal. I think that the role we have played has been very constructive.'

The then Speaker Baroness Boothroyd did try and make the new 1997

MPs feel welcome: 'I think it took them probably quite a while to settle in. Should they be guided and mentored more? As far as I know, it really is the duty of the Whips for the particular region they're in to sort of take care of them, to look after them a bit and to guide them . . . But what I did as Speaker is have them in Speaker's House, a group of them at a time – 20 or 30 of them at a time – for a glass of wine and give them a talk and suggestions like "Speak when you've really got something to say", little homilies like that, "Find whereabouts you want to sit in the Chamber, and although there are no booked seats, stay in that area once you've decided where to sit because I'll know where to look for you if I want to call you", and I would give them tips like that as best I could as Speaker.'

Women MPs sometimes identify one another as being loyal. Gwyneth Dunwoody recalls a clash with her government: 'They didn't just rally round me, they rallied round Parliament. This is the important thing to realise. Women are very loyal. Women are astonishingly loyal. They feel they shouldn't rock the boat, they shouldn't argue, they shouldn't make it difficult. But I think a lot of new people realised it was not in Parliament's interest to be dictated to in that manner.'

Joan Ruddock, the first Women's Minister, believes that being a woman politician helps her to identify with other women: 'I feel empathy with women in general. There are some women who wouldn't welcome that and there are some women, who in both or all the parties, I would not ever be saying hello to in a warm way, and that's because they are women who don't particularly have that empathy with other women, but I think we all recognise who we are really.'

Theresa May admits to working with women across the parties to get more women into Parliament. She says: 'I'm not somebody who naturally would claim to be a member of a great sisterhood here in the House of Commons; I think we're all here to do a job and we get on and do that job. But by definition almost, the issue of bringing women into Parliament is something that all women across parties have an interest in.'

Eleanor Laing agrees that she did liaise with women from other parties: 'You find that you have a lot in common with female colleagues, and there are quite a few women on the Labour benches, and Liberal and other benches, who I get on well with – at least, I think I do – because we have things that we talk about. I mean, it isn't all just politics in here. In the Lady Members' Room, we do quite often admire each other's shoes and jackets and say, "Where did you get that brilliant nail polish?" We do have normal girl-talk as well. There isn't much time, but if you're just passing through and getting a cup of coffee or something, we do have normal female chat, and from that point of view, it's good that there are rather more women here than there were before, and it does make it a slightly softer environment.'

Mo Mowlam admits to having appointed women colleagues to posts in order to progress them into influential positions: 'I was conscious of choosing women, because we had to push women on, because if we didn't do it, nobody would. So I consciously chose a female Parliamentary Private Secretary. Couldn't have done anything else, in my view.'

At Cabinet and ministerial level there was from 1997 onwards an alliance of Tessa Jowell, Magaret Hodge, Marie Eagle, Patricia Hewitt and Harriet Harman trying to achieve change for women. Tessa Jowell: 'Margaret Hodge, who is now Children's Minister, is doing a really fantastic job with childcare. It is now an issue whose time has come. It is now at the centre of the political agenda. It has taken years to get there, and has been the product of the campaigning of women; Harriet over the years, Margaret over the years, me over the years, Patricia Hewitt, the voluntary organisations, the kids club network and so forth. But this is a policy whose time has now come.'

Harriet Harman says she would have felt a failure if she had not mentored and tried to encourage the careers of other women politicians: 'I think it's very nice that other women MPs say that they looked to my experience and that they see me as a mentor. I think that, in a way, what they need above all is a critical mass of their own generation – I mean I'm more than happy to advise the new ones coming in, and am delighted to see more of them come in and press for more of them – but really, they need to be their own peer group, and invent the forward agenda. If basically I'd have arrived and there was three per cent women, and I'd left and there was three per cent women, I would have regarded myself as having completely failed. I think we want to change the agenda, we want to be sure the next generation is more numerous and stronger and taking it forward. So, I am happy to give them any support they want, but they're such a fantastic group of women that I'm sure they can manage without me.'

Beverley Hughes says getting to know other women politicians had been important to her: 'Information actually really did get transmitted in [a] very kind of informal and sometimes rather chaotic way. So it kind of took quite a long time to bed down, but I do really have an abiding recollection of the importance of getting to know new women as being very crucial . . . and actually, those relationships, particularly amongst 1997 women, have endured.'

Melanie Johnson agrees: 'I think women are far better at admitting that they don't know the answer than the men. And I think it gave us a head start, actually, over our new male colleagues. Also, the women are much better at networking with each other, comparing notes and saying "I haven't a clue about this, but I found out about that," and trading information all the way round. I got the impression, although it might not be right, but I got the impression men weren't quite so good at doing that. So actually, we learnt much more quickly than they did about these things.'

Marie Eagle agrees that women ministers worked together to achieve change, but says that they also approached the men for support: 'Sometimes it's based on "I get on with that minister very well, I know they have the same perspective on this issue as me, I'll go and talk. I'll just circumvent all the Whitehall and official channels." You have to do that, and I think women are particularly good at doing that, and men are much more aware, generally, of how the hierarchies work, and the "Are you above me or below me?" And they do generally have much more of an awareness about that, whereas women will think, 'Well, who's in charge? Who can I go and to talk to about this? and they'll just cut through.'

Oona King understands that coalitions are essential to be an effective politician: 'You've always got to be in a coalition to get something. Coalitions can be cross-party; they can be within their own party. It's about being more than a lone voice because a lone voice, on the whole – unless you're Nelson Mandela – isn't going to get what you want. So it is about coalitions, and it is about compromise, and some people view compromise as a dirty word. The reason they view it as a dirty word is because you have to give up something that is dear to you, otherwise it is not a compromise.'

Some believe that women's networks are still not as good as the men's. Anne McGuire: 'I used to say, "If we had unisex toilets, perhaps we could be part of the deal as well." I don't mean to say that all the Trade Union deals are done in those sorts of circumstances – but it was those informal networks that I think women didn't have, and I think most women still don't have the informal networks, and that's a more difficult thing to establish.'

Using Parliament as a platform

MPs use Parliament as a platform to champion and campaign on the issues that they believe in. Women MPs believe they have used their experiences of life to bring a more feminised agenda to the chamber. From stem cell research, to concerns over female body image, to helping other women internationally, to involving more women in the talks on Northern Ireland; they have become crusaders for social justice.

Anne Begg used her personal experiences to have an impact on the debate on stem cell research. She recalls: 'I was keen when I came in that I wasn't going to be the disabled MP, but an MP who happened to have a disability. I would take as my model David Blunkett, who makes light of his disability, and doesn't particularly address disability issues. But what I did learn once I felt I had established my identity, what I did learn after that was I had things to say, I had insights, stem cell research is an example of it, into things that other people, even with a lot of years of experience in the field of disability, didn't have that kind of personal knowledge of. And when I spoke on disabled issues, where I had that personal experience, people listened to me more than they might to someone who didn't have that extra dimension. So I realised I had something that you can't learn, and I happened to be born with the disability, and I should use it. So I do a lot more on disability now, but I really shied away from it to begin with.'

Patricia Hewitt has been working internationally to help women in Iraq, but she says the achievements are not always noticed: 'I've been working for over a year now with a group of Iraqi women. I started with women who were in exile here, many of whom have gone back. We helped to organise the first Women of Iraq conference. And it was wonderful. There are now hundreds if not thousands of women's NGOs all over Iraq, whom we have helped to support in many different ways. And it's really, really exciting. And I'm now getting male colleagues saying, "It's really good that you did that, and kept on and on and on about it." '

Another Cabinet minister who listened to women and used her skills was Mo Mowlam. She used the skills of other women to take the peace talks forward: 'I used to talk to the women on the phone and say how great it was that they were there, and they really did make a difference because everybody else had set positions; the women came with ideas. It was wonderful. They also made sitting easier, because so many people would sit next to each other around the table. They didn't sit at the table very long anyway. But the women meant you could put people either side with no problem at all. The women were a great asset. And women carried the Good Friday Agreement. I don't know if you've seen the figures for that, but we had to get a majority of Protestants, Catholics and the south, and women made it such that there was a majority in each community, so it was due to the women's vote that we got it, so women did make a difference, both in the talks and in the referendum afterwards.'

Hazel Blears says she was ambitious for her constituents and their needs: 'I'm ambitious for the people I care about and I want them to get a better deal than they've ever had in the past, and I think you can be ambitious without putting other people down. And I think that one of the things that our Labour movement lost in the eighties was a sense that it was okay to be ambitious and it was out to aspire, and if you think about traditional Labour values, families always wanted their kids to do better than they did; they were ambitious for their families, and there's nothing wrong with that. They wanted them to be doctors, lawyers, to do well. They also wanted them to be happy, but I think we lost our way a bit and we found that ambition was somehow the preserve of the Tories, so I think that it's okay to be ambitious too.'

Women MPs effectively use Parliament as a platform on many levels. They champion causes that have come to light through their constituency work, bringing these to the chamber, and into select committees. One MP believes they have 'punched above their weight.' Fiona Mactaggart: 'I think, actually, although the media have not given us credit for this, we have punched above our weight. If you look at the way in which policies which specifically advantage women have been delivered by this government, the way in which we have gone further than our manifestos on things for women, for example women's representation, then, we have done.'

Are women less confrontational?

There is a stereotypical view that women are more consensual in their approach to politics; that they do not like the confrontation and jousting. Some firmly believe that to be the case but others would take issue with this view and point out that men may also find the aggressive approach to achieving political change difficult, and that women too can enjoy con-frontational politics. After all, they say, you do not go into politics if you cannot stand a good fight.

Annette Brooke thinks the public want to see a less confrontational style of politics: 'I'm convinced if we had more women in Parliament, it would be less confrontational, and I think the public would appreciate that there was serious debate going on and would perhaps get more involved; because I think there's a big problem in the way people do perceive politicians in Parliament at the moment, and I think a key to that improvement is actually to have more women in Parliament. I think people really like having a female MP – it's certainly my experience – feeling that they listen, are approachable, of which men can have those characteristics, but it does seem to make a difference.'

Glenda Jackson thinks women have certain characteristics in common, including a loathing of 'time wasting': 'Our side asks a question that shows our party in the best possible light, the opposition asks a question in trying to reduce that. I think most women – myself included – find that a complete and utter waste of time. Westminster wastes time. Absolutely wastes time. In a way that I think is antipathetical to most women. Because most women I know, have known all my life, have to be capable of doing at least eight different things at the same time, and doing them all well.'

Margaret Hodge thinks the environment you are in can influence how you behave: 'The adversarial politics of sitting opposite each other doesn't make good consensual and grown-up debate over very difficult issues, so it's difficult to move from the committee environment, which I had in the select committee, where you're sitting actually in a semicircle, not across the chamber from each other, it's difficult to move from that to a much more confrontational, debating sort of atmosphere and environment in the chamber.'

But that confrontational environment does not worry Ann Clwyd one bit: 'I hear people say, oh, they don't like things. The men shout and they don't like the barracking. Well, I think if you give as good as you get, and if you worked in journalism or in broadcasting you look on yourself as an equal. And so that never bothered me, I mean, you just give as good as you get. And I don't think one should be particularly concerned about that, you should be a lot more robust in answering back. And I quite enjoy the barracking.'

Louise Ellman agrees: 'I think the notion that women don't want conflict, and really if it was all women, everything would be solved, is really very superficial indeed. There are conflicts, there are choices to be made in life, and there are differences, and those have to be argued through, and it does arouse passions, and having passions is not wrong, but I think that shouting out things is just plain silly; but I don't think it is true to say that if everyone just got round the table and mainly women and just spoke nicely, then it would all be solved. I think the same problems would be there.'

Ann Taylor, who stood down in 2005 and is now in the Lords, does not believe she is more consensual in approach than her male colleagues: 'I don't think I am more consensual. If I think my party is wrong on something, I like to try to sort that out behind the scenes, rather than in a confrontational way within the party, but I have no problem with confrontational politics in terms of the other parties. What I don't like is confrontation within the party in public. That is something that I have no time for.'

Harriet Harman questions the validity of stereotypical attitudes to men and women's representation in politics: 'I think there are two stereotypes, one which is sort of the macho, competitive, adversarial kind of "male" model of politics, and the other which is consensus-building, outcome-focused, collaborative working behind the scenes rather than, you know, flashing yourself around publicly, supposedly the female model. I know that's the stereotype, but I think there are many women who behave in the former model and there are many men who behave in the female model. So I don't necessarily see that stereotype working in quite the same way; there are many aggressive women who are competitive with and undercut their colleagues, and there are also many gentle, caring, sharing, and outcome – focused, collaborative, unself-aggrandising men.'

However, Angela Eagle thinks the men are 'show–offs': 'I think that men tend to show off. I mean, the number of meetings I've been in where I've been maybe the only woman, and men will just talk, constantly, even though everything's been decided, and you think, Why don't you shut up?, and then you realise they're doing the peacock thing. Well, women don't behave like that. If something's decided, that's it; they want to go on to the next thing. They're much more practical, in some ways, like that. And less egotistical, as well, I think.'

Lorna Fitzsimons who lost her seat in 2005, also relishes a battle: 'I am a very confrontational politician, who's never held back saying hard truths to colleagues, would find it very, very hard to say that we find, as a gender, adversarial politics hard. I was brought up on adversarial politics, and sometimes I find them easier than consensual politics. I think the issue is that actually Parliament shouldn't pander to one or the other. People should be allowed to express themselves in the way that they are most comfortable with. Women are perceived, or expected to be, more caring and listening. Whether we are, I think you have to take on an individual basis.'

Despite the differences of views expressed over whether or not women are more consensual and less confrontational than men, there is a view that the way women do politics is more appealing to the public. Christine Russell: 'Well, I just don't think women resort to personality politics. I think, to be honest, there's a lot more integrity about women's politics. I think we seriously want to have intelligent discussions about the pros and cons of different policies, and not to indulge in sort of silly 'yah-boo' slanging matches between politicians. I think our nature is to actually try to do our best, and perhaps be collaborative and conciliatory and all these other qualities.'

Differences from men and fitting in

Women do perceive significant differences in their approach to politics from that of men. The women do not like political grandstanding as much as their male colleagues; they do not see themselves as being as 'clubbable', and they are not always as ambitious. That lack of ambition has been identified as a weakness. However, some believe that they do prepare more for debates and committees, and that they are more conscientious, but surprisingly less confident.

Estelle Morris did not want to fit in and become part of a 'blame culture'. 'So what happens if something goes wrong, you either blame the Civil Service, or you blame predecessors or you blame someone else. I could have done that with most of the incidences that led to my downfall, certainly the A-levels, which I never had ministerial responsibility for. I never did that in the whole of the three months. I might have gone to friends and said "Sod it, I didn't actually cause this," I never once during those three months said it publicly, I've never said it since, and I've never got anybody to tell the press that that was the case. I don't brief anyway. But we never did that; and I'm actually quite proud of that because shifting the blame to someone else could have been a way of surviving during those three months. It could have been a way of surviving, and I didn't do it and I didn't survive, but what it meant was when I walked out of the DFES, it was with huge affection; and they felt the sense of loss because I was somebody they enjoyed working with.'

Cheryl Gillan thinks women stick at it: 'Women are very persistent and tenacious, and I think that women – far more than men – when they hit their brick wall, stand back and think, Hmm now, can I tunnel under this brick wall, can I go round this brick wall; if I take a run at it can I get over it in one go? I think we're actually slightly better at working our way towards a goal after we've been initially told we can't do that, or it cannot be done.'

Vera Baird says: 'Don't be misled by the apparent, false confidence that men put on. A lot of women tend to downgrade their own abilities because they see men looking very confident. I have found in this place, men often act confident when they don't know anything about what they're talking about. I've heard people say the silliest things with sublime male confidence on their faces. Whereas I wouldn't dream of intervening or contributing to a debate unless I'd researched it to the nth degree.'

Claire Curtis-Thomas says women have a more direct approach to politics than men: 'Well, we're very different from the men, I think we're far more direct. It's not a coincidence that you've got a significant number of women running the committees, and we're seeing more of them as ministers, I mean we've got a far greater proportion of women as ministers than we should have. Now that may be – it probably is – a conscious decision to send clear messages that women are multi-tasked or multi-purposed individuals capable of doing many things at one time. It shows here.'

Julia Drown thinks women are good at getting people to work together: 'I've seen it in meetings where a man is getting everybody antagonistic over something, and I've been able to say the same thing, but calm people and bring people together, and maybe get people to come to more of an agreement on something. We're less scary. I obviously replaced a man, being the first woman MP for Swindon. I remember a few people coming to me saying, "I've always wanted to raise this, but I've never felt able to approach a man on it," but I think men could learn from that.'

Some believe that the women could learn from the approach of men too. Gisela Stuart: 'By and large, the men seem to be more successful in actually enjoying what this place [Westminster] has got to offer. And I really do think the women need to learn from that a bit more, and where I think the men could learn from the women is the competitive edge on always having to win; there are some things where it is important, but on others just ease up a bit.'

Theresa May thinks the differences attributed to the sexes are real: 'I would hope that there wasn't that much difference about it. I've always taken the view that women tend to be more interested in delivery, and less interested in talking about things. There's an obvious advantage to that, and the disadvantage to that is that when you're dealing with a lot of men, they prefer to have all the talking done; and I think that's one of the problems. Certainly I found in the past that I didn't probably do enough sort of going into corners with people and sitting down and talking to them about what was happening because I just wanted to get on with it and get it done.'

Some feel those marked differences work against women. Jenny Tonge: 'I'm now going to utter a heresy. I think sometimes women are their own worst enemy. I think they can back down very easily; they can take the easy line sometimes. They're not as combative or as competitive as men. We have so many other things in our lives; we have much more interesting lives than men anyway because of the emphasis on children and education, as well as all the other things we can do. So I think women are sometimes their own worst enemy.'

Mo Mowlam said that her experiences in Northern Ireland had taught her that it was not being a woman that made a difference to how she was perceived, but the social class she came from: 'It made it easier in the comparative sense, because before me, there'd only been patrician Tories and patrician Labour, and they weren't liked by the Irish, north or south. Well some of them were: there was the odd minister like Brian Mawhinney that people liked; the odd single one. But almost to a man, they had been patrician: "Blah, blah, blah, blah, very good to meet you," and that used to get right up Irish people's noses.'

Some see women as being less egotistical than their male colleagues. Helen Liddell, who stood down in 2005, says: 'Many of the women who came in, particularly in 1997, fought extremely hard to get in here, and they come from constituencies that have not traditionally been Labour. They work very hard in their constituencies, and know what their constituents want, and I think women have less of an ego than men do. Men usually have to have their ego stroked and they don't like the idea of having to be taken in and talked to; whereas I think that women make their mind up and get on with it.'

Others believe women are better at team working. Christine Russell thinks: 'There is the gender difference of how women and men operate, and I just feel in general that women are much better at teamworking. And if you want to get something through it's, "Well, we need to get Education supporting this, we need to get Social Services supporting this, we need to get Health supporting it, we need to get other public agencies supporting it."'

Anne Begg agrees: 'I think women probably are more collegiate, and I think women will also look for solutions. I don't think we always necessarily dig our heels in and say, "Right, we either get our way or we're not shifting." I think women are much more open to negotiation than the men are. Men sometimes see that as a weakness. I'm generalising here, of course; but I think women are more interested in getting a result and getting something solved rather than necessarily standing on their dignity.'

Those changes have often been felt most in the select committees where women feel they have brought a new approach to conducting business, asking questions and setting the agenda. Dari Taylor: 'I do think that to feminise the arguments in Defence has been very valuable. I think Rachel Squires now does a very good job in Defence. So I think the debates needed feminising. I think the debates need to be far less aggressive. I think the debates need to be a lot more constructive.'

Sally Keeble thinks that generation is as important as gender: 'I think there's a generational issue about the men, really, because I don't notice huge differences in the attitudes in quite a lot of the younger men. Of course, some people are going to have different views because some people are always different. But, comparing notes with a lot of the men who came in, in 1997, the younger men have got a lot of the same issues, and a lot of the same attitudes.'

Anne McGuire thinks women in the Commons have made men 'softer'. They even praise one another now: 'I think they've softened a bit – I don't mean that they go round giving people cuddles – but I think that there's a bit more praise going around sometimes. I think, for the most part, women are keen to say, "Well done." I think women are quite good at giving compliments to each other and to male colleagues, and I think a bit of that's rubbed off. I mean, that almost sounds superficial, but it changes the culture a wee bit.'

Barbara Follett thinks men have constructed the political game to be 'dangerous' and that women do not warm to this approach: 'Politics is a male game, and I use that word "game" very advisedly. What people do is they pad it out, the joust, and it was quite unusual when they had that many women in, that the women did not do what most men do. When you talk to a man, they say, 'oh, you've got to make it really dangerous for X to do something you disagree with.' Now for a woman; women don't think like that. Women think, we've got to make you see why what you're doing is wrong, not make it dangerous for you to do it.'

Eleanor Laing is surprised that women are not more ambitious: 'If you were to ask most men who are MPs "Do you want to be in the Cabinet?" most of them would say, "Of course I do," but women, being rather more self-deprecating, don't say, "Yes, I want to be in the Cabinet, yes, I'm going to be in the Cabinet." I find it quite hard to say that, because it seems quite arrogant somehow, and I don't think I am arrogant, but if I'm being honest, I would like to be in the Cabinet, yes. I would like to play an important role in the future government of my country.'

Angela Eagle also thinks it is time that women started to build a 'power base' within their parties to further their ambitions: 'If you look at Estelle [Morris] and what's happened to her, if you look at particularly Mo Mowlam and what happened to her – I mean, there was a period of time after the Northern Ireland Good Friday Agreement, when she had a chance to do organisation in the party . . . she wasn't prepared to do it because she had got where she had got by always nominating the man who was going to be the leader of the party and being around and being useful in that way. But at some stage, you have to strike out on your own to establish a base. I don't think it comes naturally to women to think, "Okay, right, now I've got to go off and factionalise." '

Gwyneth Dunwoody remembers her battle when she walked into the smoke room, a room even Margaret Thatcher found difficult to gain acceptance in: 'When I walked into the smoke room, this was regarded as very odd, that women should come into the smoke room, and all sorts of jocular remarks were made that indicated that women didn't normally come in there . . . they didn't want me there. But I said, "Tough. I'm coming in," and I made it very clear to them; I went in every day. So of course they stopped bothering about it.'

Helen Liddell now uses the smoke room, much as the men once did: 'The smoke room is a room that looks very much like a room in a London club, it's all leather sofas, and it's where the grandees used to retire for their cigars after dinner. But it's actually the only place where you can just sit in a sofa and be comfortable with your friends; maybe have a glass of wine or something. There's no other place where as Members you can do that because once you're in the public bits of the building you are on parade, there is no place you can really relax with your own colleagues. So now it is very much colonised by women who use it as freely as the men do. But all the grandees have taken themselves off elsewhere, and I have no idea where they've gone and no desire to find out.'

Some have at times found that 'club' atmosphere lonely. Ann Cryer: 'Sometimes it is a lonely place. It just happens, sometimes you get here, and you don't seem to see anyone who is a friend of yours, or a colleague that you work with on a particular issue. And next day can be the complete opposite, you can't move for people that you need to have a chat with about this or about that. I suppose it's like working in a biggish factory really, there are a lot of people, but at any given time you might or might not be surrounded by people who you feel comfortable talking to.'

Tessa Jowell explains how the appearance of a woman can make it hard for her to gain acceptance: 'Wearing the wrong clothes, having the wrong kind of voice, having wet consonants; all those kinds of things. The level of occupational abuse is – if you really take it seriously – well, you'd never get out of bed. So you don't take it seriously. But it is an occupational hazard.'

Eventually acceptance is achieved. Jean Corston, who is now in the Lords, says: 'I remember one particular day, I had drafted an Early Day Motion, and I was taking it round the tearoom to get my Labour colleagues to sign it, and it was being passed round the tables as I stood there, and they were carrying on with their conversations and they were all signing it. So I said to one of them, "Don't you want to read it?" and he said, "Did you draft it?" and I said "Yes," and he said, "That's what we thought, so it will be all right." And I suddenly realised this was about acceptance, and in a sense that somehow I and others had got to a place beyond gender.'

Virginia Bottomley knew when she had crossed the threshold with her male colleagues and been accepted: 'I was accepted by a kind of boys' club: Ian Gough MP, Nicholas Soames MP, various others, who didn't really approve of having women in the regiment, somehow, took me under their wing and I was thought to be acceptable.'

Some point to a very 'male' way of doing politics, which involves being a member of a club that is almost sycophantic in its support for each other. Teresa Gorman is blunt about how she first perceived the club worked: 'How you get on in politics is this: you don't offend, you butter people up, you get to be made their factotum, which is therir so-called parliamentary private secretary [PPS], which is slave labour, it's not a paid job. You stand around pouring their drinks when they have little get-togethers with their backbenchers who they want to get onside, and then you gradually get made into somebody else's PPS, a ministerial PPS, and so on. But the whole system depends on you being able to butter up people along the line. Because nobody wants somebody in their wake who is going to put them into the shadows. You have to suppress your personality in the hopes of getting promotion. That's how it's done.'

Baroness Golding learnt from a man that it is best not to be seen as being too clever: 'I learnt his [my father's] technique for taking people with you who were against you. Being pleasant, and not too clever, and always giving them a way out, so that they feel they've won a little bit, even though you've won the most.'

The increased visual representation of women in Westminster is important to women both inside and outside Parliament, and undoubtedly helps them to gain acceptance. Lorna Fitzsimons: 'I think that we bring a very important dimension to Parliament, because Parliament now looks a bit more like society, and when I first got elected, there was a wonderful group of women, that had never been involved in politics before, held a street party for me in 1997, and they said to me, "Look, Lorna, politics now looks like us. The House of Commons looks like us." '

Ann Taylor has worked slowly to establish her political career and to fit in: 'I've kind of taken it incrementally, it had to be possible to live in the north and be a woman, it had to be possible to live in the north, be a woman and have children . . . and be on the front bench, it had to be possible to do all that and then be in government. You just add and juggle. Yes, you need a cooperative partner and maybe not everybody's as lucky as I've been in that respect, but it is also a question of juggling and being willing to make your own priorities that allow all of those things to take place.'

Nagging ministers to achieve change

It may be a male word that is applied as a derogatory term to women but women MPs themselves admit that they 'nag' when they want to change their ministers' minds on an issue. They collar them in the lobby, they request meetings with them and they persist in putting across their point of view.

Vera Baird explains: 'How do I persuade them to come round to my side? Well I think I just nag. I find the right people who are likely to be interested in the issue; I marshal outside lobbyists so that it's not just some quirky idea from Redcar, and try to present cogent arguments to my friends and colleagues who are in the government at all levels – with a measure of success. It's a listening government, truly, whatever everyone says.'

Fiona Mactaggart doesn't mind using the word 'nag' either: 'I'm still an advocate of the way that women go about these things, which is by nagging. You know, that's a very male word to describe it, but just being quietly persistent and banging on for a long time, and adapting a bit and just being a bore about something. Actually, it's one of the reasons why we've got such significant changes on family-friendly working, on child benefit, on things that really, really make a profound difference.'

The Lobby is one place that nagging works best, and working out where to stand is advisable. Maria Eagle: 'When we had a chance to vote for electronic voting by pressing buttons in Lobbies, I voted against it, and that's because the thing about voting through the Lobby is it's the only time when you can see ministers . . . There are a couple of places to stand in the Lobbies where, if you need to see a minister, they cannot get past you without you being able to grab them. You can only get that happening when votes occur and everybody has to go through the Lobby, and I believe in that very strongly. I know from some of the things I did as a backbencher, I couldn't have done it without being able to grab ministers in the Lobby, so I think it's tremendously important that everybody has to go there at the same time to vote.'

Women have gradually developed a distinct and different way of doing politics from their male colleagues. Early on, they began to see themselves as 'social entrepreneurs' who listen to what their constituents have to say and work hard to develop strategies to bring about the desired improvements. That may mean they have to nag, collar ministers in the Lobby or write letters and request meetings with the relevant secretaries of state, talk to other ministers, or network with one another to bring about those changes. By listening and learning from people's real experiences and then translating them, they have strived to change policy. It may not be an entirely new approach, but the number of women in Westminster since 1997 has allowed it to flourish.

FOUR

Overcoming sexism

Battle of the sexes

The 120 women MPs of 1997 represented a sea change for British politics. Labour's policy of all-women shortlists had not only succeeded at getting a record 101 Labour women into the Commons but also a significant number of younger women. It was not just their gender that threatened some of their older male colleagues but also their age. However it was their sheer number that proved most threatening to an institution that had a reputation for being a London gentleman's club, or as some would allege, the biggest boys drinking club in the West.

Joan Ruddock thinks 1997 was definitely a watershed both for women and for some male MPs too: 'There has been slow incremental change during the whole of the time I have been in Parliament. But the very big significant change was the election of the 120 women in 1997, and that was a turning point. It just meant that in sheer force of numbers there were more women to stand up for women. There were more women always in the chamber at any time, there were more women on committees, and so it was less easy for men to express their sexist remarks. Also, it shouldn't be forgotten that there were a lot of newer younger men with different attitudes coming into the Commons.'

That sexism begins even before women politicians get to Westminster and is inherent in the parties' election procedures. Research on selection systems has concluded that British political parties are 'institutionally sexist' and that the Conservative culture was the most hostile to women. [14]

Biographies and autobiographies of some of our best-known politicians record how women politicians of the past were treated in the chamber.

Barbara Castle once wrote of the time when George Brown had tried to 'unbutton the back of my blouse' during a 10 p.m. vote on her Transport Bill.[15] Certainly in 1997 it was clear that some of those sexist attitudes still prevailed. Women MPs from earlier intakes have numerous stories to tell.

Teresa Gorman had been an MP for ten years when Labour's landslide victory of 1997 put more women into Westminster than ever before: 'I was chatted up, I might tell you, by any number; because, by 10 p.m. some of these blokes are desperate. On one occasion, I had a wonderful bright red, shiny raincoat and I ran through the chamber late, I ran over from my house . . . and of course it was raining. I came in with this red, shiny raincoat, and as I pushed my way through the Lobby, which was crammed with men waiting to vote, it was electric. Every eye swivelled to look at me in that raincoat. And on another occasion, I came back from a do. I was at a function, wearing some eveningy thing that had quite a low décolleté, if that's the right word. And so my cleavage was showing. And again, the same thing; the eyes of all those middle-aged men as I passed swivelled. It was extraordinary. I think because by that time, they're sex-starved by ten or eleven in the evening. It's a case of any port in a storm.'

Jean Corston recalls how men resented the presence of women in the House: 'I heard one say to the other, "Look at this, the place is filling up with women." Now, there were about 600 men and 50 women, and it really astonished me that he resented the fact that there were just a few of us there. God knows what he would have made of today. It was April 1992 and he sounded just like Sir Basil on *The Herbs*, and I just thought, This is bizarre, I didn't think people like this still existed. I thought they were characters in Anthony Powell's books.'

Dawn Primarolo came into the Commons in 1987. She was the target of so many sexist taunts and jibes that even women from other parties made a point of sitting with her when she was in the chamber to support her: 'Well, it is a culture of intimidation that some Members of the House, for some strange reason, thought that that's how Members of Parliament should behave. I wouldn't want to subscribe that view to all Members of the House of Commons, because that simply isn't the case, but of course you only needed a few to behave like that.' The taunting was so serious on occasions that Dawn came close to resigning from her seat: 'I think actually my worst experiences were when I came close to thinking that I should walk away, that I could not stand the constant barracking and attempts to undermine me as a new minister . . . They are shocking, but I just cannot allow it to get any credence and my own personal view is that I cannot allow a scintilla of doubt or for them to see me hesitate or to think that they've actually got to me, and so I don't then repeat stories, but I've been well supported by women in the chamber.'

Julia Drown was 35 years old when she was elected to Westminster in 1997. It seems the younger women MPs were picked on most: 'I was certainly subject to the louder noise that comes from the opposition when women stand up, compared with equivalent men. And that was noticeable, and relatively more jeers . . .' Julia thinks those sexist taunts are still present today: 'I wouldn't be surprised if someone measured the decibels on average, and you looked at equivalent men and women in terms of how long they've been here, you would still see it. It was absolutely clear in 1997, absolutely clear.'

Patricia Hewitt also believes it was younger women who received most of the sexist banter: 'Now by the time I became an MP I was a bit old for this stuff. But my younger colleagues, young attractive women, particularly in the first term, were getting these – well, I'd better not be rude about other Members of Parliament – but you know, would get particularly Conservative male MPs who'd had a good dinner, coming in and making the most offensive, sexist remarks. There's less of that now that we stop at 7 p.m., and I think it's a great advantage.'

Rosemary McKenna noticed how bad the behaviour was: '. . . no names, no, but it was clear where it originated and what was happening, and some of our young women suffered very badly from that; gestures across the chamber, quite offensive, especially if you're trying to make a speech and make a serious speech, so there were a lot of difficulties over that first year, and the women sort of hung together a lot, gave each other strength and support that you really need to have to face up to that. This is a big, big world; this is a big, big chamber where the eyes of the world are on what happens in the House of Commons, so you're very conscious of that all the time, so it was very, very difficult coming in.'

Barbara Follett recalls how some Conservative men resorted to sexist gestures as well as remarks: 'I do remember some Conservatives, whenever a

Labour woman got up to speak, they would take their breasts – their imaginary breasts in their hands and wiggle them and say, "Melons" as we spoke.'

Phyllis Starkey thought the sexist behaviour was unacceptable: 'They also said things which would be inappropriate on a building site and certainly totally inappropriate in the House of Commons . . . It was surprising rather than difficult. I mean in my professional background, I've always worked in an environment where there's a majority of men in a scientific set-up, but I'd influenced that sort of behaviour, and it was a shock, it was shocking, literally shocking to me, to have such remarks made by people I perceived to be professional persons.'

Beverley Hughes remembers how personal those remarks were: '. . . Some of the comments that were made at that time were very, very personal, about a woman's shape, or her hair, or her face, or her clothes, and that's not normal, that's not done *vis-à-vis* men. But it was done about women; the size of their breasts and things like that.'

Gisela Stuart experienced problems over a pair of shoes: 'I came into the House and I was wearing red shoes, and one of the officers of the House said, '"Remind me, is it red shoes no knickers or red hat no knickers?" At the time I said nothing and just walked on. I thought it was so unbelievably outrageous. And then I thought, What would my predecessor have done? and I thought she would have done a coquettish giggle, and my instincts were to come back like the harridan, and I thought then I would have completely fallen into what they thought we were. But that was in the first six months when this place was quite horrified at the sheer numbers of us, and they didn't know what to do with all these women. I remember one moment in the library, the Members' library when someone turned round and said, "God, there are women everywhere now." But that's completely, utterly, totally gone. And so it was a brief shock where, I suppose, I thought it was horrible. But you couldn't even imagine it now.'

Helen Liddell recalls how they used video footage of the chamber to show Conservative whips what was happening in order to get them to stop the sexist behaviour: 'I think having more women has made a definite difference, the place is less macho than it was when I first came in, in 1994. There are no "no-go" areas for women. When I first came in I didn't dare go into the smoke room, for example, and it was the Labour women who sort of occupied that and got squatters rights. But you don't have that terribly negative macho environment. When we were first elected in 1997, such a huge number of women, it was sometimes very difficult for some of my younger colleagues who were getting cat-called every time they stood up to speak. But some of the older hands used the videos that we have running here all the time to show opposition whips just what their members were doing, and it's got a bit easier since then.'

Some thought the Speaker Betty Boothroyd should have taken a firmer line on it. Rosemary McKenna was shocked by the behaviour: 'It was gestures and comments across the chamber, and unfortunately, the Speaker and Deputy-Speakers didn't deal with it firmly and quickly enough.'

The Labour women were in no doubt as to who made the most sexist taunts. The behaviour of the Conservative MP Nicholas Soames shocked many of them. Jackie Ballard: 'Oh, he often made jibes at women that didn't get into Hansard, because they were muttered in a low voice that you could hear if you were sitting alongside, but the Hansard writers wouldn't hear, or the Speaker wouldn't hear.' Those sexist remarks were of a very personal nature: 'Sexist remarks, maybe about someone's legs or someone being a lesbian – the sort of thing that if he worked for me he'd probably be sacked, actually. And that's the thing about Westminster and the chamber, that the behaviour falls way below the standards that you would allow in any workplace, particularly in terms of use of sexist language and so on. Maybe it's changed in the last few years, but that was how it was when I was there.'

Jackie has one particularly vivid memory of Nicholas Soames' behaviour. 'The worst was a debate in the evening, I can't remember what on earth it was about, and Nicholas Soames sprawled across the benches, obviously having had, as they say, "a very good dinner", and interrupting this debate with meaningless drivel.' She goes on to say that Nicholas Soames was not the only culprit.

Dawn Primarolo says that the sexist behaviour upset her: 'In any other workplace, it would fall into one of two categories: bullying or harassment, and that's sexual harassment . . . I suppose it's a responsibility; it's not that I don't talk privately to my friends, it's not that it's not reduced me to tears in the past, because it has in private, but a responsibility to confront and stop that form of action, because we absolutely have to demonstrate that this is not how people should behave, we're not putting up with it and it's going to stop.' She continues: 'So, I've developed strategies, as other women have, for dealing with it, and I have to say, on the whole – I mean, sometimes they say things now, but it's moved much more into jest, and it's now on that thin line, "You haven't got a sense of humour if you think that." I think they would accuse you of not having a sense of humour if you took umbrage at it.'

Dawn's colleagues across the parties also wanted to put a stop to the behaviour of Nicholas Soames. They took to taunting him with comments his ex-wife had made about their love life together. Barbara Follett explains: 'We devised the little click gesture, because . . . his ex-wife had this story that being made love to by Nicholas Soames was like having a very large wardrobe with a very small key falling on top of you. So we'd go, "Click", and it stopped.'

Jean Corston encountered sexism early in her parliamentary career: 'I don't think the sexism shocked me, because I was born in the 1940s, but it was something I hadn't heard for quite a long time. I suppose part of me thought I was going to be coming to something halfway between a public school and a gentlemen's club, and I was right, because that's how it was.'

Baroness Boothroyd says she did not witness some of the worst of Nicholas Soames' behaviour: 'I didn't see that. If I did, I would stop it right away. I can't comment because I didn't see, but I do remember on one occasion . . . I don't know whether it was anything to do with the women, I don't think it was, but Nicholas rather misbehaved. I don't know what he said, but I reprimanded him and he came to the Chair to apologise . . .'

The sexism directed at women can take other forms too. Sometimes it can be downright tasteless remarks like an occasion when Lady Hermon was talking about Alzheimer's disease: 'I was very displeased and irritated to have a gentleman colleague say to me, "Oh yes, but you're experienced in that." And I just thought, first of all, it was an unnecessary slur on my dear husband, who has Alzheimer's, but it was completely unnecessary in the context; but the fact that that was joined with laughter and banter from other colleagues did not entertain or amuse me at all. And I had it repeated later. It was most unfortunate. I rise above it. I said, "Well actually, that would never be the case," and I was very stony-faced as the remark was made. It was very ill judged, but as I say, to have it repeated later was most unfortunate. I just refuse – refuse – to go down to that sort of level and to be diminished by those sorts of petty, nasty little comments.'

Glenda Jackson found that some male MPs had problems with her past career in acting: 'I had a double-edged whammy here, because I was not only female, I was also an ex-actress. And those are two contemptible positions to be in, in this place. And I think that certainly, this is still the case, and this cuts across all parties; there is absolutely no difference. I don't care how much the party may proselytise or present it is committed to equal opportunity, that it wants, whatever is, "affirmative action" to increase the number of women members. There is no basic fundamental change, as far as this place is concerned. Now there may be fundamental changes in the relevant political parties in the country, although I have to say I haven't come across it very markedly, but certainly within this chamber, if there is an opportunity for a male to make some remark which is based on an MP's gender, they will make it.' Glenda gives a first-hand account: 'What I'm talking about is on the actual exchanges in the chamber, where if a male Member of Parliament disagrees with a point, or simply wants to make some kind of a cheap point for themselves, they will use gender. I mean, the most recent example happened directly to myself. It was a debate – no, I think it was – it might have been defence questions, and it had to do with whether we were going to change one of our radar facilities to accommodate Bush's sky-wars project. And someone had made a point that radar had won the second world war, or won the Battle of Britain for us. And I stood up and said that I understood that it wasn't only radar, but it was also the pilots. And somebody then stood up and countered that. And a Conservative MP, from a sedentary position which as you know means they're sitting down, said, "Stick to what you know, Glenda." Now, I have never spoken to that MP directly. I would never address him by his Christian name. I would expect him to address me in the way that I think people should. But . . . none of those things apply. And, you know, there've been far worse things said to women in the chamber.'

Dari Taylor had a similar experience to Glenda in a defence debate when she intervened on one male MP who was speaking about women on the front lines: '. . . I made the point to him that he was speaking from a very chauvinistic perspective that didn't reference the way that the armed forces were there to select the talented and the best, whether they were women or men, black or white was irrelevant, and wouldn't he agree? I sat down and his response was, "I would only choose to quote a medieval monk to the Honourable Lady, who said, 'To be with a woman for 24 hours and not to make love to her was an outrageous proposition.'" I was up on my feet like you didn't know and I said, "Would the Honourable Gentleman give way?" and of course he did, and this time, I really gave him what for.'

Parties and sexism

The sexism that the Labour women MPs of 1997 experienced did not just come from the Conservative Party but from their own side too. One woman MP of 1997 said off-the-record how a member of her own government had attacked her when she and other women were elected to the committee that represents Labour backbench politicians, the Parliamentary Labour Party or PLP. The domination of women on the committee had not been done deliberately. She explains: 'The Parliamentary Committee is a committee that's elected in the Labour Party of six of your peers to represent the Parliamentary Labour Party on an annual basis to the prime minister and the government and the party. So, every year we have an election and six backbench colleagues are elected, and they sit on the committee for a year, and at the first ever election . . . five women were elected and Chris Mullin was the only man . . . [one MP] came up to me and literally pinned me by my neck up against the wall in the lobby and screamed at me and he said, "You've done it now, you've done it now!"'

There were similar hostilities expressed in Wales when Labour's women MPs had fought for a system of 'twinning' to allow more women into the Welsh Assembly. Parliamentary seats are paired so that one constituency must select a man and the other a woman. One Welsh woman MP said off-the-record: 'Well, of course it was a hard fight. We were fighting the establishment, effectively, in Wales . . . I remember distinctly at the debate in the Conference at the time, working with my colleagues, running around talking to people . . . We had one or two other notables, and heads of trade unions, in a huddle, absolutely working frantically to stop this vote going for twinning. And we won. And we won narrowly. And it was a tremendous victory . . . But I think historically, that will be seen as a tremendous achievement.'

Harriet Harman says there was an attitude that the women MPs were only in Westminster by virtue of their sex: 'I think there are a lot of sexist attitudes. One of the sexist attitudes I met was, "Well, you've only succeeded because you're a woman", not, "You've succeeded despite being a woman and having young children", that somehow this gave me a "privileged" status. I remember one of my colleagues, who currently is actually in the Cabinet, said, "Oh well, I'll never be in the Cabinet because I'm not wearing a skirt." And I thought, 'That's very odd because most Cabinets include everybody except people wearing skirts.'

Teresa Gorman noted how sexist her own Conservative Party was to women. She says a colleague once said to her: '"the Tory Party hates women, Teresa, they hate women." I can remember her saying that to me, and that was someone who was a classical middle-class, well-connected, orthodox Tory type individual.'

Conservative women have looked to their Labour colleagues for support at times. Jean Corston: 'The worst remarks that I heard of were relayed to me by one particular Conservative woman . . . Teresa Gorman – who used to talk to me, and I remember Edwina Currie once saying to me, "You're quite lucky, you're a Labour Member. You don't have to put up with some of the crap that we put up with," and I do think that they have got a bigger problem than us. But personally, I don't think I was ever the butt of a sexist remark.'

Angela Eagle thinks the Labour Party began to defeat such attitudes to women in the mid-eighties: 'I think the big wave against racism happened in the seventies, led by people like Joan Lester, and the big feminisation began to happen, led by the following generation, in the mid-eighties onwards, and that has become accepted. It helps when it's led, but I think it's part of a process – it's like pushing on an open door; it's great to do it, but you have to push on it, you can't just leave it, you've got to press ahead.'

Jenny Tonge thinks there is some degree of sexism in her party [Liberal Democrat] still: 'There's a bit of resistance to putting women into the key posts, I think. That might be being a bit unfair. But I think there is a bit of resistance. And I think the Labour Party have been magnificent about that.

Absolutely magnificent. Like them or not, Blair has made sure that women have gone into key posts and key roles, they've all had their chance. He's been very good.'

Sandra Gidley refuses to 'cluster' next to her leader so that there appears to be more women in the Liberal Democrat Party than there really are: 'We were always being asked – the women – to stand close to Charles [Kennedy] so that it looked like we had more women in the party, and I refused to do that. I will stand naturally where I end up, which may on occasion be close or not, but if anyone asks me to move to the centre, I refuse. And it may sound petty, but hey, you know, there are other ways of appealing to women. We've only got one woman, that's myself, in the shadow Cabinet.'

Jackie Ballard tells how two women from other parties, Labour's Harriet Harman and the Conservative's Gillian Shephard came to support her when she encountered sexism in her own party when she stood for the leadership of the Liberal Democrats: 'I felt that it was important for the party that there was a woman candidate, that it wasn't the same old few men standing and that that was the image that should be portrayed of the Party. And when I did that, there were some men – both within my party and outside my party – whose attitude was: "what sort of upstart are you to think after you've been in Parliament for five minutes you can stand for the leadership of the party?" and were quite dismissive. But there were women – and I would single out Gillian Shepherd from the Conservatives and Harriet Harman from Labour, and quite a lot of other Labour people – who were particularly supportive and would put an arm on your shoulder and say, "Well done, go for it, good luck," and I found that very encouraging.'

Vera Baird thinks that discrimination is often based on class as well as gender but says that in the Commons she has found more support among women colleagues than she did as a barrister at the Bar. She says: 'I'm a working-class woman, unskilled working-class. And most of the Bar is not; most of the bar is fairly posh. And here, in the Labour Party, a lot of the women are like me. And so you've got more friends than you have at the Bar. Because fairly posh women who've had a silver-spoon upbringing don't really appreciate the difficulties women face because they fit that kind of Margaret Thatcher mould. But here, women from working-class backgrounds who are now successful do appreciate the difficulties women face. So I think there's a broader range of support here than there ever was for women at the Bar.'

Virginia Bottomley thinks that Margaret Thatcher was a role model for women in her party and for other politicians: 'The role model of Margaret Thatcher was characteristic of that type who is the first one to break through all the barriers, and in nearly every profession, the first woman through is not somebody who has spent all their time supporting others, in the same way as David Blunkett doesn't spend his time developing opportunities for people with disabilities. It's an interesting phenomenon that the first person through does it on their own, without making heavy weather of human rights and equal opportunities. But the fact that they've got through that ceiling is a fantastic opportunity for everybody else that comes behind. And the next wave are people who are much more likely to spend time thinking about their peer group, coaching, supporting, mentoring . . .'

Labour's Ann Clwyd has mixed feelings about the image of Margaret Thatcher as a typical woman: 'I remember one time they were peddling a myth that Margaret Thatcher had succeeded; that when she was a young working chemist, she used to come home and look after the twins . . . I remember this particular quote, that she'd put her apron on over her hat and her coat. Now, for the wife of a man who was then a millionaire, the idea that this was the sort of Thatcher household at work, was clearly ludicrous, and one wanted to poke a big pin into that kind of myth . . . She had no women on her Cabinet, and there were some good Tory women who should have had a place in that Cabinet.'

Two women who have experienced personal difficulties with their constituency Labour Party think that sexist attitudes are still present. Helen Clark, who survived de-selection attempts by her own party but lost her seat in 2005, says: 'They [party members] may well say, "Oh, we'd like a woman. We'd like a woman, you know, that makes us look all modern and trendy on the doorstep." Soon as they've got the woman, they then try, and it's quite universal . . . They then try and go about controlling you and getting what they want, etc. And when you actually turn out to have that independence of mind, for which they selected you in the first place, then it's scheming, undermining, trying to get rid of you . . . It's just bloody appalling, quite frankly. I mean, basically, what's happening now is the reselection procedure is being used as a wonderful opportunity for institutionalised bullying, and particularly against women.'

Jane Griffiths, who was deselected as a candidate by her own Labour Party, has had similar difficulties: 'Scratch the surface of I think any political party and what they want is white men to do their bidding, and when they get uppity women, they don't like it. They would deny it, but that's how it is.'

Conservative women in the John Major government of the 1990s thought he was very supportive of women in general. Virginia Bottomley: 'John Major was somebody who supported women, promoted women, was comfortable with women, and in his Cabinet there was always a lesser sense of the sort of macho environment, albeit they discussed cricket scores rather than football.' Gillian Shephard says: 'John Major was one of those men who truly did not see the difference between men and women. He really, really was a new man in that respect. There was no anti-women trace of attitude in him.'

Sexism then and now

The sexist remarks do not just come from men; they are also sometimes made by women too. One Cabinet minister told how her rise in the ministerial ranks was met with scepticism by one of her female colleagues. Off-the-record she says: 'When I first became a parliamentary secretary . . . [a female colleague] did say to me, "Oh, you've had a very fast rise", something like, "Who have you been sleeping with?"'

It shocked Gillian Shephard to be called 'Betty' by her male colleagues when she first entered the House in 1987. She was even more shocked to find that the women did it too. She recalls: 'This is a rather horrid story, but it is true. When I was first here, there was a Conservative MP who was a back-bencher, but rather a prominent one, and he called us all Betty. And when I said, "Look, you know, my name isn't Betty," he said, "Ah but you're all the same, so I call you all Betty, it's easier." However, I can cap this because for the first two years I was in Parliament, my contemporary, who entered with me as a Conservative MP, Emma Nicholson, called me Elizabeth; I suppose because she couldn't be bothered to find out what my real name was.'

Glenda Jackson notices how women are trivialised by her male colleagues because attention is paid to what they are wearing rather than what they are saying: 'I can remember one of my own colleagues saying to me one day, "Did you see Margaret Beckett at the dispatch box today?" and I said, "Yes." And he said, "Do you think she should have worn short-sleeves?" and I looked at this guy, a supposed adult. Margaret Beckett, standing at a dispatch box, in a short-sleeved suit jacket, and that was deemed to be worthy of comment or concern? I mean, come on.'

Other women MPs new to the House in the 1980s were also shocked by the sexism they encountered in their own parties. Virginia Bottomley: 'As a woman, it was extraordinary; I'd always worked, I'd always worked with blokes. I didn't see that the difference between a man and a woman was very great. I wore a grey suit, a black suit or a navy-blue suit with three buttons at the wrist, or four, and a small tie, you know, with a tidy bow; but I felt like an alien person, and people like Keith Joseph would always say things like, "That's a very pretty dress you're wearing," as opposed to, "What did you think about the speech?" and I understood how excessive gallantry is really a form of sexual harassment.'

Sue Doughty, who lost her seat in 2005, thinks sexist attitudes still prevail today particularly in the north: 'From the past, both in time and in geography . . . they [men] would be saying, "but who's going to look after the children? Who's going to cook the dinner? I will expect the food on the table at this time." And I've had that. But I think in the north still, somehow, you're doing things because a man lets you. I think that still exists in some parts of the north, as it exists in some parts of the south, I think particularly amongst certain age groups; less so with younger people. I think men realise that women have a choice, and you know, they may very well say, "I'd rather do what I want to do than do it with you." And that's a thing that men have had to get used to. But certainly it's been a lot longer coming in the north.'

Those sexist attitudes in a household can mean that some women don't vote. Jackie Lawrence: 'If there's one thing that gets me annoyed, when I go out campaigning on the doorstep, is when you knock on someone's door and a woman comes to the door, and says, "Oh, I don't bother voting." It makes my blood boil, because I'd love to drag them to this place, and show them the history, and take them round to the cupboard in the Chapel, St Mary Undercroft, and show them the cupboard that Emily Wilding Dayton hid in so that she could put on the census that her address in 1911 was the House of Commons. And the fight that's gone on.'

Men too can be disadvantaged by sexist attitudes; Meg Munn points out: 'Two things I would say about being a woman: one is that, as you can see today, here I am in a dress on a hot day, sleeveless dress and no tights and all the rest of it, I can go in the chamber and I can sit there and nobody will say a word. If a man goes in without his tie or without his jacket on he will be told to leave the chamber, which demonstrates that as far as the codes are traditional and stuffy and all the rest of it, what they demonstrate is that as far as the traditions of Westminster are concerned, women still don't exist.'

Margaret Hodge remembers how sexist the attitudes were when she stood for selection as a candidate: "When I went for my seat, I was the only person asked – because the children were still relatively young – how I would manage. I was actually asked, at the selection meeting, how I would manage with the children if I became an MP. No man was asked that.'

Christine Russell had her all-women shortlist nomination contested but was still selected by her party. Even so, she still experiences sexism today. She explains: 'I was selected twice; I was selected first of all from an all-women shortlist, but then, before my nomination was ratified by the NEC, the successful challenge came from the two guys at the employment tribunal, so the contest in Chester was re-opened. So, of course, I then had men throwing their hats in the ring, and I actually won the second, so I was selected twice, but there are still those that persist in saying that, "Oh, all these women have just catapulted, parachuted into Parliament, didn't deserve to get there because all of these good men were denied the opportunity," and that is such a load of baloney . . . The accusation is still made, and it's still made locally by male members of the Labour Party in Chester today.'

Jane Griffiths thinks the Labour Party is still openly sexist: 'My former Constituency Party Chair went to the senior officials of the Labour Party nationally and said they didn't want to have a woman MP any more, because they didn't really feel that Reading was really ready for a woman MP, and they should just stick with one male MP. They were sent away with a flea in their ear, but that was in 2000 that was said, so those attitudes are still there.'

Bridget Prentice came up against sexism in the corridors of Westminster: 'Along came one of the security guards . . . I was on one side of the corridor, he was on the other, and he looked at me and said, "Can I help you, madam?" and I said "No, no, it's fine, no problem," and he said, "Do you have a pass, madam?" And I said, "Yes, I do, but it's in my bag because I lost it a few weeks ago and now I kind of keep it in a safe place." I know that sounds daft, but that was what I did. And then he said, "And is your husband a Member, madam?" At which point Jim [my husband] said, "Bridget, just go," because he could see me just about to explode . . . it would be highly unlikely that they'd say something like that now.'

Some women MPs don't think they have experienced sexism in their careers. Gwyneth Dunwoody: 'I was always treated with equality by my colleagues in the Labour Party, even some of the men who were subsequently damned as being sexist were really very fair in their treatment, because they treated you as an equal. They didn't treat you as a sort of special quality that had to be handled with kid gloves.'

Hilary Armstrong thinks the sexist attitudes in the Commons are also represented in society at large: 'We don't come here as innocents. You've been involved in cut and thrust political activity all your life, and I don't expect this place to be any different, partly because it is part of a democracy, and in a democratic organisation, you're going to get a reflection of the world out there, and if we didn't get a reflection of the world out there, there'd be something wrong with this place. And of course, at times there is something wrong. At times, we're too protected from what's going on outside, so I don't complain about it in here at all.'

Oona King notices how the media too picks on young women MPs because they are attractive and sell papers: 'I think the media in general trades on women as an attractive commodity basically. We all know that the majority of British papers, certainly the tabloids, and even the broadsheets, have to have female bodies selling those papers because women in terms of their attractiveness – their perceived attractiveness – sells or moves products. And I don't think politics is any different in terms of what the media's going to pick up on. The media will concentrate on attractive film stars, singers, pop stars, authors – especially lately – and politics is no different because they can have the article and have a picture of a young woman next to it.'

Candy Atherton, who lost her seat in 2005, thinks that the reputation of women MPs still rests on how they all perform: 'I always die when we've had occasional women lapses in Prime Minister's Question Time, because I always feel that we have this collective responsibility, that somehow collectively all women are [responsible]. So I hate it when one of my sisters has a brain–dead moment or something, and let's face it, we all do – or a senior moment.'

However, Westminster has certainly come a long way from the days in the 1980s when some Conservative male MPs felt uncomfortable merely sitting next to a woman. Teresa Gorman talks about a particular male colleague: 'One of my great amusing hobbies is body language. And he would sit next to me with his arms crossed and his legs crossed. I would go to sit next to him, because he was quite entertaining. And I said to him one day, "Why is it you feel threatened by me?" and he said, "What do you mean, Teresa? Absolutely not, absolutely not." I said, "But your body language says you are." And he said, "What's the matter? What have I got to do?" I said, "Well, uncross your arms, and stretch one along the bench behind me, now uncross your legs and put them slightly apart."'

Is the battle won?

Some of the most overt examples of sexism in the chamber have undoubtedly subsided but women MPs are divided as to the level of prejudice still in existence.

Ann Widdecombe thinks too much is made of gender and more attention should be focused on the individual. She can't see what all the fuss is about: 'Of all the men who are competing for these selections, at least thousands every year are failing to get selection. You don't think it's because they're a man, we would say they didn't quite have the personality or the luck – luck plays a big part in this. You know, it's horses for courses – the personality, or the luck, or whatever it was, to make it. Now, if you say that about the men, and you make the same statement about the women, you're not saying anything. Why on earth can we not relax about this, and understand that all these matters are down to the individual, be that individual male or female. There is not some hidden agenda that militates against women.'

Jackie Lawrence thinks there has been change but that change is not necessarily permanent: 'I don't think we have changed it for good, no. I don't think that anything is permanent, I really don't. I think we've got to keep up the pressure, and get more women here. And that involves actually getting more women out there interested in coming in here to serve. I think we've made good incremental progress, but we mustn't be complacent. It would revert to type at the drop of a hat, I'm sure.'

However, Angela Eagle thinks that a new influx of younger members to the House since 1997 and later has markedly changed attitudes: 'I think it is generational. I think the younger generation of male politicians are actually good on a whole range of these progressive issues, too. They take the equality arguments basically for granted and want to see what they can do to make it better. They aren't ashamed to admit that they want a reasonable family-life themselves. For example, I remember how, whether they're on the right or the left of the party, large numbers of them were very good on gay rights and a range of issues like that.'

Dawn Primarolo thinks the Labour Party has passed a turning point: 'I've often wondered whether 1997 gave us a critical mass. I think that's what we thought in 1997, just because it was such a change, but actually, I think that political change is more complicated than just the number. It's about the type of women that came in, their age, how they added to the women that were already elected and bringing in those new, fresh perspectives that wanted to change how politics was conducted. Change has been slow, but I think 1997 has been a turning point.'

Gwyneth Dunwoody thinks that women now are much the same as the men, and that represents progress: 'In a sense, women MPs are more representative of women now, because you get every size and shape and type and age-group and background. So you get the same mix that you get amongst the men. You don't get the same numbers, but you get the same sort of mix. Some of them are very bright, some of them are not terribly bright. Some of them are funny and good and clever. Some of them have got enormous abilities.'

Dari Taylor knew she had broken through an important ceiling when men supported her in one defence debate: 'After I had spoken on the Territorial Army, people like Julian Brazier, who knew exactly where I was coming from, because he was on the Defence Select with me, said to his colleagues, "Shut up! Listen to what she's saying," and it was really quite powerful, because he was telling his own to shut up, and there was a real sense of not only respect, but a sense of – they wanted now to participate in the debate, and they appreciated my participation in the debate. The veracity of what I was saying, the sincerity of what I was saying.'

May 1997 was a culture shock to the Commons and a culture shock to the many new women MPs who took up their seats. Most had come from professional backgrounds and were not prepared for the cheap jibes and remarks that were made to them simply because they were women. It wouldn't have been allowed in any other workplace. It also seems that some of the new intake of male MPs too were taken aback by the sexist attitudes shown by some of the older members of the Commons. The new MPs found support and camaraderie in talking to and befriending one another. What is remarkable is that this happened across party too. It wasn't that they couldn't fit into the male culture of the Commons, some simply didn't want to. The attitudes they encountered belonged to a bygone age. There were enough indignant women now to fight back.

FIVE

Work/home-life balance

A busy time

MPs live busy lives. Over and over again the women MPs in Westminster across all parties, mention how difficult it is to juggle the many different commitments they have. They live Monday to Thursday night in Westminster, when they may be up late voting in the chamber. They then have to make arrangements with husbands, partners and families, as to how their households are to be run. Some have to take or arrange for children to go to school and be collected. In fact a feature of the increased representation of women in Westminster is that they are becoming more like the populations they serve and represent. Their lives can be much the same as ours, and balancing work and home-life is a problem. Some say their job is not a job at all, that being an MP is a vocation.

They then return to their constituencies on a Friday afternoon where they meet with their constituents in their regular surgeries. Most of Saturday can be taken up with constituency business too, meetings with the local party, and talks with local pressure and campaign groups. Then on a Sunday they may be campaigning on the doorsteps, knocking on doors to ensure they are re-elected in a future general election, or doing the same for a council colleague or fellow MP in a neighbouring constituency who is worried about the size of their majority. Some are expected to attend church services or open a village fete on a sunday too. There's little private time in an MP's life that others would recognise private time to be.

However, they agree that London MPs do have a relatively easier time of it than others who may have constituencies and families hundreds of miles away from Westminster in Scotland, Wales and the north of England. Some move their families to London in order to see them, whereas others make the decision to bring their families up outside London where there is fresh air and green grass and local accents.

The number of hours MPs actually work each week is astounding. Some clock up over 90 hours – that is a 13-hour day, seven days a week. Contrast this story with the ridicule they often receive publicly for being 'scroungers' or 'wasters' of taxpayers' money. Sue Doughty explains the outcome of a survey of MP's working hours: 'We got something like 90 hours per week. When we had it measured, that's what it generally comes out at, so it doesn't leave much time for anything else but sleep.'

Candy Atherton has taken to living on a narrowboat in London to cope with her working week: 'We live on a narrowboat in London, so Monday, Tuesday, maybe Wednesday nights we sleep on the narrowboat in Islington. Friday is a constituency day and I will usually do a school/business/constituency meeting, an appointment surgery – perhaps a supermarket surgery . . . meeting with health officials; all the different ranges. I mean, people think you only do surgeries, but actually it's a tiny drop of what you do.'

Theresa May says the job does take over your life: 'You think MPs have a private life? It's very difficult to achieve a balance. I always say it's not a job, it's a way of life, being an MP, and it can take over. Some colleagues I know will say things like, "We never do things on a Sunday," I don't think that's practical. People have events on Sundays, they like you to be there. It does take over in a sense.'

Julie Kirkbride agrees but says MPs can control their own timetable and that is a big advantage over other working women: 'Well, busy doesn't quite fit the description . . . you think . . . Can everything just stop and I'll step off a minute and get my head around it, and I'll come back on again? But everybody feels like that . . . so whilst I have a huge amount to do if I'm going to be doing my job properly and responsibly, and that involves being out in the evening a huge amount, being out at the weekends, it's sort of a 24-hour commitment in that sense, the thing where I benefit from other women who are equally busy, but don't have the same kind of workload, is that I choose a lot of the time when I want to do things.'

Some see the job of an MP as being a vocation. Maria Eagle says the Commons reforms of the hours MPs sit each week have not helped her either: 'I don't think that being an MP is like an ordinary job, it's more of a vocation than a job. My constituency is in Liverpool. Just because I finish at 7 p.m. instead of 10 p.m., it doesn't mean I can get home earlier. I can get to my London flat earlier, which is good. It means I can go and see my friends . . . [There are] I think a lot of red herrings about family-friendly hours and all that, about MPs' lives, because most MPs do not have their families in London, and it's an all-consuming kind of thing to do, and it always will be, so you can't change that by changing the hours.'

Gwyneth Dunwoody recalls how difficult it was bringing her family up: 'At that time, for instance, my husband and I had a home in Devon, and we used to pick the kids up from school and drive like mad, and work all weekend, and drive back on Sunday night so they could be at school on Monday morning. So it wasn't exactly ideal. It was quite hard work.' But she thinks she may have passed onto them the trait of being a workaholic . . . 'Looking back, I'm quite appalled to find I've produced three children who are all workaholics. I don't want to work out where they got that example. I mean, I enjoy work, and I enjoy the things I do, and therefore I don't find it a hardship. And I like music and I like my friends, and I like a lot of my family, to go to things with. But work is still very fundamental to me, and it's very foolish to pretend it isn't.'

However, some would like to have a different work home–life balance today. Harriet Harman: 'I don't get any time for leisure and recharging my batteries, but no doubt in due course I will, at some distant decade, but I'm lucky because my constituency is in London, it's just the other side of the river . . . The three balls in the air are children and wider family, constituency and Parliament, and my front bench work, and I feel really I can just about keep those balls in the air because everything's very close at hand, everything's about fifteen minutes away from everything else.'

Harriet's colleagues share her enthusiasm for a more rounded family life. Margaret Beckett explains: '. . . this is related really to the political career rather than to the House itself; . . . how impossible it would be for any human being to do all the things people would like an MP to do, and that nobody who wasn't an MP would ever really understand how you could ever say to somebody and mean it, "Sorry, I don't have half an hour to spare" . . . so in that sense, there's a camaraderie between MPs of any party that there's an understanding of their common life. Because it's a way of life, it's neither a job nor a profession. It is literally a way of life.'

Hazel Blears asks: 'What's life/work balance, tell me? I come into the office at 8.30 a.m.; I very rarely leave this office until 7 p.m. I always have a box to do. I do papers at midnight, I work Saturdays in the party, and I do constituency work on a Friday. As well as being a minister, I'm a member of the National Executive Committee, I do a lot of other Party meetings up and down the country; it's barmy and it's unhealthy and I know it, and I keep meaning to change it.'

Rosie Winterton misses simple things like her friends: 'What I find is that it is sometimes difficult to find the time you need to see all your friends and to do the things that you used to have, because, you know, it is busy. There's no doubt about it, you know, it is very time-consuming . . . It's enjoyable, but I do sort of miss the ability to be able to just kind of drop everything and say, just go away for the weekend, or whatever. But you just learn to live with it.'

Ruth Kelly is married with four children and early in her career gained a reputation for never taking her red boxes home with her. Since being promoted to the Cabinet, that's changed. She explains that when she was a Treasury minister it helped to have had one job for a good length of time: 'I was incredibly privileged to have been in one job for quite a long length of time, which allowed me the opportunity to really come to terms with the job, get on top of it, push it forward, and during that time I had a number of months off for maternity leave, which was wonderful, because I seem to have had the best of both worlds. I was able to spend some more time at home with the family as well. So in a way, I've been lucky.'

Patricia Hewitt thinks the job is manageable because of the long recesses: 'The hours are very long when Parliament is sitting, especially, but against that, you have to balance the fact that there is quite a long recess when Parliament is not sitting, eighteen or twenty weeks of the year, whatever it is. Obviously, you're not on holiday then, but constituency, certain amounts of departmental work, family – that's perfectly manageable.'

Ann Cryer had a husband who was an MP (he died in 1994) and thinks she has more juggling to do than her husband once did: 'I never anticipated being a Member of Parliament through all those years when I was married to Bob, and he was a Member of Parliament. It never ever entered my consciousness to think that one day I will do this job. So once I did start doing it, yeah, it was stressful, and it was, I think, as with all women, you do a lot more of the juggling than men MPs do. Juggling with family, running a house, coming down here, and of course, for some women, it gets too much.'

There is a great deal of resentment about all-night sittings and votes. Karen Buck: 'Well, let's just talk about the bad one, which is completely unexceptional, which even with the majority we had in 1997, it was sleeping in a sleeping bag in my office all through the night and getting up at 6.30 a.m. in the morning and getting the first tube home to get my boy off to school, and then come back down here. I mean now, it's almost impossible to remember how we did that. What's that all about?'

Linda Perham is blunt in her opinion of how Westminster is run: 'It's a stupid way of running a government, and we actually sit longer hours than most Western democracies . . . some Parliaments only sit for a couple of months a year, so all this stuff about, "Oh, the long holidays".'

Husbands and househusbands

The long hours that MPs work are known to have serious repercussions on their family lives. Understandably the divorce rate amongst politicians is high. Joan Ruddock attributes the failure of her marriage to the life in Westminster: 'I don't have children and I think that whereas that was my loss, not having children, at the same time, of course, especially for when I came into Parliament, it was much easier to come in as a childless woman. Undoubtedly, my marriage broke up as a result of my coming into Parliament. That was my inability really to manage my personal life and my parliamentary life.'

Barbara Follett explains why she thinks marriages break up: '. . . there were 21 divorces by 1999, I think . . . and almost all of them ascribed it to the hours and the way of life. There are also other things you have to take into account. When you become an MP, you become much more important. Your whole space in the world shifts, so it's difficult for your relationship. But the

Hansard Society has done some very interesting work into how many hours MPs work a week. It is a minimum of 72. And that's all the time. People ask me all the time, was I enjoying it? I've never enjoyed it here. I have found it worthwhile doing it, but it is relentless. Just relentless.'

But some think being an MP has improved their marriages. Anne McGuire: 'I find it reasonably easy. I have a very supportive husband, who I've now been married to for 32 years, and probably our marriage over the last seven years has been more interesting.'

Some of the woman MPs of 1997 have decided to juggle their work/home-life balance by getting their husbands to work for them in their offices, as many of their male colleagues have done with their wives, or by enlisting the help of their husbands to look after their children at home and share the running of the home and the school run. Rosemary McKenna now employs her husband: 'In the middle of the week, my husband comes down and joins me. He works for me, so he works between the constituency and here, so we can go down and see our family in the south-east and the south-west.'

So does Linda Gilroy: '. . . it's very important that although he works with me, and I used to think that wasn't a good thing, but when you understand the hours of the week that we're up here, and then when you go back to your constituency, your constituents naturally expect to see you, and for you to be involved in the life that's going on in the constituency, so it's important to sort of have a separate life. But I'm sure other people work it out very well . . . he works in my Plymouth office, occasionally up here, and that's very important to me because actually, it keeps me in touch with my constituency. It's one way of doing it, I'm sure there are other ways of doing it. So we do work very carefully together.'

Like other modern working women, Lorna Fitzsimons enlists the help of her husband to look after the children: 'My husband's a househusband. I'm away half the week for 36 weeks of the year.' And Jane Griffiths explains: 'My husband works for me in Westminster, so we're sharing the same agenda day by day. I think that's good for marriages, actually. Fortunately we don't mind seeing a lot of each other!'

Joan Walley says her husband forfeited his career for hers: 'I think it's really hard, and my boys were four and six when I first came in, and the only reason it was possible to do it is because my husband gave up his job to be at home with the children. That was in the days when we sat up all night long, and we were working Monday until Friday relentlessly and tripping through the division lobbies and never overturning anything, so it was all a bit sort of destructive in that sense, but I think that it's really difficult, for any parent.'

Other husbands prove similarly adaptable. Hilary Armstrong: 'My husband simply books time out in the diary, so that we have good holidays where we do nothing, and we have the occasional weekend where we do nothing. The only thing we commit ourselves to otherwise is that we always try to spend Sunday evenings together, so we try and be in the same place on a Sunday evening.'

Those who have husbands or partners as MPs find it easier to juggle their lives than many, particularly if both are MPs living in London. Virginia Bottomley is married to the MP Peter Bottomley. She advises: 'When I advise young women going into Parliament who have a clean piece of paper, my advice is, Do everything you can to try and get your children to London, because, in general, it makes domestic life easier; it stops you and your partner drifting in different directions. Now that is not a message that people in the constituencies completely understand, but I think if you did a kind of survey of the health and happiness of Members of Parliament, and their families, you'd probably find the ones where the husband and wife could share more of the London, Westminster interest and then go to the constituency for weekends and holidays, I suspect that's an easier way of living. Now, it may be that I'm dated, old-fashioned, and because of the new hours and the way the allowance is changing, people are going to interpret that differently. But from my generation, being close to work's important.'

Julie Morgan is married to Rhodri Morgan who represents the neighbouring constituency of Cardiff West. She says: 'The fact that we're two politicians, that doesn't matter that much. It's probably an advantage because I think that with the job that Rhodri has got now, which is 24-hours-a-day, a very high-profile job in Wales, I would have found it quite difficult if I didn't have a similar demanding job . . . So on a personal level it's good, otherwise it might have been quite difficult; I couldn't have been the partner or the spouse, you know. I mean I do occasionally go with him to things, and he comes with me, but that's not the nature of our relationship.'

Joan Ruddock now has a partner who is an MP too, Frank Doran: 'It helps in that we understand entirely the pressures and we're able to accommodate each other, support each other at the times when it matters, and so on and so forth. Occasionally if both of us are under pressure as in any other field, it's unpleasant; but mainly it's the understanding and an ability to work together. And, you know, we do things together when we can in Parliament. And it's interesting. The constituencies are totally different; his is one of the wealthiest parts of the UK, hardly any unemployment, mine is one of poorest parts of the UK. The contrast makes it of great interest actually. But it's hard at the end of the week when you want to relax.'

Phyllis Starkey thinks an MP's work/homelife balance is more difficult to juggle than most because of the constant changes to their timetable: 'The thing about an MP's life is that things keep changing at the last minute. So you think you've got it all sorted out, and then something comes up that you have to do, and everything else has to be rearranged. I'm lucky in that my children are grown up and don't live with us anymore, so there's only my husband and I to sort out. But it has been very difficult to arrange things so that we do have quality time together, and you have to, in a sense, timetable in your family commitments, because if you don't then they just get squeezed out completely, so you have to put it in your diary that you're going to spend time together and make sure you keep that sacrosanct.'

Families and children

Women MPs find it hard not seeing or being with their children, whether those children are under five or in their teens. Those who put off coming into Westminster until their children are older still miss them. Some feel in retrospect that they have worked too hard and the cost had been to their families. Several women MPs have now taken maternity leave from their roles as ministers.

Ruth Kelly says her family are always her main priority: 'I think my family keeps me sane. It imposes, of course it imposes huge demands, but I wouldn't want it any other way. I have a very, very close relationship; a very close-knit family and I think it keeps me a well-rounded individual. It imposes constraints on my work time, which is probably good, actually. It makes me much more disciplined and focused, and my family always has the priority.'

Tessa Jowell also puts her family first: 'I think you have to start by accepting the basic rule, which I always did, which is, "I'm only irreplaceable to my children. In almost every other circumstance, I am replaceable" and that has actually, for me, been a very good rule by which to live, because it sort of separates the really difficult decisions from those which are a matter of course, and most of them are just a matter of course.'

Yvette Cooper says having a young family does make an MP's life complicated: 'This is the second time I've taken maternity leave as a minister, that's do-able; Ruth [Kelly] took maternity leave as a minister. That's possible, actually, but how do you take maternity leave from being an MP? You can't really because all the constituency things need to carry on; and you can take maternity leave from voting if there aren't close votes . . . We travel back every weekend, so we just go to and fro every week; so it does become complicated, and, you know, small children and trains and things can become very difficult, and things just go wrong . . . the logistics can become very difficult, and you can find yourself trying to do interviews with small children in the back of a car, just things that don't work as smoothly as they ought to.'

Claire Curtis-Thomas says juggling parliamentary life and a young family is difficult: 'It's been immensely difficult, it's been awful. I mean my daughter with a learning difficulty, big, big responsibility, and my husband had to give his job up in order for me to be able to do this one, so he was dealing with a young woman going through all sorts of stages of her life, all the sort of intimate stuff that you would normally associate with someone with severe difficulties, to be undertaken by him, and he found it very difficult to be able to manage that, and therefore you look to your place of work to be supporting you in that regard, and that support simply wasn't available, so it put a tremendous strain on our family.' Her second child, a boy, was born six months after she was elected to her seat. She continues: 'My son was born in the November, I came here in the May, and he was born three weeks early in the November, and we just had to sort him out. But to give you some idea of what it was like, he was born at 6.50 p.m. on a Wednesday night and on Thursday morning, I was back at work, I was opening mail in my house, opening the letters because, as I said earlier on, it wasn't possible to have a maternity leave . . . I needed some acknowledgement that I had duties at home, which were imperative and needed to be addressed, and there had to be some flexibility here to allow me to do those duties, to execute those duties.'

Julia Drown is now standing down as an MP to spend more time with her family: 'I will miss it, but you can't be in two places at once and, you know, so many of my constituents tell me quite rightly, "You only have the children once," I love them and my family to bits, and I want to have more time with them. And some of my colleagues have said, "No, stay, stay, stay, do the job badly, we'd rather have you for two days than somebody else who's not as good for four here in Westminster." But I can't. I have to do it; I have to do it to the best of my ability. I'm that sort of person; you try and give your all to it, and I can't commit myself now to do that.'

Hazel Blears has watched her parliamentary colleagues try to juggle work and young families and thinks it is heart-rending: 'All I would say is that something stuck in my mind once when I was in the Lady Members' Room and there was a woman MP on the end of the phone trying to do maths homework down the phone with one of her children. There was another occasion when a young woman MP, not long since had a baby, and the baby was on the other end of the phone, just gurgling and crying on the other end of the phone, and she just went to listen, and that was quite heart-rending anyway, to be in that position.'

Dawn Primarolo knows how difficult it is pursuing a career in Westminster and having a young child at home: 'It is tough. I wouldn't like to underestimate how difficult it is to have young children and be a Member of Parliament, particularly if your constituency is not in London, because then balancing your time with your children, wanting to be there is very difficult, and each Member of Parliament will manage that in their own way. My son was eight, nearly nine, when I was elected, and I felt I could make that change then, but I do think yes, you do need Members of Parliament who are reflecting all experiences. But to be perfectly honest, when you're trying to balance work and family life, it is so difficult you don't forget it quickly.'

Caroline Spelman says her children are now getting clued up to the Westminster calendar: 'It's about knowing what those priorities are in your heart, before you start applying that to the system. My children are very savvy now. They know all the differences between three-lines and two-lines and one-line whips, and they know what latitudes I have on each of those whips.'

Melanie Johnson, who continued her parliamentary career after having breast cancer, says life for the families of MPs is tough: 'I think my children, all families of MPs suffer as a result of them being MPs. You know, they're probably not getting much of a sympathy vote from the public, but I think they ought to be, because they do all actually pay more of a sacrifice. I mean, those of us who love doing the job, go off and do the job we love and that's fine. The families haven't necessarily chosen the job, they don't necessarily love the job, but they are the people who see less of you, who when they do see you, you're probably likely to be very tired, or very busy still even if you're at home.'

Helen Liddell also thinks the children of MPs have a tough time because their life becomes public too: 'I deliberately don't live in my constituency to try to give [my daughter] some privacy. The children of MPs do get quite a rough time. She was bullied at school because of my job, and I've heard other colleagues say, "I feel the same." And of course you get a lot of press intrusion. When I was a Cabinet minister, it was not unusual for me late on a Friday afternoon to find myself on to the Press Complaints Commission because of some silly, usually wrong, story about my kids liable to appear in an anti-Labour Sunday newspaper, and that's the downside of this life. I can always remember, when I was elected I got a letter from a man whose name I didn't recognise saying that he was the son of a Member of Parliament, and that it had wrecked his life. And I've always borne that in mind, and been a bit cautious about the consequences for my children.'

Baroness Boothroyd says those who do not have children to care for find their parliamentary lives easier, but she respects those women that do take on both: 'I think that the reason I didn't find it difficult was because I don't have a family. I'm not married; I've no partner. In that sense, I've no family, so I had a selfish life to some extent. I could take off and do those things whenever I wanted to. I had nobody else to consider, but I always have great respect and admiration for particularly young women in the Commons who have a home life, who have a husband and who have children; how they balance it, goodness only knows. I don't think I could have done it, quite frankly. But, you know, how they manage to balance it is to be hugely respected.'

Gwyneth Dunwoody remembers her parents taking her with them to party meetings when she was young: 'I went to every Labour Party conference from the time I was born, because they took us everywhere. Everywhere they went, we went. And when I got in here we deliberately lived quite close and my children came in here when they came out of school. They went to school round the corner, two of them went to the primary school at the back of the Army and Navy [store] and one went to a comprehensive in Putney. But we all did everything together. That's the way it has to work.'

Helen Clark thinks there is an issue about childcare in Westminster and not just for young children: 'Now, we talk about "family-friendly" and children, and my children were older when I came in, which made it worse. It's all very well to be having baby after baby in this place and carrying your moses basket round, but you can carry it round, that's the point, you know: babies are very portable. Well, when they get older, what is there here for them? There's nowhere that older children can come; there's no games room, nowhere they can do their homework, do a bit of IT, no library, you know, that might have interesting things for them to look at, so, you don't see them unless it's basically at a weekend or on high days and holidays.'

Christine Russell feels the issues of caring for elderly parents also needs to be taken into account, much the same as caring for young families: 'I mean, my 84-year-old mum is permanently on my conscience because she lives in Lincolnshire and it's not en route between the constituency and Westminster, so even though my two kids are now independent, I do feel guilty that I just can't get across as often as I would like to Lincolnshire. She's got macular degeneration, she's got sight problems, so she's no longer got the confidence to use public transport, and obviously she can't drive any more, and so she's sort of marooned in rural Lincolnshire, but fortunately I do have a younger sister who lives relatively near to her. But again, I feel guilty because now it's my kid sister who's doing all the caring.'

But some mums do see more of their families when they come to Westminster. Ann Cryer was elected as an MP on the same night as her son: 'Amazingly my son John was elected on the same night . . . a sort of mother-and-son team to be elected together, it was unheard of. So it is nice. I don't see John every day, but we nearly always have dinner one night a week to exchange notes, mainly about family matters rather than political matters, because he represents Hornchurch and lives at Upminster, and therefore I don't see as much of those three grandchildren as I do of my three Yorkshire grandchildren. It's worked out all right. I'm enjoying it. If I'm defeated next year, I'll cope with that. I'll be 65 by then, and I hope to go gracefully into retirement.'

Managing two homes – Westminster and the constituency

How to organise their lives so that they can work from Westminster but keep the home fires burning in the constituency is a dilemma for all the women MPs.

Christine Russell points out that an MP is never off duty in their constituency and sometimes their constituents think they are never in the right place: 'There are times when, okay, you go round the supermarket, and you feel that you should have a little tag saying, "I'm off duty". I think we have to be honest and say that it is actually quite tough because you simply cannot be – I was going to say in two places at one time – but obviously if you include your family home, it's three places. And the public unfortunately; half of them assume that when you're not in your constituency, you're somehow failing them because you're spending too long in Westminster, and when you're in the constituency, you get people saying to you, "Well, what are you doing here? Because Parliament's sitting today."'

Judy Mallaber also thinks it's hard to please your constituents: 'You just need to be able to do the constituency stuff and do your work here [Westminster], you know, and combining those two is always difficult, and if you're not in your constituency, people want to know why, and if you're not in the House of Commons Chamber people want to know why, so it's always juggling, and you always get some things right and some things wrong.'

Angela Eagle has a family life in London with her partner and they both travel to and from her Wallasey constituency: 'I understand why constituencies want MPs to have their families living in the constituency, but it's very, very difficult for families who, when the MP is actually away in Westminster for the vast majority of the week, and they're sort of holding the fort up there, but also being on show and sort of representing the MP up there, and it's not something that I would have liked to impose on any family I have. My partner lives in London, as it happens, and I tend to go up there myself, although she comes up on occasion, so there's nobody up there having to hold the fort for me. We don't have a sort of old-fashioned marriage like that. I would have thought it was appallingly difficult for the vast majority of wives, and let's face it, that's what we're talking about, and what's expected of them in the constituency.'

Charlotte Atkins allowed her daughter to decide whether she wanted to live in London or in the constituency: 'Well, it has not been too bad because my first year, I was actually down in London because Emma was at school in London in 1997. She had another year to go and we had to decide as a family whether to live in London or whether to live in Leek. Now, everyone said to me, "Well, nine-year-olds don't make these decisions", but they do. Because I said to Emma, "Well, what do you want to do? Do you want to do your secondary education in London? Or do you want to move up to Staffordshire?" She actually liked Staffordshire, she said things like, "Oh, it doesn't feel so dirty up here," and everything else . . . But in fact she finally decided that she wanted to finish doing her final year, year six in primary school [London], then come up to the middle school system [in Staffordshire].'

Anne Begg is so used to being in Westminster now that she misses the social life of London when she is not there: 'Most of my social life is actually down here because a lot of my friends are here now, and these are my close friends now. And during the long summer recess, I actually miss this place, you may not believe that, because I miss my friends and I miss the social side of things. And even when I'm up in the constituency, even if I'm going out on a Friday or Saturday night, it will probably be because there is some kind of constituency event on. I do have a bit of a social life, but I'm too tired a lot of the rest of the time because the life is unrelenting. So if I get an evening to myself, rather than socialising with my friends, I'm more likely to fall asleep in front of the TV.'

Women MPs have adapted their family lives to life in Westminster. They have invented solutions to the many problems that long unpredictable working hours can bring. They have managed to carve out special time for themselves and their families and friends. Some have regrets that they did not see enough of their families in the early days, but the challenging nature of the work and the job satisfaction they obviously feel provides compensation. Having a supportive partner and supportive children is mentioned by many. However Westminster has some way to go if it does want to attract more women with young families to work there. The location and working hours may not be appealing to a younger generation of women who have become articulate at expressing their wish for a more balanced home- and work-life. This could well apply to men too.

SIX

Party loyalty and the Lone Parent vote

Voting with your party and voting against your party

The new Labour women MPs of 1997 have been shown to be slightly more loyal in their voting record with the government than their male colleagues.[16] Critics have used this to denigrate their contribution to British political life and Ann Widdecombe accuses them of 'having the obedience of puppy dogs'.[17] However they may have forgotten that the one woman politician who got a reputation for toughness, the former prime minister, Margaret Thatcher, was herself loyal to her party when she was a backbench MP and also as a government minister. In her first ministerial post as the new Secretary of State for Education, Margaret Thatcher oversaw the closure of grammar schools and ploughed on with the programme of comprehensive education even though she was personally opposed to it.[18] Barbara Castle recognised that compromise was important. She wrote: 'Fundamental change isn't created overnight. Meantime you've got to live with the reality.'[19] Or the critics could have noted that Margaret Bondfield, Labour's first woman Cabinet Minister, had to cut the dole in the midst of the Depression and then resigned over it.[20]

It is also the case that new MPs are more likely to vote with their party, simply because they are new and haven't fully learnt the ropes to be confident enough to vote against their party. In 1997 women may have achieved significant numbers, but they lacked experience of Westminster.[21]

Baroness Golding takes a pragmatic approach to party loyalty: 'I always vote with the government . . . That's why I'm here. They elected me as a Labour Member, they elected me to support Labour Party policy; if in the end the policy has been agreed, you vote for it. I'm a good trade unionist. You may not approve of all the things that go on, but when they've been decided, you get behind it.'

The vote on the cut in Lone Parent Benefit in December 1997 worried many. Sandra Osborne: 'I'll never forget it, it was an absolute nightmare, it was very, very difficult. I voted with the government to my eternal shame; I would not do that now, at all. I think we had only been elected a week when it came in, and I think I took the view that having come down here, I didn't want the first thing that I did to be to vote against my own government. But I should have done, I should have done.' However, as research shows,[22] she attributes her loyalty to being new to the Commons: 'I think it was because I was new. I do have strong views about party discipline; I wouldn't vote against the government just at the drop of a hat, it's a serious thing to vote against the government. Our party was divided for at least ten years to such an extent that we made ourselves completely unelectable, and I don't want to go back to those days. So I am quite a loyal person.'

Anne Campbell campaigned against top-up university fees in the vote in January 2004 but eventually voted with her government: 'The thing that worried me most was the variable fee, and I was worried about that because I thought that if universities started charging, some universities, such as Cambridge, would charge very high fees and others charge very low fees. So a student applying to university would have to make a decision about whether they could afford the Cambridge fees or whether they went for a cheaper university, and I thought we might finish up here with even more discrimination against lower-income groups than we have at present. However, in the course of the Bill, we managed to get several changes to it.'

Christine Russell was eventually persuaded by a colleague to support the Government in the votes on Iraq in 2003: 'I voted with the government, and I have to say – I will give her all the credit for it – the person who eventually convinced me that it was the right thing to do was Ann Clwyd. I'd been prepared to listen. Obviously my constituency felt very strongly against any military intervention, and I'd had meetings with them, and I'd taken every opportunity to go and listen, whether it was Jack Straw, whether it was the PM, whether it was Geoff Hoon; and it was an issue where I think a lot of us just wanted to talk together about it. I'd met a few Kurdish families, but I hadn't heard many first-hand brutal experiences, but then Ann told me about all the work she'd done over the years, and then, as it turned out, on the Saturday morning, I think, before the vote, I had this young Iraqi who came to the surgery who had literally seen his father being butchered by Saddam Hussein, you know, this young man in his early twenties who was still having real psychological problems. Maybe as a mother, I looked at him and thought, That could be my son. I thought, This brutal guy has just got to be got rid of, so I voted with the government in the end.'

Vera Baird also has misgivings about her decisions to vote against the government: 'I have voted against the party, I think three times, always in issues close to my heart from my past in the criminal-justice system. I don't believe that the right to trial by jury should be eroded as was proposed, and I voted against that. And I didn't think either that people's previous conviction should automatically be put in front of a jury when they were tried, which was the import of a clause that I voted against as well.'

Louise Ellman believes that she became more confident to vote against the government after being elected for a second term: 'I started to think that this really was a very different structure, and it was a loyalty demanded, and then a loyalty taken for granted, and I decided then to take a different attitude, and that is why when other issues came along in the second Parliament I was here, which I felt strongly about, I felt much more inclined to vote against the government.'

Glenda Jackson says: 'It was undoubtedly for me the war [in Iraq], and up to that point I had abstained, if not actively voted against the government, on issues to do with immigration and asylum. But, it isn't easy to vote against your own government. I mean, that goes without saying. But the first time you do it, you've done it.'

Some believe that pragmatism may be the best long-term approach to politics and that you maintain more influence as an MP when you stay in the fold. Dawn Primarolo: 'Ultimately, you can vote against your party, and if that was necessary and you felt very deeply about it you would have to, but my view is that you've already lost if the only thing that's left to you is to vote against . . . I've voted against, but in the end, I just felt good about the fact that I'd voted against; nothing changes.'

Staying loyal to your party and keeping your party in power is raised as an issue by some. Helen Liddell: 'I work on the premise that I have been elected to this place not because of my baby-blue eyes. I have been elected to this place as a Labour Member of Parliament, and my constituents would lynch me if I were just to cause problems for a Labour government, because they voted Labour for year after year after year and didn't have a government, and now we have got a Labour government.'

It is not easy for politicians to vote against their own parties when those parties. Betty Williams: 'Some of us have voted against the Government. You do that with a great deal of soul-searching. You do it with a heavy heart as well. And the first time I did it, I remember I was in the wheelchair at the time. I was wheeled into the lobby, and being wheeled in a wheelchair facing Cabinet Members and the Prime Minister and the Chancellor and so on, it wasn't easy to do it. It wasn't a nice thing to do. But it was to do with welfare reform, and I didn't agree with what the government were doing on Incapacity Benefit and so on. But I do honestly believe, looking back now, that because the government changed course on some of those policies later, I like to think it was because some of us had the courage of our conviction, to vote in a certain way, and we made the government think.'

Gisela Stuart believes that voting against your government is a 'nuclear' option: 'I did on one occasion vote against a private member's bill on pensions. Voting against your government is a kind of nuclear option, and what it usually means is that you've lost the argument inside your own party. Now if there are 60 of you, then it's actually quite significant. But the kind of voting against your government when there are five or ten of you on your side, it's almost finding the indulgence of grandstanding. If an issue comes and you disagree with it, at that point you really need to engage with your ministers, with other colleagues. If you make your case and you win it, then quite often you see policy changes.'

Some share Tony Benn's belief that Westminster is a forum for 'consensus'[23] and that the conflicts should be fought in the party at large. Christine Russell: 'I do feel very strongly that if you are unhappy with any aspect of government policy or anything that the government puts in the manifesto, then you use the forums within the party. You go to the Parliamentary Labour Party meeting. What infuriates me enormously is that so many of the disaffected MPs just don't take the opportunity to come out, they never take the opportunity to come and publicly express their views to party meetings, they just go running to the media.'

Voting against your government is obviously a stressful thing for some politicians to do and they may lose sleep over it. Ann Cryer voted against the government on Iraq: 'I find it very difficult. I don't go lightly into a lobby opposing my own government. I think there there's a touch of machismo in some men, and there's a group of men – one or two women, but mainly men – who will vote against the government at almost every opportunity . . . Now, I'm not in that category, it has to be something that I feel fairly strongly about. I rarely sleep the night before I vote against the government, and don't sleep the night afterwards. It's a very traumatic thing for me to do. I'm basically a very loyal person, and having been in the Labour Party since I was 18 . . . I find it quite hard to do. But if it's something I had a strong conscience about, as I did about Iraq, I just felt that the Prime Minister was misguided, I thought he was wrong, I wrote him letters about it, I spoke at Parliamentary Labour Party meetings, I spoke at private meetings with him in small groups, and I just couldn't have done any more than I did.'

Anne Campbell, who resigned her PPS position over Iraq, also found the vote difficult. 'Well, that was quite traumatic, really. I'd been very worried about the whole Iraq situation. I'd been to see the Prime Minister on two occasions, actually, to express my doubts and concerns about it. I'd spoken to Patricia [Hewitt] about it, so she knew how I felt . . . What I was questioning was whether the US and the UK had the right to take the matter into their own hands, and to go in in an isolated way, without the backing of the United Nations. So, if we'd had that second UN resolution, I would have voted with the government, actually. But it was that that I did feel very, very strongly about.'

Anne Begg says: 'On the war, actually it was the Prime Minister that we went to. A small group of us Scottish MPs went to the Prime Minister and said, "Well, we're very unhappy," and again it was a group of people that would normally be regarded as loyalists. We went together, so again you couldn't say that these are people who enjoy voting against the government or make a habit of it and it is in the hope that our concerns will be taken more seriously.'

Helen Jackson pressed hard, finally taking her concerns over Iraq to the Prime Minister too: 'I've only fundamentally disagreed with the government on the Iraq issue, and the fact that we went to war without the second United Nations resolution. That was a big disagreement, and so I went about it by asking questions of the Prime Minister, by writing to the Prime Minister, by speaking to the Prime Minister in the Parliamentary Labour Party Executive, by talking to constituents, by opening that issue up in the constituency, having public meetings, encouraging people to write what they felt about it in the lead-up to the war.'

Karen Buck worked hard behind the scenes to lobby for change on Iraq. 'But if, you know, on the issue of Iraq, and on the issue of asylum and immigration, which I've also voted against this government on a number of occasions, you know, you talk to ministers, you write letters, you make a decision about how much you do it privately, how much you do it publicly. Well, I've done both over the years. But, you know, you use every access possible that you've got, if necessary right up to the top, which I've also done some time on occasions . . . You will make a judgement as what is likely to be most effective, and sometimes the public disagreement comes if the private negotiation has failed. But it depends very much on the stage in which a policy is developing, you know.'

Conservative women, too, see voting against their government as a last resort. Virginia Bottomley: 'Voting against in the chamber is a last resort. It's rather like having a fierce row with your partner in public. You have many fierce rows in private before you have one in public. And it was always said when I came in that you can vote against on one thing at a time, and so long as you've given warning in advance.'

Voting against your party can be unproductive in terms of securing change. Fiona Mactaggart: 'Let me tell you: voting against your party is the most ineffective way I know of getting change. I can't think of anything where votes against have delivered change, except to some degree . . . where actually the kind of debate and negotiation went and became relatively public . . . But just going and voting against is really stupid . . . it's a good way of being a hero in the eyes of the media, but it doesn't change things.'

What the Lone Parent vote was about

The honeymoon of the 1997 government ended on 10 December 1997 when 47 Labour MPs defied a three-line whip to vote against the Lone Parent Benefit cut. There were eight women MPs among the 47 rebels, but only one came from the 1997 intake and was new to Westminster: Ann Cyrer. The fact that the Labour government consisted of more women MPs than ever before but that its first rebellion revolved round a cut to the benefits of lone parents seemed incongruous to most people. It was not what a socialist government was supposed to do. From that moment on, the 101 Labour women of 1997 were marked out as being 'loyalists' or more cruelly 'Blair's poodles'. Women MPs voting for cuts in the benefits of some of the poorest women in society shocked many of their supporters in and outside Westminster. Some women MPs came to regret it, others genuinely thought they were supporting a policy shift that would take women off benefits and into work. Many now believe that what was perceived as an ill-fated vote has led to a better deal for lone parents in the long term, because of subsequent rule-changes.

The Labour amendment to the Social Security Bill, which cut the benefits to lone parents, was carried with support from the Conservatives. It was never in danger of being defeated, but the rebellion was embarrassing to the government, particularly to the Prime Minister. The vote was taken just seven months after the new Labour government had been elected with a Commons majority of 179, and it took the gloss off the victory for those who were idealistic about the values a new Labour Government would champion once in office. The government wanted to stick to its strict spending limits to overcome any impression that Labour was not fit to govern or was reckless with taxpayers' money – an image that had harmed Labour governments in the past.

Three male MPs had resigned from their government posts to join the first backbench revolt of the Blair era. Apart from those who voted against, another fourteen abstained. The Government Chief Whip, Nick Brown, said all 'No' voters would be interviewed and given a 'yellow card'. Abstainer Diana Organ grew to realise just how much that yellow card would affect her parliamentary career in years to come. Alice Mahon had raised her children alone and was later fired as Chris Smith's Parliamentary Private Secretary for voting with the rebels. The papers reported that it was a 'grim night' for the Prime Minister, Tony Blair. The cash saving from the benefit cut, which would affect lone parents most, was likely to be £50 million in the first year, and approximately £395 million over three years. Lone parents, usually mothers, would lose about £10 a week in their benefits, a crucial sum to most. It was ironic that the former Conservative Prime Minister John Major was able to denounce 'Treasury-driven' welfare reform as inhumane.

The story had another sting in its tail. The Secretary of State for Social Security was Harriet Harman, her portfolio included Women. The first Woman's Minister, Joan Ruddock, reported to her. Both feminists, their presence in the Blair government had been symbolic for women. However, the blemishes to the reputation for women began when Joan Ruddock was attacked for accepting her role as the Women's Minister without pay. That the cuts in Lone Parent Benefit were thought to be done to women by women at the highest level damaged the government and led to much anger at its women MPs.

One of the rebels, Ann Cryer, says that vote was traumatic for her: 'The first vote against was in 1997 against the reduction in payments to single parents; and I was the only new woman MP who voted against that. I felt terribly strongly about it, and we'd been arguing about it for at least five months. The argument had started just after the election, when we knew that that was what the Chancellor was going to do, going to reduce benefits of various guises to single parents . . . And I think that was the most traumatic thing I ever did, that first vote against the government. They say it gets easier each time you vote against them, but I don't find it that way.'

Diana Organ, another Labour woman from the 1997 intake who stood down in 2005, says she abstained and did not, at the time, realise the implications for her career of not voting with the government: 'I voted against the government in December 1997 about the Lone Parent Benefit because this was for me just unacceptable. And I don't think I really understood what the implication of that was; and the implication of that was that the mark was against you and the mark would stay against you.'

Her naïveté was due to her lack of experience of Westminster politics. Diana continues: 'I had no experience, and because I had no experience I did it on "this was a political issue that for me was like a rubicon," and this was a

New Labour government, wonderful, great stuff, that's what I wanted, but this was something that I felt they were erring on the wrong side.'

Ann Clwyd was an old hand by the time of the vote in 1997 on lone parents: 'On that vote, I voted against the government. And you know that was very difficult. We'd been eighteen years in opposition, and to have to vote against the government in the first few months of a new government for which we waited eighteen years was a very difficult thing to do. And I know people on both sides, people who voted with the government, and who didn't want to vote with the government, were very upset about having to make that decision at that time.'

Gwyneth Dunwoody also voted against her own government: 'Oh, I didn't support the idea. I made it very clear from the beginning. I just think the government had the best reasons, the best possible reasons. They want people to get out of the poverty trap of being reliant on benefits. Who doesn't? But it's one of those occasions where you have to think these things through very carefully.'

Others voted with the Government with a heavy heart. Dari Taylor explains: 'The pulse of the policy was not losing the £10, the pulse of the policy was, "Can you damn well make work appear so that we can all feel we've got childcare provision intact, in place, and work there." I knew that was the argument, and I sat there like a dummy. I felt so wretched. I thought it was an extraordinarily mean and unnecessary policy that the government pursued. £10? Are we serious?'

Jean Corston says she went along with it reluctantly: 'I did [vote for it]. I was David Blunkett's parliamentary private secretary at the time, so in that sense I was part of what's called the payroll vote, and I remember David saying to me, "Look Jean, this might be difficult for you, but I would find it really hard to, you know . . ." so I thought, Yeah, I'll go along with it.'

Louise Ellman says the government got her vote because it was important for Labour just to be in power: 'I did vote with the government. That issue came with the very early stages in that new Parliament, and I think at that stage, and for most of the Parliament, the strongest thing in my mind was that we'd been in the wilderness for eighteen years, that we had become as a party during that time, non–electable, mainly because we were arguing internally, fighting one another, and the public did not like division, and instead of that producing good policies and making things better just weren't there at all, and the Tories were wreaking havoc. So I had very firmly in my mind that I didn't want to be rocking boats, that I didn't want to be jeopardising government, and I didn't want to be voting against the government.'

Anne Campbell still doesn't know if the cut was the right decision: 'Well, I wasn't happy about it, obviously, but I had spoken to Harriet [Harman] about it quite a lot. It came from her, although the Treasury drove it; and what I was reassured by, at the end of the day, was the fact that the government would bring in the changes . . . We couldn't reverse it without actually finding some extra money, and there wasn't any extra money around, and that was a really, really, tough decision to make. I don't know whether it was right, even now, but, as I say, I was reassured by the fact that we were going to reverse it and actually make lone parents much better off after a year.'

Tessa Jowell thinks the whole issue was badly handled by her government: 'I think that we should have had the alternative in place at the time that we withdrew the Lone Parent Premium. I think that we took an unnecessary political hit, and although I think the damage was short-term, it was unnecessary to inflict that damage. We could have announced that we were going to remove the premium, but replace it with a programme that would be supporting lone parents into work at the same time.'

Harriet Harman and the Lone Parent vote

Some believe that Harriet Harman was put in a compromising position over the Lone Parent Benefit vote and only decided to cut the benefit with a reluctant heart. Off the record, three women MPs insisted that the Chancellor, Gordon Brown, put pressure on Harriet into going along with the cuts. One said: 'Gordon [put pressure] on Harriet into giving in, I think, in effect.' Another commented: 'As far as Gordon saw it, opportunities for lone parents couldn't just be about how much you paid them to not do anything when so many of them were desperate to be in a position where they could be supported if they went to work, where they wouldn't lose benefit, where they often wanted to get training.'

Watching from across the benches, Jackie Ballard, the former Liberal Democrat MP, thought it was unfair that a woman was left to take the blame for the cut: 'Initially, I was really angry at Harriet Harman for having anything to do with it. Then I began to feel sorry for her and my impression, from my perspective, was that she was dumped on, that they thought, Stick a woman up there to front this bloody awful policy and she'll get away with it, and I think that was a tragedy for Harriet and a tragedy for women.'

Harriet's minister, Joan Ruddock, said she and Harriet wanted to help women get back to work: 'It was her [Harriet Harman's] department, she was responsible for it, but I was a Minister for Women as well. We both came from constituencies with exceptionally high numbers of lone parents and yet in those constituencies, the constant demand I had from my constituents, and indeed Harriett from hers, was not to increase the level of benefits but to help the women to work . . . I wanted to see universal improvements, universal improvements in the level of Child Benefit and universal improvements in the level of childcare provision, and it was that failure to project that package in the round that caused the problems that were encountered and obviously led to Harriet being removed from the department.'

Harriet's fellow Cabinet minister, Tessa Jowell, thinks Harriet took too much of the blame for the cut: 'The Lone Parent vote was a bad moment for Harriet who I think . . . bore far too much of the responsibility for that when Harriet has campaigned all her political life for lone parents, but it was a bad moment that was then very quickly followed by the introduction of the New Deal for Lone Parents and the Lone Parents Premium. So, actually, there was six bad months and then things got better, and Harriet is very largely responsible for the fact, that in the end, we got the National Childcare Strategy and we got the deal for lone parents.'

Harriet Harman herself says her overriding priority as a Cabinet minister, was to stick to the government's spending plans: 'We had promised the electorate that we would stick to the spending limits laid down by the Conservatives. You have to cast your mind back to the situation. At the moment, people regard us as highly economically competent, both domestically and internationally the money markets and everybody regard the Labour government as being economically highly competent and stable, but you have to remember, when we were trying to get back into government, we had a reputation as being the party that would wreck the economy. Our absolute first goal was to say to the public when we asked them to vote for us, you can trust us with your money, we will not put up taxes and throw the money down the drain.' She continues: '. . . Now we made a solemn promise to the electorate, and that economic reassurance was very pivotal in getting us elected with such a majority. Then when we got into government, we had to stick to it. When I was Secretary of State for Social Security, I had to carry out that promise, and that meant sticking to the Tory spending cuts and they had already taken that money out of the budget. But since then, we have increased the money for lone parents not in work and also for families with young children where they're a couple not in work. So since then, the amount of money and benefits available to families not in work, with children, has hugely increased. So that was a sort of, immediate expediency to deliver our election promise.' Harriet declined to comment any further on this topic.

Changing the way policy is made

There is a strong body of belief among Labour women MPs that what some regarded as a disastrous vote for lone parents has now been turned round by better policies in the long term. Fiona Mactaggart believes that women MPs went round to the back door, lobbied and achieved some of the most important policy changes this Government has made in the way welfare benefits are now administered: '. . . on Lone Parent Benefits, every Labour MP who voted for that did it with blood running down their chin, but the women had actually, at the point of the vote, basically got the deal, which more than remedied the result of it, which wasn't announced until much later.'

Dawn Primarolo: It made me determined, to say, 'Right, I'm not having this. Single parents are not some sub-standard [group] . . . So we moved to what was first working families' tax credit and then on through into now the tax credits, introducing the paying for childcare, which frankly, I thought there'd be a huge row on.'

Claire Curtis-Thomas agrees that good can come out of bad decisions: 'We wouldn't have got some of the legislation, some of the benefits that we see today because the Child Tax Credit came directly off that whole episode. So some things that looked absolutely disastrous turned out to be fantastic opportunities of change, and that's one of the tricks you learn here.'

Many Labour women were attacked personally in their constituencies for supporting the government on the vote, but they have since lived to see the benefits of the long-term changes that that decision resulted in. Linda Gilroy says: 'I have to say I go round my constituency, and I see women all over it who are liberated by those policies.'

More help for lone parents now

One theme that occurs over and over again amongst Labour's women MPs is how much better off lone parents are now than when Labour came into government in 1997. The New Deal for Lone Parents, the new system of Child Tax Credits and Sure Start are three policies that have made a difference to lone parents and others struggling to bring up a family.

When Melanie Johnson goes round her constituency she says she can see the difference Labour policies have made: 'I've met constituents, single parents who said . . . how it has absolutely transformed their lives to be able to receive the additional support that we've made available. It's enabled them to get out and earn a living, whilst making sure their children are still looked after properly.'

Oona King observes the policy changes on her doorstep too: 'I represent the poorest constituency in the United Kingdom. I know exactly what's going on in that constituency, I know that the poorest children in the UK, some of those poorest children have been pulled out of poverty because of what this government has done, because of the Sure Start, because of some of the reforms to the benefit system, which has meant more money going to families with children, but just not in the old way. That is why we reformed it. I fully support those reforms. I was brought up in a single-parent family myself, and I know how hard some single parents have struggled. Single parents with children are undoubtedly, undoubtedly better off now in financial terms than they were in 1997.'

Tessa Jowell thinks the negative impact of the decision on Lone Parent

Benefit was quickly turned round: 'I think that was short-lived to be absolutely frank, I mean I think that the removal of the Lone Parent Premium was very quickly – I think it was the budget after – replaced by the early stages of the New Deal for lone parents, which actually made Lone Parents better off than they were with the Lone Parent Premium. So I think that the sense that we were somehow victimising lone parents was very short-lived, and I think now one of the most strongly developed areas of policy is the support for lone mothers to get out to work, to support, to have their children well cared for while they are out at work, and making work pay.'

Rebellion

Women MPs do lead rebellions against their own party's policies, and often these will lead to changes in the law. Ann Widdecombe recalls: 'I particularly led a rebellion – in fact it was the only rebellion that succeeded on the floor of the House under the Thatcher government – I led a rebellion over the level of Income Support for people who were in residential homes, because I had constituents who were very severely affected by the cost of having to live in these homes. And indeed as a result of that rebellion an amendment was made to the Bill; not an amendment in terms of amounts, but amendments in terms of how the assessments were going to be made. One can change emphasis, change direction, change a bit of law as I did with that particular rebellion.'

Rebelling is seen as a last resort. Sally Keeble: 'If you get really upset with your party, then the obvious thing for you to do is to leave it. And the only times I've ever thought of doing that was long before I came in here, and there were a couple of things on race issues where I thought the party was going to be racist. And I thought, If it does that, then I'm off. And it didn't.'

Julia Drown, who is sometimes called a rebel, thinks loyalty is a good word: 'Loyalty's a good thing, so I think we all celebrate it, but of course it's not blind loyalty. I think it's sort of seen as not good, and it really irritates me about how the press do that. I'm called a 'loyalist' by some papers, and then I'm called a rebel by others. And the labels are just completely unhelpful, I think. It's no surprise, is it, if you've been in a party, and you're almost giving your life if you become an MP for your party and for those beliefs, that generally you will support them.'

Party loyalty is a far more complex issue than it might at first appear. There are a range of views on how strategic an MP should be in sacrificing influence for taking a stand on issues of conscience against their own party. While the media views party loyalty as a weak link in an MPs armoury it is clear that MPs themselves across party do not share that view. Labour women do not believe the Lone Parent vote was handled well by their own party but they say that women have subsequently been beneficiaries of many new Labour policies that have brought advantage to them. They argue that increases to child benefit and tax credits for children have more than compensated for what the cut had done. Many would argue that liberating women was always the long-term plan.

SEVEN

Women MPs and their public image

The initial poor public image

Westminster was not the only institution not prepared for the record number of women MPs coming into the Commons in 1997. The media and the general public took time to adjust and to absorb not just the scale of the Labour victory but also the significance it would have on an institution that until then had mainly been dominated by men. In retrospect some of the women MPs admit that they should have been more prepared for the attention they would receive simply because in May 1997 when they arrived in Westminster a woman MP was still regarded as a novelty. Their clothes, their hairstyles, their fashion accessories, rather than their political skills or backgrounds, became the source of the stories written about them. Many of the women MPs of 1997 started their careers in local government as councillors or county councillors and were to some extent used to the sexist attitudes that others had towards them, however, nothing had prepared them for the full scale attention and eventually derision that they would receive from the national media.

There was one act that defined Labour's 101 women MPs of 1997 more than any other and still it lives to haunt them today. On 7 May the Prime Minister Tony Blair lined up on the steps of Church House with all but two of the women MPs for a publicity photograph. Clare Short and Kate Hoey did not take part. The *Mirror* was the first newspaper to use the catchphrase 'Blair's Babes' in April 1997, when it pictured a group of fashion models who had expressed the intention of voting Labour. Others, such as Roy Greenslade in the *Media Guardian*, called its page-three tactic 'pathetic'.

114

When on 8 May 1997 the *Mirror* ran the picture of Tony Blair and the new Labour women, its headline read: 'Blair's Babes (Sorry . . . we mean Labour's Brilliant 101 Women MPs)'. The story went on to say: 'Labour's new generation of women MPs lined up for the first time yesterday. The magnificent 101 have already rejected the title "Blair's Babes" and are determined to end the male domination of British politics for ever.' The newspaper continues: 'Parliament's first wheelchair-bound MP, Labour's Anne Begg, had pride of place in front of the line-up. The 41-year-old English teacher, newly elected to Aberdeen South, said her inspiration was blind Education Secretary David Blunkett – known for his abilities as a politician, not his handicap.'

It is clear now that while some women MPs still really object to the 'Blair's Babes' title, believing that it demeaned them and their achievements, many do not. It probably had more significance for those under 50 years old than those over. Some think that to be called a 'Blair's Babe' is a compliment and Anne Begg believed that the alliteration could have been worse: 'It could have been "Tony's Tarts".'

However there are those who believe the party should have been more prepared for the attention the new women MPs would receive. Fiona Mactaggart: 'That photograph of us all like pilot fish around Tony Blair would have been fine if he hadn't been in it, but he was in it, and he was in it because he'd led the victory, but actually it was, I think, the image which created a whole load of problems. One of the things about us making so much of electing so many women was we didn't name what difference we'd make, and therefore, everyone could pin on the election of women their personal ambition for more women being elected, and so we were guaranteed to disappoint, because we didn't say, "The election of women is going to deliver this and that and the other," we said "Look how we've changed the world: all these women have been elected." And, of course, we didn't manage to get everything that everyone imagined that having 101 women in Parliament would do.'

Conservatives also agree with Mactaggart; Gillian Shephard thinks they should have received better advice from their party. Remarkably she wrote to *The Times* complaining about the press treatment of women in her rival party, but *The Times* did not believe it was her, even though it was on Commons-headed notepaper: 'The women should have been advised not to play ball, I think, because it trivialised them and what they represented, and the achievement that they had had. There was an article in *The Times* by Jane Shilling – I shall never forget it – there was a picture of the New Labour women, and Jane Shilling said, "Isn't it awful, they're wearing synthetic fibres and strangely coloured shoes, and somebody should have done this and done that . . ." and I thought, How can you so miss the point? And how can you so trivialise all this? And do you not know that those women have spent six weeks on the campaign trail, and they don't care a damn whether they're wearing artificial fibres or not, and you try an eighteen-hour day and see how a linen suit looks at the end of it, and you in it, moreover. And I was so moved, I faxed to *The Times* a letter, and *The Times* said, "Who are you?" . . . and they didn't publish it because they said they didn't believe that I was myself . . . despite the fact that it was faxed on a piece of paper saying "The Right Honourable Gillian Shephard, MP for South West Norfolk'. Well, you wouldn't know, would you?'

In a way they should have expected the criticisms and unwanted attention to their fashion accessories. After all, wasn't Margaret Thatcher known for her handbag, Shirley Williams for her wind-blown hairstyle, and Barbara Castle for her flaming-red hair? Castle was often referred to as 'Leather Knickers', by a male Labour MP,[24] and Jennie Lee was dubbed 'Lady Macbeth' as Nye Bevan's wife.[25] Mo Mowlam comments on her own 'dishevelled appearance'[26] and Ann Widdecombe won the nickname 'Doris Karloff' by referring to herself as 'short and fat'.[27]

The belittling headlines that have troubled New Labour women also haunted Margaret Thatcher. 'Mark's Mummy is an MP now' was the headline in the *Evening Standard* when she was first elected to Westminster.[28] Tellingly Margaret Thatcher, who was known for her 'not for turning' toughness as a Prime Minister, had a 'stubborn adherence' to her party line as a new MP.[29] That same party loyalty has been an albatross around the necks of the New Labour women.

Women MPs often have to overcome a poor or prejudiced public image. Vera Baird thinks the media can only deal with stereotypes of women: 'I am sure they treat [women] with stereotypes. The most notable thing is the incapacity of the media, particularly the red-tops, to contemplate a woman who is a complex character. She has to be either a mother, or a hard-nosed career girl, or a tart, or a failure, or an emotional mess. You know, she cannot be as complex as men are.'

Gillian Shephard encountered such prejudices many years before when she was Secretary of State for Agriculture in the Conservative government of the early 1990s. Working in a male environment, Gillian made sure she wore skirts below her knees but tellingly received hate-mail from a woman: 'I hardly noticed the attitudes at central office, but they were there. When I became the Minister for Agriculture, I was the first woman, I actually did think about that fairly carefully. After all, the agricultural community's rather conservative, and I was pretty careful about what I wore; even then, I got some hate letters, from some woman, obviously saying, "Who do you think you are doing flashing your legs" . . . I mean, as if, at my age . . . Anyway, I became rather startled by those. But it was from a woman.'

Margaret Hodge thinks the poor public image of MPs is perpetuated by the media: 'We have to change the culture of politics and we have to change the role of the media in how it relates to politicians and the political class, and the deprecation of politicians and the sort of *Today*-style conversations that go on between interviewers and politicians I think has helped bring politicians into disrepute. And that means people don't listen to what you say, all they do is take that two-second look at what you're looking like.'

Harriet Harman thinks the public image is unfair on MPs: 'It's kind of the down-side of public office; sometimes I think it's unfair, and sometimes I think it's downright unfair and nothing to do with them and private, and sometimes I think it's unjustified. But I don't spend too much time contemplating that, if there's nothing I can do about it, so I basically just find myself getting on with going to the next objective.'

One Labour MP tried to change the image of the Labour Party to make its prospective parliamentary candidates more electable before Labour's 1997 election victory. Barbara Follett changed the stereotypical image of what a Labour MP should look like: 'What I did in the late 1980s, early 1990s, Labour was seen – we did research into what people's perceptions of Labour were – and it was woolly-hatted and woolly-headed. They felt – if you look at that gentleman over there, you wouldn't trust him to run a government . . . people have a stereotype of how you should look. And it certainly wouldn't be looking as I am right now, with just a shirt on and sandals. But we didn't fit into that in any way at all. Basically, I got people to clean up. I said, "Don't go on a doorstep with egg on your shirt, your hair all messy, and your glasses all smeared; you may be the one Labour person people see in their whole life." And at that point, in the early 1980s, people didn't think Labour could manage anything, let alone their personal hygiene and – actually they weren't far wrong. Most of what I said was along the lines of, "Go to a hygienist, brush your hair, and clean your shoes." '

From the outset, image was a problem for the Labour women MPs. In the September after they were elected, Rosemary McKenna intervened to stop one photo-shoot taking place: 'On one occasion, we almost fell into a trap. We were asked to go along to a photo-shoot for women MPs at the first Labour Party Conference, and I walked into the area where the photograph was taken, and it was in a bar. The bar was empty apart from us, but they had all the young women lined up, sitting on the bar with legs crossed, and I was able to go in and say, "I don't think this is a very good idea." ' The more experienced women MPs wanted to prevent the media portraying them as political eye-candy.

Harriet Harman says she hates being regarded as a trophy woman politician: 'I'm seen as having been invented by New Labour instead of the part of a team that invented New Labour. So that is a way of looking at women as if they are simply trophy politicians who have been moved forward, and really it's not to do with their ability or what they've got to contribute. And that is sexism, basically, that you see women having got there . . . by [a] kind of gender preferment, and that's wrong because I had to really struggle, I had to really struggle to get the issues that I was concerned about raised.'

Other women MPs simply refused to do interviews. Fiona Mactaggart remembers: 'I refused to do interviews early on. I mean, I've always been a feminist. One of the reasons I'm in Parliament is because I'm a feminist. I refused to get involved in the interviews for one book, because I thought, Actually, this is worrying, that we're sort of being seen as a separate class. I mean, nobody would ask somebody of my weight to be doing the kind of fashion stories, but I always wanted to avoid that kind of thing. I'm afraid what happened was that we got a lot of attention, and one of the things about Members of Parliament, we are an attention-seeking lot, actually.'

But deep-rooted prejudices about women MPs were also present in society at large then, and for a subsequent generation of women who were elected to Westminster. Conservative and Liberal Democrat MPs noticed them. When Labour's Meg Munn won her Sheffield Heeley seat in June 2001 she took the remarkable step of knocking on the door of every Labour Party member who could vote for her selection to overcome the prejudices there may be about her: 'You've got to persuade them to take part in the process, you've got to persuade them that individually you are the person who will best represent them and you've got to get over the kind of rumours which might be flying around, like, "She lives in Barnsley," which I do, and, "You're not from round here," and actually I was the most local person because I was born and grew up [in Sheffield]. So there's all that to counteract, that's what you are dealing with, which is why it is so difficult, is not blatant outright discrimination, it is individual people making their decisions, so you are dealing with 300 people's expectations, and prejudices . . . All of them, all 300, I knocked on all their doors, yes . . . you have to go and knock on their doors. I mean, I probably didn't manage to get to talk to all 300, in the end about 200 of which will have taken part in the selection process, but I will have spoken to the vast majority.'

Patsy Calton thinks MPs are not seen as being hard-working or even normal: 'We're like a funny little group of people, who aren't seen as being normal people at all, unless they happen to know us, in which case they say, "Oh, you're all right, Patsy, you're one of us," when they are your constituents. But the constituents from another constituency wouldn't think that, they'd see me as being part of this rather strange group who come here, seem to spend a lot of time on foreign trips and they don't see the work actually that goes on here.'

Annette Brooke agrees: 'My feeling is, in terms of when you do get a bad reception on the doorstep, when people are just against politicians in general, that it is because of the impressions that they've got from the television, and I think all the scandals did quite a lot of harm, and I think Alastair Campbell [and spin doctors] will be shown in history to have contributed to the lack of trust and confidence in politicians.'

Karen Buck thinks the real issue was not about the dress sense of women MPs but about the calibre of candidates elected to Westminster: 'Unfair as it can be, the one that really struck me more than anything else I've known – and it reverberates now to this day – is the Lyn Barber interview with Harriet Harman, which I will never forget as an object lesson . . . and [she is an] absorbing journalist, so it's not conventional sexism in that sense, but how Lyn Barber opened an interview with Harriet Harman by saying that, "She's in government sat on top of her MP's salary, what does she spend all her money on? She certainly doesn't spend it on clothes." '

Jacqui Lait joined the media in condemning the quality of MPs elected under Labour's all-women short-list policy: 'I think the sad thing is that so many of the women who did come in are not the calibre that one would wish, and I think it's actually done us damage. I'm a great believer in the right person for the right job, certainly in the Conservative Party we have improved our systems to get more women selected, that's absolutely right . . .'

Theresa May says the Labour women MPs failed to make a mark and that contributed to the poor public image: 'I think that there was flack directed in a particular party's direction because . . . the Labour Party made a very great deal of the fact that it had got 101 women MPs and obviously that was the biggest single leap forward we've had in terms of the number of women sitting in the House, but then I think there was a perception that they had not come in and made a mark in the way that they had implied they were going to; and that's when the media tended to be pretty dismissive of them.'

But Ann Taylor believes it is the media which polarises issues and gives MPs a poor name: 'I just think that too many MPs fall for the trap of having to talk to the press when actually they don't need to, because they fear what the press will say. I think if we could just calm that down and slow that down a bit, more people would realise that they can influence decisions.'

Linda Perham was one of those trivialised by the media when the 'Blair's Babes' photograph was taken, down to most items of clothing and the colour that she was wearing: 'I think the media trivialised us, and to some extent the tabloids still do, because my memory of that "Blair's Babes" photograph is that, first of all, I got that question about why I was wearing a trouser suit, which I think was the *Mail*. *The Times*, I think, referred to my blouse, which was orange, as a 'cruel French marigold colour'. The *Telegraph* commented on my brooch. I saw a television programme where – I have to say, I was wearing a green trouser suit – it sounds awful, but I thought I looked nice and

I'm in autumn colours – I was wearing a green trouser suit and an orange blouse and Margaret Beckett, who was wearing shocking pink, came and stood next to me, because she came down the steps with Ann Taylor and Blair and stood in the middle where I was, just next to me.' Linda continues: 'They actually scanned the both of us with the camera and were saying, "God, isn't this awful" and there were remarks like, "Oh we look like a convention of Avon Ladies" . . . and I said, "People are not asking me what I came to Parliament for, what my policies are, my issues that I care about, causes I support; they are focusing on our clothes," and you know, if it had been a picture of all the men, it would be grey or dark blue suits.'

Betty Williams says that up until she and her female colleagues from Wales were elected in 1997 there had only ever been one woman Welsh MP. She recalls: 'In fact there was quite an interest within Wales from the media, and HTV did a programme called *Now We Are Four*, and they followed us and they interviewed us and showed what we were doing here and back in the constituency. So we did have a profile, in 1997, 1998, in that time, which is good, I think. Because I'm very conscious that women sometimes are a bit reluctant to have enough faith in themselves, and I think the fact that so many of us came here not only were we able to persuade women to put their names forward to become Members of Parliament . . .' Even so, constituents can still be surprised to see her going about her normal household duties. She continues: 'But it is rather nice when people stop you in the supermarket. And this again was a novelty for the people of Conwy, because they'd had a man for all these years, and a Labour politician had never held onto the seat for a second term until I did in 2001.'

Valerie Davey thinks women constituents feel more at home talking to women MPs than they would do to a male colleague. 'Just the fact that I'm a woman MP has enabled a lot of women to come forward and talk to me . . . I was surprised how many people came to my surgery and said, "It's really good to have a woman, and indeed to have a Labour MP," because it was the first time ever in Bristol West. "We may now have somebody who understands what it's like caring for a disabled child, what it's like to be vulnerable, what's it like to be bullied at work . . ."'

For some of the 1997 intake, racial identity has also been an important influence in how they are judged and received. Oona King was a reluctant role model for others: 'I remember quite early on, a black woman coming up to me on the street with her eight-year-old daughter, and shaking my hand, kissing me, saying, "All our hopes are on you, and I want my daughter to see you as her role model because she hasn't had one before because she's mixed race, and all our hopes are on you." I got it quite a few times – and I got to a point when I almost wanted to shake these people and say, "Well, I'm so grateful to you for having so many warm wishes and all the rest of it, but don't pin all your hopes on me because it's too much pressure!" you know, and, "I can't deliver necessarily every dream and wish and hope for your daughter and for every black child in Britain, and little mixed-race girls up and down the country," that sort of thing. So I did feel that. I don't feel that pressure any more.'

Women MPs feel the regional media is much more balanced in its representation of them and their job. Diana Organ sums up what a number of her female colleagues feel: 'I have to say I love the regional media because they never really did the "Blair Babe" thing. They didn't, partly because you go to your regional media, your local media about constituency issues or what you're campaigning on for your local area. And that's what they want. They want the good local story, don't they, about the MP fighting for miners' rights, or the MP fighting for the foot-and-mouth disaster in the Forest of Dean, or whatever. And so it doesn't service their end or their story to write about "Blairite" or "Blair Babe, Diana Organ", it's much more about what's happening from this local issue.'

The 'Blair's Babes' photograph

While many Labour women protested at the 'Blair's Babe' tag, others were really not offended. Cabinet member, Ruth Kelly, thinks the name was symbolic of the new Labour victory that had just been achieved: 'The press attention about the influx of women MPs was bound up with the image of a New Labour government, which was exciting and new and modern and young, and it was all part and parcel of the same phenomenon, I think, and that we were branded as a part of that, and hence the "Blair Babes" image came along. But it wasn't just the fact that there were so many women, as I say. It just was bound in with this whole view, with the huge majority as well, of change that was represented by the New Labour government.'

Joan Ruddock was surprised by the hostile reaction to women MPs: 'There was a huge backlash, which was led, of course, by the tabloid press against the women, making all kinds of accusations about the "Blair Babes", about not being up to the job, it was absolutely incredible to me, because most MPs take time to find their feet, anybody does, in a new job; this is a particularly daunting job, nobody was looking at how the new men were performing.'

There were women amongst the most senior ranks of the government of the time who didn't mind the 'Blair's Babes' label. The former Cabinet Minister Mo Mowlam: 'I have the unfortunate notoriety of having worked out "Blair Babes", because somebody said something, and I said, "Well, 'Blair Babes', that's what we are," which I'm not proud of, and it's been used against us. But I think we needed to do that. I think we needed to do other things to show that we were there in such large numbers, because you very rarely understand how little the public know about Parliament, how little they know about their MP, how little they know about what's going on, and I think it's very important to get whatever method you can to get that message across, and I think that was a good one.'

Barbara Follett also had no objections: 'I have no problem. I was 52, I didn't mind being anybody's babe! . . . It was a very potent picture. It was meant to show how many women had come in, and we only clustered around the Prime Minister because he was the Prime Minister. But – and for the other parties, and for the basically quite conservative press – remember, we represent a change in the established order. And they reacted by belittling it, and that is the way, in Britain, we deal with that kind of change. We make it slightly ridiculous, and that view persisted for quite a long time. I think it's now been dropped.'

Others remember the occasion as being historic and something they will never forget. Melanie Johnson recalls: 'I hadn't realised how many of us there were until we all sat down there; to have Tony Blair come in and be the Prime Minister was amazing as well after all these years of opposition. Then to go out on the steps and do this photograph where there were all these women with Tony Blair in the middle as one man, and then this wall of media – which was almost all men, of course – on stepladders; the photograph of them is almost as interesting as the photograph of us, in a way. And that was almost all a male bank of photographers, all clicking like that, that was an occasion you'll never forget.'

Sally Keeble has actually kept the bright pink outfit she wore for the photograph: 'It was the first photo-call, which everybody decries, and thinks was, you know, Tony and the women and the fuchsia-coloured suits, and mine was actually fuchsia-coloured. But my husband's grandmother, who was in her nineties, when she died, the family . . . found that she'd ordered up that copy, you know, she was Labour, Labour through and through in South Wales . . . she had that picture in a frame in her house, and I was absolutely astounded, and I've still got it . . . I actually kept the pink suit as well.'

Anne Begg was in her wheelchair at the front of the group in the photograph: 'The Scottish media knew that I was likely to be elected in a wheelchair, but it hadn't registered with the English media that somebody in a wheelchair was going to be elected as an MP. The shot had been set up because everyone had come out of Church House down the steps, but I had to come out a different way, come round, and I trundled up to the front and spoiled the shot for them because I'm sitting there in the front. Somebody had written in later and said, "Oh, you're stuck on the front," and I said, "Well, you see me. Disabled people have been invisible for generations and now you see I'm there." . . . If you're a 40-year-old woman who is disabled, being called a 'babe' is not a bad thing, you know, I've got a bit of "street-cred".'

Others also thought the 'Blair's Babe' nickname was amusing. Gisela Stuart: 'Well, if the cap fits I wear it. I have nothing on how we respond to this . . . I always remember when first the phrase of "Blair's Babes" came out, one of my sons said, "Well, look, Mum, I'm really sorry I know what a babe looks like, but you ain't one."'

Claire Curtis-Thomas thinks it is a compliment to be called a 'babe': 'I have had instances of it, I mean I had a constituent who wrote recently to me and said I was a "Blair Babe", and I wrote back saying I was absolutely delighted with the description because of course it's been years since anyone called me a babe, and the notion that I'm still young enough to be fitted with that adjective is fantastic, you know.'

However, very many Labour women thought the 'Blair's Babes' photograph was a mistake. Ann Clwyd remembers taking part but not liking it: 'I can remember turning my face away from the camera. I don't think you can see me in the picture, actually. Because I actually didn't like the stunt, and I thought that it might have repercussions.'

Yvette Cooper thinks it led to women MPs being caricatured: 'There is always a problem with caricatures. I think politicians will always get caricatured . . . I think, the more that women journalists are able to challenge those, the easier it will be.'

Helen Liddell thinks the 'Blair's Babes' caption accompanying the photograph has been very unhelpful: 'I think it's been very unhelpful, and it has been, I think, a conscious attempt to undermine the fact that the body politic is changing; and women do have much greater influence now than they have ever had.'

Harriet Harman thought the title 'Blair's Babes' demeaned the women MPs and treated them like groupies: 'I wish I knew who had invented that. I just think it's absolutely silly because the irony is that we got those women in from the women's efforts, it was not – I mean of course Tony Blair was a fantastic leader of the Labour Party that led us into a great victory – but the reason why it was a team of women as well as men is because women had fought to get in there, so the idea that all of us had been brought there by Tony Blair, that's not the truth of the situation. The reality is that women had fought for women to get into Parliament in order to deliver for women. And yet the media turned round and implied that we were just a whole load of groupies.'

Jean Corston thought the derision was symptomatic of attitudes in society: 'I thought the whole thing was uniquely patronising. At the time I was called a "Blair Babe", I had two grandchildren, which was kind of bizarre; nobody ever called me a "Blair's Granny", but I suppose they could have done.'

Women MPs in other political parties also thought the picture was a mistake. Jackie Ballard, the former Liberal Democrat MP, says: 'I think the "Blair Babes" picture – most people would think, in retrospect – was a terrible mistake. It was meant to give a message that there was now a greater, huge group of women in Parliament, but I think it gave a message instead that this was something quite sort of fluffy and light and started the media looking at things like what people were wearing and what their hairstyles were, instead of looking at serious issues.'

Julie Kirkbride, the Conservative MP, identifies sycophancy as a problem: 'The "Blair's Babes" have allowed themselves to be portrayed as being sycophantic to the Prime Minister, often because they do ask the most sycophantic questions, which, you know, "pass the sick bucket". I mean, there are some very good, very impressive women on the Labour benches, who would no more fit the "Blair Babe" description than any of the rest of us, and you know, they also get unfairly tarnished with it. But the media is going to pick up on the caricature.'

Cheryl Gillan thinks the raised profile of women MPs caused the problems: 'Well, when you go out of your way to ram down the public's throat that you've got such a large number of women MPs, come hell or high water, then you can expect a reaction. That was the reaction that they got and it was rather poor.'

The media on women MPs

There is a clear and persistent resentment of the national media amongst a large number of women MPs of all parties. That dislike or loathing may have been caused by comments on their legs, clothes or hairstyles, or by what they see to be an unacceptable invasion of their family life and privacy.

Barbara Follet calls remarks her South African mother-in-law made about her being paraded across one Sunday paper: 'I remember the *Daily Mail* or *Sunday Mail* going to South Africa and going to my 85-year-old ex-mother-in-law, pretending they were going to interview her about her son who was shot dead in South Africa – my husband. So she was really pleased because she always wanted publicity for him. And she said, laughingly, "Oh, Barbara, she was a bit of a man-eater when she was young." She was 85 and they spread that right across the front of the banner headline when I was getting elected in Stevenage. Fortunately, people don't read the *Daily Mail* in Stevenage, they read the *Evening Standard*!'

But often it is the clothes they wear that get written about. Melanie Johnson recalls: 'I remember one occasion when Dawn Primarolo and I turned up to Parliamentary Questions both wearing, as it happened, brown suits and some sort of similar coloured top. It was completely coincidental and it had absolutely no significance whatsoever. But, you know, it gets written up by the sketch-writers, as it were, and you just get used to shrugging these things off. But I think that's something – if two men turned up in a dark blue suit together to do Questions, then there would be absolutely no interest in it whatsoever.'

Claire Curtis-Thomas had the same attention paid to her dress sense by the local media: 'For the first two years I was a Member of Parliament, the local newspapers, the regional newspapers used to ring my office and say, "Can you tell us what Claire will be wearing this autumn?" You know, well, my husband is really the wrong person to ask that question to because his normal answer was, "Haven't you got anything better to do with your time?" '

Other women from other political parties also receive the same hostile attention from the media. Ann Widdecombe has been subject to much derision but she says so are the men: 'People say that they've commented on my looks, which they have, ad nauseam. But on the other hand they've commented on William Hague's bald head, Ken Clarke's Hush Puppies, there's always something to be commented on. Though I think if one were to be absolutely objective about it, I have probably had a lot more comment about my circumference than John Prescott has had about his circumference. So I mean there may be a slight dual standard, but what is that except a reflection of the importance that women attach to their looks? I mean, you know, pick up any woman's magazine – what's it all about? "Lose a stone in a fortnight." I mean, as if.'

Others have not experienced any negative media attention. Angela Watkinson thinks the media's approach depends on how the individual MP behaves: 'They've never given me a hard time. I think that people treat you the way that you allow them to treat you, and they're probably more critical of women, and that's why I'm very careful never to play the women part.'

But it does upset other Conservative women. Theresa May feels it taints the whole approach to politics: 'I think the other frustration in terms of the media is related to comments about me as well as others, is about this culture of politics and how you do it. I would argue that I tend to do politics differently from a lot of the men, and that's partly about not taking a "ya-boo" approach, it's about not thinking that when you're in the chamber, you're only there to deliver killer blows, whereas from the media point of view, if you do not deliver a killer punch or a killer blow then, "You're not up to it dear," and I think that's where there needs to be a different understanding of what the job is actually about . . .'

Caroline Spelman is angered by how the media treats women politicians: 'Well, it infuriates me, and I think that there are enough female journalists actually in the lobby as well, who if they wanted to do their sisterhood in politics a good turn, would stop writing up all the trivia. I always remember, almost within my first month or so, Patricia Hewitt was given an incredibly hard time in a parliamentary sketch about some multi-coloured jacket she was wearing.'

Jacqui Lait thinks the approach of the media to women MPs is beginning to change: 'I always thought the best definition of feminism was when a female managing director was allowed to fail and nobody commented, and I think there is still that element. But a lot of it is, by definition, because we are an MP, the media will take an interest. And it doesn't matter how junior a backbencher you are. If they've decided to take against you, suddenly you're a senior backbencher, and "How can we make maximum grief out of this?"'

Cheryl Gillan gets weary of how the media treats women: 'What I get tired of, which the boys don't get, but we do get, is the moment we do television, it's, "What are you wearing? What does your hair look like? And do you in fact have a double chin?" and I was actually told by a man in the party that I shouldn't do any work on television until I'd had my teeth fixed and a face-lift. And I thought he was joking, but he wasn't.'

However, her colleague, Virginia Bottomley thinks the increased media profile women MPs attract creates envy amongst male politicians: 'On the way up, there was quite a lot of envy of the women, because the women get quite a lot of publicity. They're on the *Today* programme, they're on *Newsnight*, they're on *Question Time*; if you have six politicians quoted in the paper, you get a picture of the woman. Now, this is a real problem for the women, because they become over-publicised. They can't just get on and do their job. They become sort of celebrities too soon, so if you look at, whether it was Harriet Harman or Mo Mowlem or, you know, all manner of women, you get this great focus, which is not always helpful at all; Edwina Currie – I mean, she moved into that world. But, you know, initially, it's out of all proportion.'

Harriet Harman thinks that women MPs are still judged on how one another perform: 'I think that if you're a woman, you carry the flag for your gender; if you're a man, you just carry the flag for yourself. So if a woman fails, then all women are failures, whereas if a man fails, he's a failure; and I think that women are more visible in the media than men politicians, but they're also more vulnerable, so it's swings and roundabouts really.'

Helen Liddell thinks female journalists adopt some of the worst stereotypes: 'I think it's been negative . . . The sad thing is it's often by women journalists who have the worst stereotypes, or comment on hair or figure or clothes or make-up, which really demeans women in public life. Yet these are the very ones that portray themselves as great heroines of women's liberation. And they're actually the worst people in terms of the attacks they make on other women.'

Helen Jackson thinks there needs to be more interaction between female politicians and female journalists: 'I think there have been times when we've had useful meetings with women journalists, and we ought to perhaps do more of that, and I think women journalists think they have a role to meet up with women MPs and create a bit of a front there, and perhaps we could do more in that line, and not forgetting to include in that group the sympathetic male journalists and male MPs.'

Hazel Blears doesn't like her media nickname, 'Blears-the-bike', and says that the same headline is used over and over again when journalists write about her: 'The thing that kind of enraged me recently was I did a feature piece for one of the dailies, and in my private life, I ride a motorbike, and I said to them, "Don't use the motorbike picture, it's been used to death," and they brought a photographer with them, took photographs all the way through, and what do they do? They use the motorbike picture, and I just think it's a bit pathetic.'

Valerie Davey thinks the media hounds women more than men. She saw it happen when Estelle Morris resigned as Secretary of State for Education: 'By and large, I think they are still less respectful of women politicians, and I think, for example, one of the saddest moments for me in the House was when Estelle Morris resigned. And I could see a woman, who I admire enormously, of complete integrity, for whom the intimidation by the media on aspects of her wider family life had become intolerable; and for whom the quality of what she was doing was not understood by the media, hounded out, virtually. And that was just symbolic for me of women finding it particularly difficult with the media.'

Angela Eagle says that when as an MP you attract negative media coverage it is also hurtful to your family: 'They're nasty to every woman who's ever said anything in the chamber, and, in fact, yes, I have been treated to some pretty rancid coverage by those sorts of people. I mean, there was when I came out, yes, but I expected that. So yes, there has been a bit, and it's nasty when it happens and it's nasty for friends and family as well.'

Jackie Ballard talks of the impact the media can have on your surrounding family and children: 'My daughter, who's now 25, but when I got into Parliament, she was 18, and she was incredibly upset and hurt by some of the things that she read in the press, and she was in some ways quite glad when I lost my seat. I mean, in general she'd have preferred me to win, but there was some reasons why she wasn't sorry about it.'

The media has also 'mythologised' why some of the women MPs of 1997 are giving up their jobs in Westminster to pursue other interests. Jackie Lawrence explains what happened to her when she said she was giving up her seat: 'I'll have been here eight years, I'll be 57 just around the time of when we expect the election to be next time. I now have three grandchildren. I've decided to stand down after two terms. Now I have been harangued by one newspaper at one stage, and I know the line that they're wanting to take, and that is that "Blair's Babes" of 1997 are giving up the ghost. I'm giving up my job because . . . I'm 57 at the next election, there are other things to do out there.'

Gwyneth Dunwoody thinks the cheap jibes made at women's expense mean the media misses the real story: 'I'm afraid that their representation of women is very easy. You know, "Blair's Babes", and people sometimes lend themselves to that. But behind the "Blair's Babes" thing are a lot of talented and intelligent women who never got the chance, because they're not media people.'

Some of the women MPs accuse the media of being misogynistic. Tessa Jowell: 'I think there are very particular journalists and particular commentators that are absolutely vile about women. I mean, they are misogynist, and I think that you've just got to discount them, and you have to grow a thick skin, not read their stuff. And support friends and colleagues when they feel undermined and hurt by what they write. More generally I think that the tension between Westminster politicians and the media is an occupational hazard.'

She believes that MPs survive the hostility by a belief in their convictions: 'I think you have to engage with the media, I think that you have to be willing to explain, but also you just have to feel routed in your own convictions, and if you feel routed in your own conviction, your own passion that what you're trying to do is right, it's a wonderful immunity to the rubbish that you have to put up with.'

Baroness Boothroyd agrees with Tessa Jowell that women have to be tough: 'I think you have to have a thick skin here, and if they're going to do that, that's tough, but Ann Widdecombe is a most popular individual, in the nation and in this House, and I think it's just water off a duck's back with people like that.'

One MP who has experience of the need for a thick skin is Theresa May, who was catcalled by the press when she once wore a certain type of shoe to her Conservative Party Conference. She recalls: 'I guess it just comes with the territory. I don't mind about the shoes, I like buying shoes, I love shoes, so I'm quite happy on the shoe front. I wasn't so happy at being described as an old crone the other day by somebody in the media. Yes, it's frustrating to the extent that there tends to be talk about what you look like, how you dress, rather than what you're saying; and obviously that happens more for the women than it does for the men, so there's a frustration there.'

Some believe that the confrontational way politics is reported begins in Westminster itself with the weekly Wednesday Prime Minister's Questions when the leader of the government and the leader of the opposition joust with each other, stabbing away at each other's arguments. Lady Sylvia Hermon: 'I really dislike Prime Minister's Questions. I really dislike that half-hour each week from 12 p.m. until 12.30 p.m., I sort of sit and grin and bear it, because it is so, so uncharacteristic of the rest of the business that's done during the week. It is a set piece, the press gallery of course is full, and I'm sorry to say that both the Prime Minister, for whom I have considerable regard . . . but I don't see him at his best at Prime Minister's Questions. He's acting much better when he's making a statement to the House and responding to meaningful questions. I hate the rough and tumble of that half-hour; I dread it each week.'

Vera Baird does not let herself be pushed around by the media and thinks her professional background in the law helped her cope with the media when she became an MP. She recalls: 'I have to tell you, I'm very resistant to being bullied. I've been interviewed by various interviewers who I do think – and I'm not naming them – but I think it's pretty clear that there are various interviewers in the media who think they can bully women and set out to bully women, to show that women are too weak really to be in this hard-edged job. And I don't bully easy.'

Angela Eagle didn't like her private life rather than her political views becoming the subject of interviews: 'I'm a politician before I'm gay, believe it or not, and I have a whole range of other issues that I care about, and I was approached for loads of interviews at the time, which I turned down, because I wanted to make the one statement and leave it at that.'

Changing how others see them

One of Labour's 1997 MPs did her own research and published a Fabian paper to counter the negative media image that was being put out that the new Labour women MPs were somehow ineffectual. Fiona Mactaggart explains: 'It was just cold research on what difference have the women made, and actually, it was really striking how much difference we'd made. We changed the culture of this place, we changed various select committees hugely, we got specific legislative reform; women had done much better out of the budgets than men; we'd got, you know, even VAT lifted from sanitary protection, even really simple things like that, but they hadn't actually been publicised. The lifting of VAT from sanitary protection was, I think, the only stealth tax cut on earth. The Chancellor didn't even mention it when he announced it. It was in a press release, as opposed to actually trumpeted, and why was it not trumpeted? Firstly because I think he's embarrassed talking about menstruation in public, but actually, more seriously, it was not trumpeted because we'd sort of lost our nerve from having trumpeted hot air.'

Glenda Jackson says that whatever the media may or may not have said about women MPs, nearly all of them got re-elected. She does not think the general public takes too much notice of the media anyway: 'Their own constituents know their value and their worth. And I think there's only one woman elected in 1997 who wasn't re-elected in 2001.'

Ruth Kelly thinks attitudes to women MPs are shifting: 'I think the mood has changed in a slightly more positive direction recently. At the beginning there was huge excitement. After a while that lead to an enormous amount of cynicism about whether women MPs were just toadying, toeing the line, on message, etc. One of the results of having had a second term and having had difficult issues for the parliamentary Labour Party to deal with inevitably, as part of that time in government, is that all MPs have come to be seen, and rightly so, as individuals with their own ideas and beliefs, but committed to the Labour Party, and I think that's been to the benefit for them.'

Margaret Beckett points to the time when travelling with a colleague on a train as a new MP she realised she would always be on display. She explains how she told him: 'The thing I find a bit disconcerting is, I mean, here on the train, I'm sitting on the train and talking to you and so on and I'm realising that actually I don't know any of the people on this train except you; they probably don't know me, but on the other hand, if some of them are my constituents, maybe they do know me and so maybe I'm on display,' and he said, 'Oh, my dear girl, didn't you realise? This is your life from now on. You are never not on display.' That was disconcerting for Margaret, as she had not appreciated her public profile in quite that way before.

Ann Clwyd remembers how it was not until after she persisted in getting a parliamentary seat that she was told why she had been rejected ten years earlier. She explains: 'Somebody offered the opinion that the reason they hadn't selected me ten years previously was "because of the funny clothes I was wearing". And they remembered exactly what they were, and I remember too, and I suppose they were quite funny clothes; emerald green jacket, and cream trousers, and they thought that was very peculiar.'

Helen Jackson says you have to gain the respect of people both inside and outside the party: 'You have to live with yourself in the end, and to live with yourself you have to feel that you have the respect of the people that you're working with, which means the people within the party at every level, because they're all doing such very important things; but to live with yourself, you also have to feel that you have the respect of the people you represent. And you can't do that unless you are being pretty true, and speaking honestly to them about what you're working, on their behalf, to do in Parliament.'

Helen Clark changed the way others viewed her by employing a good firm of solicitors so that she could sue the press when it printed an inaccurate story about her: 'I've sued. I've sued successfully eight times out of eight . . . I never do any legal stuff unless my libel lawyer says, "This is definitely defamatory." Not irritating, but defamatory. And I'm very glad I did. I've got a new basement out of it, I've got a new garden, I've furnished my lounge and my bedroom. But, you know, seriously, you have to challenge if they're writing stuff that is wrong, and I actually am very concerned and worried about the standards of journalism nowadays.'

Conservative women MPs think that women give a party a more modern and approachable look. Eleanor Laing: 'People in my constituency, I think, see me as a real person, not as some sort of cardboard cut-out Member of Parliament who you're afraid to talk to.'

Sometimes the way people see you may be a case of mistaken identity. Dari Taylor recalls the time when travelling abroad with the Defence Select Committee, a wrong name badge led to a queue of people waiting to see her: 'I hadn't noticed that they were queuing up to speak to me, frankly, I was in a group, you know, it was pretty chatty and all the rest of it, so as I turned I said, "I am sticking to the brief." And as I did, she saw my name-plate and she said, "Dari, have you seen your name-plate?" and I looked down. I was "Air Vice-Marshall", "Taylor" was right, that was the only bit that was. I had every commendation that you could possibly have and there it was, on my chest. It was not a bit of a wonder they were queuing up to speak to me.'

Dari is not the only women MP who has learnt to laugh at how they are portrayed by others. The humour helps to counter what can be incredibly cruel jibes made about them. There is strong resentment across all three parties of the way women are represented in the national media. Many mention the fact that the regional media is far more fair and balanced in their reporting. There is concern that journalistic standards have slipped, that facts are not checked and that untruths are perpetuated by journalists lifting stories from other sources without speaking to the MPs concerned. However, while some think the 'Blair's Babes' picture was a mistake, it is clear that others are quite prepared to view this moment in their history with good hearted humour. The picture served an important purpose but perhaps the participants should have been more prepared for the media attention that would subsequently focus on them as women MPs.

EIGHT

Women MPs and their careers

The rise and fall of women in politics

In an age when the predominant public perception of MPs is as self-seeking and self-serving individuals, who have brought into disrepute those who follow a career path in politics, the general public might be forgiven for thinking that this is definitely not a profession they would want their children to follow. The music hall phrase that you must not 'put your daughter on the stage, Mrs Worthington' could well be applied to political life today. This is advice that you might expect parents to pass on to their children, particularly if they believe all that they read about politicians. Conflict and controversy, often between politicians in the same party, dominate the headlines rather than the issues the politicians are fighting for, even if the policies they will pursue might result in beneficial outcomes for some or many people.

Politicians themselves understand this is the game they have to engage in to make a name for themselves or the views they represent, but most would argue that they started their political careers to change society for the better, particularly for the constituents they represent. They may harbour different ambitions and aims to achieve those objectives and they may follow different political philosophies in order that they might 'do good' towards others, but it is clear that when they set out on the road of a political career they feel they are embarking on a path that will help them to help others. Whether they are a socialist, a free-marketer, a neo-conservative, a libertarian, a follower of the 'Third Way' or a crossbencher, it is those belief systems, convictions and ideals that get the politician out of bed in the morning. In pursuit of these convictions they find themselves speaking in the Commons chamber or knocking on doors in their constituency on a Sunday morning when most people would rather be tucked up in bed.

There are three main grades of ministers. The first step on the career ladder begins as a parliamentary private secretary, who acts as an assistant to a minister and they have some specific responsibilities within a department. If they prove themselves in this the most junior of all ministerial roles, they may be lucky enough to be promoted to the position of a minister of state within a government department, such as Education, Health, Trade and Industry, the Treasury or the Cabinet Office. A minister of state holds responsibility for a part of a department's work, and the number of junior ministers within each government department varies. They will be given a specific job to do and a title such as Schools Minister or Consumer Affairs Minister. At the top of the career ladder is the job of the secretary of state, when they will then be known as 'the' minister in charge. They are almost always members of the Cabinet. A secretary of state has ultimate responsibility for all of their department's work. The ministers of state in a department report to the secretary of state.

Being ambitious and getting to the top in this competitive career path will help a politician promote their beliefs and ideals. A Cabinet minister would have more influence than a backbencher, but even so politicians might like to fit into the role of a diligent backbencher or see themselves as someone whose career path may be to serve as a member of an influential select committee, where they may be an outspoken critic of their own government, rather than the loyal party member who is going to climb the ladder from parliamentary private secretary, through to minister and then move on to heading a government department as a secretary of state and member of the Cabinet. Then, for the very few, there is that one-off possibility that you may be in the right place at the right time and your own party kindly asks you to step forward to be their leader. Luck might play a large part in whether a politician does or does not make it to the very top.

Mo Mowlam certainly attributes her success as a female politician to luck: 'Luck is so important in politics: getting the seat was luck for me . . . getting the Cabinet job was lucky for me, because I became a shadow minister and then Tony was convinced that Kevin had to go because he was a very strong Catholic, very supportive of the Catholic Nationalist side. You couldn't have that where you needed someone neutral. So I was lucky all the way.' Others might think she is being unduly modest about the success of her career. However, she says she was task-focused, something other women politicians talk about, and that she was never after a top job in politics: 'I'm not interested in power-plays. What I'm interested in is getting policy delivered and changes delivered on the ground, and if I have to take part in power-plays to do that, then I would do it, but I didn't.'

So where do female politicians get their political ideals from? Ann Widdecombe says her religious beliefs are more important than being seen as a female politician: 'My defining characteristic isn't that I'm a woman. I'm a Catholic, I'm a Conservative, and those things are part of my definition. Being a woman? It's a biological fact of life and nothing more than that.'

Being a woman politician and the only woman in her party is important to Ulster Unionist Lady Hermon: 'Women do politics very differently from men. We try to find a way forward. I think that in fact we tend to focus less on what has gone on in the past. We are what we are, but we are trying to find a common way forward. We women, I think, are less confrontational, though I have to say that it is because I am a minority of one I find myself arguing frequently with my male colleagues to try and change the agenda . . .'

Politicians' ambitions, squabbles and intrigues are what we read about in the headlines of the daily newspapers. Day to day, from the broadsheets to the tabloids, newspapers relish covering the rise and fall and personal follies of MPs, ministers and prime ministers. The stories are human and we can at times feel empathy with them. We like to read of the rising stars, the promotions and the dismissals.

Individuals may go into politics to achieve change on behalf of others but after their rise often comes their fall. Former MP Mo Mowlam warns that being a 'popular woman' was problematic for her ambitious rivals, particularly after she got a standing ovation at one Labour Party Conference. She recalls: 'After my first six months in Ireland, at the party conference, I got my standing ovation in the middle of Tony's speech, which I think was a wonderful recognition of the work that we've been doing in Ireland, but at the same time was probably the beginning of my kiss-of-death, because that is not something that leaders appreciate.'

She said she found the spin about her supposed poor health, after she was treated for a brain tumour, hurtful and unnecessary: 'Oh, it was painful, of course. If you keep reading in the paper that you were not up to the job and you'd been brain-damaged by your tumour and therefore you're not capable, and your ill health makes it impossible for you to work, and I mean, just plain lies. You do get angry, but I wasn't prepared to go in the press against them, because if you go in the press you just hype the story, and I was in no way going to do that.'

Harriet Harman recalls her sacking following that vote in the cut in Lone Parent Benefits. Her minister and Labour colleague Joan Ruddock was sacked too. Harriet later regained a government position after spending time on the backbenches: 'I'd been sacked. That was very difficult, but there were advantages to finding myself on the backbenches because I then did a research project called "Mothers in Manufacturing", which I wouldn't have been able to do . . . I was able to step back and think more broadly and reflect more, and so actually, although being sacked is a horrible thing and I wouldn't recommend it to anybody, the actual outcome of it was it gave me a chance to look at things from the backbenches, which is a different perspective, and to regroup, and think strategically, and now I'm back in government so . . .'

Joan Ruddock, a former Woman's Minister, remembers the sacking: 'We had our priorities set, we had our mechanisms, we had our structures of Government and we were beginning to deliver and then . . . we were sacked, which was a time of terrible trauma.' She says she had not been aware that she would be sacked, and that she was never given a reason for it, something that still rankles: 'I had been doing quite a lot of quite high-powered things and so on and so forth, and anyway, it was all a case of clearly being sensitive to the fact I could be sacked . . . but nobody at any time suggested to me that I would be sacked and my own civil servants seemed to feel quite strongly that I wouldn't be and then I was without any kind of warning, I was just asked to go and see Tony and he said, "I am sorry but I have got to let you go."'

Joan thinks there was hostility to the work she was doing as Women's Minister: 'I just think that I was dispensable as an individual, I wasn't needed any longer in "the project", and there was a lot of hostility to there being a significant gender focus to the government, hostility which I think has gone away now. I think now the extent, to which the government has delivered for women, is considered to be important and I think will be sustained. But then there was a lot of hostility.' She initially found being a backbencher difficult but has focused on promoting the causes that she believes in, like a freeze on GM food products and helping women in Afghanistan, and she has continued to work influentially behind the scenes.

Dame Marion Roe got sacked from Margaret Thatcher's government. She recalls feeling much the same as Joan Ruddock: 'The biggest knock to the ego is when you cease to be a minister. That was quite a blow, but it happens to us all, but you have to swallow hard. I was obviously disappointed; I thought I had done a good job, we all do, but then Margaret moved me to the backbenches, and that was a disappointment, and then I said to myself, I am going to be here a long time and I am now going to make my contribution to Parliament in a different way, which is what I did and I became a representative of the Council of Europe.'

Elsewhere in the Labour Party ranks, the former Home Office Minister Beverley Hughes was forced to resign after she made a gaff on *Newsnight* about immigration applications from eastern Europe. Other women in Westminster supported her during this difficult time: 'The whole of the parliamentary Labour Party was just incredibly supportive and angry, you know, in a way that was positive for me, and indeed after I had resigned, I got . . . well, I stopped counting at 300, letters from colleagues and people all over the country I didn't know, and people I'd worked with, again expressing their anger and so on, support, and that was really helpful.'

Standing down

Not only are there more women in Westminster and more women in the Cabinet, but also as a consequence of women's increased representation, more women gave up too; sixteen in all, before the 2005 election.[30] However even though the number of women who have resigned in the last parliament is more or less in line with the proportion of women in their parties in Westminster – twelve Labour, three Conservative and one Liberal Democrat, it is the Labour women who have been singled out by the media for 'throwing in the towel' or somehow not being up to the job because they have not seen their job as an MP as being one that you necessarily needed to keep for life.

This view has, in the main, been held by their male colleagues. It is evident that women politicians see their political careers as more flexible than men. If they came into the Commons when they were younger, after eight years they might want to be with their young families more, or if they entered later in life in their 50s, they may want to be at home more to look after their grandchildren. They see no loss of virility in admitting to these emotions. Some men have also done similar things, such as the former Cabinet minister Alan Milburn, who did not step down as an MP but did step back in his career and resign as Secretary of State for Health so that he could see more of his young sons. Conservative men have also made similar decisions, Norman Fowler MP being one.

The career ambitions of politicians often falter at the ballot box when they are voted out. Jackie Ballard does not, in retrospect, regret losing her seat. She is now Chief Executive of the RSPCA: 'I had decided some time before the 2001 general election that I would stand in that election purely because I wanted to prove that I could hold the seat, but then I wouldn't stand at the next election, that two terms would be enough for me. I actually think that two terms is enough for anybody and I have a firm belief that after two terms people should be chucked out like they are in many other legislatures, and have to serve at least one term in the outside world before they can go back in again. I think that would be really good for our democracy, because I think that any institution institutionalises people, but Parliament institutionalises people more than most, because it's designed to do that.'

Another Labour MP who has had to fight prejudice as a woman but despite her battle has been deselected is Jane Griffiths: 'I haven't had any problems with the constituency. I have a personal vote, I'm popular, I increased the majority in 2001 from 1997, so the constituency is no problem at all. And, in fact, the constituency party is by and large no problem, but there is a small group within it who decided that, because I wasn't doing as they said, they were going to get rid of me. They made three attempts and succeeded the third time.'

Jane says she did feel bullied: 'I may try for another seat. I'm in discussions with a couple of them at the moment. We'll see; it's too soon to say. But unlike quite a lot of people, I mean, I didn't come in to the House until I was 43, so I had had another life and raised children and so on before that, and I did have other skills and other interests. Politics has not been my whole life, and I have had a proper job from time to time, so I can do another proper job again.'

Other's career paths wane when MPs are forced to resign from shadow Cabinet positions over issues. Jenny Tonge did just that following remarks she made in support of the Palestinians. She is also giving up her seat of Richmond Park: 'I'm not standing at the next election anyway, my husband and I are both retiring, and we'd long decided that, and I'd already stood down from the front bench. So, you know, the fact that I was still a frontbencher taking on another brief, it didn't really bother me personally, I mean, I've since discovered that it is a great disgrace, and I've fallen from grace, and, you know, I should be thoroughly ashamed of myself. But I'm not actually, I'm quite pleased that it happened.' She says she has enjoyed her parliamentary career: 'When I got into Parliament, I was already 57 years old, you see, so I came in very late. There was never really going to be a serious career in politics, it was just a sort of wonderful, wonderful experience to end my career in medicine, really. I don't regret a minute of it; it's fabulous.'

Sometimes MPs resign their ministerial roles on points of principle or because they want to be free to vote against their own government rather than, as ministers, being forced to follow the ministerial whip. Anne Campbell resigned her role as a parliamentary private secretary over her deep feelings on the government's position on Iraq: '. . . because obviously I had to resign my parliamentary private secretary role, and I was sad about that because I had got on very well with Patricia [Hewitt] and I liked being in the centre of things. I couldn't really envisage what life was going to be like not being a parliamentary private secretary.'

Others have also decided that two terms in Westminster is enough and that they want to be with their families while they grow up. Julia Drown: 'Okay, I'm stepping down, and I'll have done it for seven or eight years, and I think that's a long time to do any job . . . but now that my children are getting older I have to leave them behind all the time in the constituency, and it feels just completely wrong for me to take my children to school on Monday morning and then not see them again until Friday. And I'd be happy to do it, I've shown you I can do it, but I don't want to commit myself now, at this point, to do it [for what] could be another seven years at this point. That just feels wrong. I might come back to it at some future time, but it just feels right for me to now do something different for a while.'

The careerist, the campaigner, the rebel, the loyalist, the sister

The trait of loyalty is not one that many MPs would find offensive. Others might criticise them for it but they themselves talk openly about why they see loyalty as a good trait not a bad one. Being an MP, says Ann Taylor, is a tough but satisfying career for a woman and deflecting criticism is part of that: 'It can be a tough career for a woman; it can be a tough career for a man. It can also be a very satisfying career, because you can help people very directly, and there is a great deal of satisfaction in that.'

Loyalty is important to some. Jackie Lawrence says she is loyal to her Government: 'I mean, the public see that as the public face of Parliament, but my role in being here I've seen as twofold. Firstly to represent the interests of my constituents and secondly to support and maintain the Labour government, in whose philosophy I believe.'

Anne McGuire also takes pride in being loyal to a Labour government: 'I certainly would be labelled a loyalist, and I don't just mean that in terms of the current prime minister or the current Cabinet, the current leadership. I mean that in terms of all my history in the party. I have been loyal to the party through all its leaders since the 1960s. That's not to say that I don't have my criticisms, but I would voice those criticisms in an appropriate manner.'

However, Ann Cryer does not mind having earned a reputation as a Labour rebel: 'I wouldn't like to think of myself as being an ultra-loyalist. But I hope it's a rebel in a constructive sort of way, in that I think almost all the things I have rebelled against – except Iraq, but we can't put back the clock, what's done is done – but on other issues, often changes have come about subsequently, such as the single-parent changes.'

Glenda Jackson rebels on some issues but not others. She did not want to become a figurehead in any way: 'I'm a firm believer in exercising your franchise. I think if you disaffect the electorate, nature abhors a vacuum, so you're going to see something far worse . . . to come rushing in, and to dismiss parliament as being just something to get your name in the papers, I find deeply, deeply shocking.'

Harriet Harman says she is someone who wants to effect change for society generally and for women: 'I think you've either got to do it or not do it, and I didn't do it in order to support the status quo, I did it to get in there and change the status quo, change the hours, change the climate, change the number of women MPs so that even if I'd found it a struggle, then it would be less of a struggle for others . . . I got in there not because I wanted to struggle and struggle in the system, but actually change it, and I think it has changed. It's still snail's pace, there's still so much more to go, it's two steps forward, one step back, but you know, the show's on the road.'

Harriet believes she is privileged to be an MP: 'To be able to work, to do something that you care about and things that matter and make a difference is a huge privilege, and you know, I can see where I've been part of a movement for progress, and it's very demanding, and it's a heavy level of responsibility, but that's a great privilege, really.'

Other women politicians would agree, Sarah Teather says: 'There are hugely rewarding aspects of the work. I mean, when you can get something done for somebody, that's the most tremendous feeling, and Parliament is where it's at. I mean it is where the influence lies. If you really want to change the system that is the only place to do it.'

Eleanor Laing is also motivated by a desire to help others. She loves her job because she can make a difference to people and society: 'Being an MP is the best job in the world. It's absolutely great and I love it to bits, because every day is different from every other day, you have a chance in your work as a constituency MP to help people and do some good, which is one of the driving forces that I had – making a difference to people's lives and trying to help them – and you have a precious opportunity to take part in the formulation of the laws which will dictate how our society develops in the future, and I think that's a really important role, and I think it's such a pity nowadays that politicians are derided in the press.'

Dawn Primarolo thinks her job is 'exciting': 'I can't think of anything more exciting to do in a job than to be able to make changes that benefit people's lives and give people the tools, the abilities, the opportunities, to make the most of themselves. There is nothing like it. It is unique.'

Maria Eagle says it is commitment not conflict that drives her: 'I'm not saying there aren't disagreements and personality clashes, there always are in politics, like in everything else, but this huge emphasis on it as a contest instead of as something that people do because they're committed to it, because they want to improve people's lives. Most people come into politics, . . . to improve life for people, to provide a public service, but [also] to change things for the better.'

Sandra Gidley, says 'making a difference' to the lives of others is her prime motivation for being a politician: 'What other job is there that gives [you] the opportunity to get involved in almost anything you like, where you can dip into an issue, see if you think it's interesting and then if not, actually, you've shown an interest, you might have helped at a certain level, but then you can walk away? If there's something that you think is a real issue, you can get involved at a much more intense level.'

Virginia Bottomley sums up the feelings of the majority when she talks of the rewards of being a constituency MP: 'Well, my constituency's like being a social worker, and I am hugely fond of my constituency and my constituents, and even though I'm stepping down from Parliament, we're staying in the house where we've been for the last twenty years and we will I hope live there for another twenty years . . . In the constituency, I've always been very straight and not been partisan, which is one of the reasons I'm so against multi-member constituencies or top-up lists because I feel the one-on-one relationship between the constituency and the MP is part of our parliamentary democracy.'

Personal convictions drive them on their particular career paths. Margaret Hodge says: 'I'm pretty clear about what I want to achieve and pretty passionate about it, and I've had that all my life. I mean, that's what's driven me in politics, I want to change the world and I want to make life better. I'm not in politics because I want power, I'm in politics because I want to improve people's life chances and life opportunities.'

Many of the women MPs in Westminster say they are driven by ambition but that ambition derives from wanting to achieve change on behalf of others, particularly women. Labour's Tessa Jowell says the pay gap is the next big issue she and some of her colleagues want to confront: 'Well, it's raising aspirations for women to be able to get into more of the higher-paid jobs, for women to be able to take time out without suffering the penalty of lower pay as a result.'

Teresa Gorman championed the issue of the menopause on behalf of other women: 'I campaigned for menopause, getting that on the map, and getting more women aware, we now have a backbench group on menopause, or something like that. I did campaign for women who were suffering life imprisonment, for what I considered were manslaughter issues, and I did that with what you might call some of the left-wing campaign groups. I certainly campaigned against lowering the age for abortion with the Labour Party women.'

A number of women MPs take pride in being backbenchers and do not raise their ambitions further. Lady Hermon has won acclaim for her work on the backbenches: 'Within the first eighteen months of finding myself at Westminster, I was nominated as the opposition backbench MP by the Channel Four awards, and then subsequently by the *House* magazine awards, and I found that absolutely nerve-wracking because I suddenly felt media attention.'

Linda Perham fulfils her ambitions through her work on a select committee: 'You can be tremendously influential as a backbencher, and not everybody can get on a select committee, and not everyone gets on the top ones, of which Trade and Industry is one, so it's seen as a parallel career, really. And that's something I welcome. I said early on to the whips that I don't expect to be a minister, because I was elected – back to ageism – but just before I was 50 . . . I think being a parliamentary private secretary is about the worst job in the world. You're not paid and you've got all the hassle of being the minister's bag carrier, sitting on standing committees and all this sort of thing, so I'm just not interested. To get on a select committee [Trade and Industry] was really something that I've enjoyed tremendously, and that's one of the good things in Parliament: you can feel that you've achieved something.'

Feminism

Across parties, women MPs felt comfortable talking about feminism and pursuing a feminist agenda. However, some make distinctions between 1970s feminism and feminism today.

Someone who feels more comfortable with today's feminist agenda is Tessa Jowell: 'I didn't feel comfortable with 1970s feminism, and in fact all of my radicalism in the 70s and 80s was focused on the rights of people with mental illness. I am now very comfortable with feminism and being a feminist, because I think that feminism now recognises choice much more, I think it expressly recognises motherhood. I think it's been highly, highly organic. Certainly being a Member of Parliament has feminised me.'

One Conservative MP prefers the feminism of the 1970s to the 'softer' feminism of today. Ann Widdecombe: 'I think it is complete tosh, all this talk about women being treated differently. I can vividly remember that after the 1997 election, one of the "Blair Babes" said to me, "Ooh, isn't it terrible how the men are so rude to us." And I said, "Yes, and isn't it so terrible how they're so rude to each other." It's absolute tosh, and I have no time at all for the so-called "feminism" approach, which says that if you're a woman, everything that ever goes wrong in your life is because you're a woman. That is not equality. I've no time for 1990s feminism. I have a lot of time for 1970s feminism which said, "Give us the equal opportunities, we'll show you that we're just as good as you, if not better than you."'

Gillian Shephard realised that prejudice still existed towards women when she first entered Parliament: 'It didn't occur to me because I was born in 1940, and when feminism burst upon the stage in the mid 1960s, it was a revelation to me. I had been to an all-girls' school, an all-women's college, I worked for two years in an all-girls' school, and then went into local education administration, where there were a lot of women in powerful positions. The squire of our village was a woman, the chairman of the local magistrates' bench was a woman, and there were powerful Norfolk women farmers. It didn't occur to me that there was a problem. I then, with everyone else, read Betty Friedan and Simone de Beauvoir and so on, and realised there must be a problem . . . I've never had a professional problem. A bit of a problem with being selected, but I just thought, Well, you know, how silly, and did not expect there to be any problems at all. There were, however, because when I got here, I found that there was an attitude towards women MPs, which was, "Dear lady, how delightful you look," or "What a clever little thing to say." There were those attitudes. But I can't honestly say they worried me in the least.'

Theresa May realises that it may not be fashionable for Conservative MPs to be feminists but she says she is one: 'Now this has always been a difficult question for Conservatives to answer because of the sort of image about what feminism is about. I think the honest answer is, Yes, I am a feminist in the sense that I think we should treat men and women equally, and we should say that the opportunities should be open to women as well as to men. And if feminism is about that, then yes, I am.'

Sandra Gidley was angry that her party did not pursue policies that would have led to positive discrimination in favour of women. She thinks the Liberal Democrat Party is still sexist: 'I mean, we put a motion to Conference, I was one of the people behind that, it was loudly decried by all and sundry, including a group of women who were nicknamed the Pink T-shirt Brigade, wearing pink T-shirts saying, "I'm not a token woman"; and I felt like getting a baggier T-shirt, because one of those would not be flattering, saying, "I am a token woman".'

Other Labour women are quite open about their feminist beliefs. Hilary Armstrong says: '[It] doesn't mean to say that I want to be confined to women's issues, or don't think that the men here have got an important role to play, and I work on them as much as I work on any women. I don't get hung up on some of the things that people associate with feminists; I don't care what people call me, so that probably means the men work with me a bit more easily.'

Gwyneth Dunwoody agrees: 'I believe that women are tremendously important and different and essential. In that sense, I'm a feminist. I don't believe in empty gestures, I believe in real advances. So that means equal pay, it means better hours, and it means support services for people that they really need. In those things, I am 100 per cent a feminist.'

Anne Campbell thinks definitions of feminism have become clouded: 'I'm never quite sure what a "feminist" means any more, but I do believe that women should have equal opportunities to become Members of Parliament, obviously, but to work, to rise to high positions, and to have a family life as well.'

Anne Begg is a feminist: 'Probably by most definitions I would be described as a feminist, but I actually think that looking back with hindsight, the biggest failure of feminism is that we forgot to take the men with us. I think we forgot that if we were going to have our independence, if we were going to have choices about whether we worked and our home/life balance, then the men had to change too.'

Claire Curtis-Thomas thinks it is a shame more men are not feminists too: 'It isn't that they won't come along with the female agenda, they just don't relate to it very well because they're still stuck in very stereotypical relationships themselves – you know, they are down here, their wives are invariably at home looking after the children. And that's how it's always been, so there are some men here who are very much switched on to a feminist agenda, and others who are not.'

Others admire the feminist struggles staged by their 'sisters' from previous generations of women politicians. Ann Clwyd recalls her encounters with Barbara Castle when she was putting up a fight in the Commons for a ladies loo: 'I know when Barbara Castle came in, there were even fewer women, and she had to fight very hard to get a ladies' loo, an extra ladies' loo, and eventually it was dubbed Barbara's Castle, because it's on the library corridor.'

Supporting each other

It is clear that prior to the victory for women in the 1997 election, women have been crossing their party lines to help, support and encourage other women. Two names are frequently mentioned, Harriet Harman for Labour and Gillian Shephard for the Conservatives. Margaret Thatcher is also mentioned.

Tessa Jowell praises Harriet's support for other women and Joan Ruddock says of her: 'There were a lot of colleagues who were helpful, but I did associate a lot with women, Harriett, who I already knew when I came in here was extremely helpful, extremely positive, looking out for the new women and making us very welcome.'

Oona King says Harriet and others helped her: 'I remember Harriet Harman, I spent a lot of time with her. When I think back to it now, thinking that she was a Cabinet Minister, it's quite amazing, you know, how helpful she was. Tessa Jowell and Joan Ruddock were the same. There were a lot of women who helped me. I have to say there were also one or two men.'

Caroline Spelman talks of the help Gillian Shephard has given her: 'Well, I beat a path to the door of Gillian Shephard, as a female and experienced Member of Parliament; in fact she [was] next door to my office. She's a wonderful sounding board, very experienced, doesn't impose her opinions on you but she opens the wealth of her experience to a relatively new Member of Parliament.'

Sarah Teather talks of a comradeship across parties: 'There was a kind of odd camaraderie with women across parties. I remember one thing that sticks in my mind; the first day I was here, and there was a note under my door from Kate Hoey who's on the same corridor. It was a lovely note, saying, "[During] a by-election, it's completely bonkers, but it will settle down, if there's anything I can do, pop round the corner." And I thought that was lovely. It was really nice. And I was very, very touched by that. There are a few of the Tory MPs, I mean, Gillian Shepherd stopped me and had a chat to me.'

Surprisingly Dame Marion Roe saw the softer side of Margaret Thatcher, as soon as she came into the Commons. She tells a remarkable story: 'I was given a welcome from Margaret Thatcher, who wondered into the tearoom, and came to the table where I was sitting drinking my tea, and you must remember, this was the Prime Minister, and so I went to stand up, and she put her hand on my shoulder, and said, "My dear, don't stand up, we are all equal here, and I have come to welcome you to Parliament." I was about to say who I was, but she obviously knew who I was, which I thought was very good, bearing in mind her other responsibilities at the time, and she was very friendly, very welcoming and she wished me success and so on. That made me feel I had arrived; that the Prime Minister actually welcomed me to the House of Commons.'

Gillian Shephard says she has consciously helped other women: 'It's because I'm very interested in them, of course, and the things they've done, because they're more diverse than the men coming in. But it's also true to say that some of the new Labour women asked things when they came in. I always say it's because I'm short, you know, I look very approachable.'

Taking the knocks

Their worst moments in careers of MPs are either embarrassment in the chamber, being sacked, losing an election, or receiving unwanted and intrusive media attention. Often they feel they are not given a reason for their sacking, that they have to rebuild their lives after an election defeat, that the media's reporting is sensationalised, or that the words simply do not come out when they begin to speak in the chamber. They have to be tough enough for the job. It's not easy but it is rewarding.

Oona King is happy to laugh at her own expense: '[My] worst moment was when I stood up and the Speaker didn't call me, so I sat down and then he did call me, but I'd forgotten what my point was. I was a new MP at that point – I would never do this now – but I said, "Sorry, I don't know what I wanted to say." I couldn't sleep for about three months, I thought, Well how can a politician say that? That was definitely my worst moment in Parliament.'

Angela Eagle has never been given a reason for her sacking, which happened by mobile phone: 'Being sacked on a mobile phone in front of 100 people just as I was about to make a speech . . . I was astonished. I hadn't expected to be sacked. I think most people thought I was a good minister. Most people were very shocked. I had no inkling of it, nobody had spoken to me, I was given different reasons as [to] why – none of them were valid – and, in fact, talking to other people who've been through that ministerial mill, they've all been given pretty similar reasons as to why they were got rid of as well.'

Hazel Blears recalls losing one election: 'The worst thing was probably losing the 1992 general election. I'd been a candidate for three years in a marginal seat. Had a fantastic campaign, we all thought we were going to win. The last week, it went away from us and we lost by 400 votes after three recounts in the middle of the night. I'd had to resign my job, so I woke up with no job, no seat, no dreams, no nothing, and then two weeks later had to go and knock on doors in the local elections.'

151

Jenny Tonge also recalls losing in the 1992 election: 'That was a terrible time. Really, it sounds pathetic. We lose an election and then it can affect you that much; but it was really terrible. The phone stops ringing, all of a sudden nothing, there was nothing after all the attention and the media and the rushing about and the interest and the policy-making and everything. It all suddenly disappeared.'

Jackie Lawrence feels the press invaded her personal privacy when they told the story of how she had once had an illegitimate child: 'When I was a young woman, I had a child before I was married. My husband knew about it when we started going out together – I told him. And I think this is a measure of how society's changed. I was seventeen, I had a child before I was married, and the child went for adoption. When she was eighteen, she found me. She's part of our family, very much part of our family now. It was not public knowledge, but the *Daily Mail* got hold of it, and decided to contact me, and I thought, Well, you know, I can be nothing but honest and open. But they splashed that all over the newspapers in such a way that it caused my family grief – the way in which it was publicised – my parents, my husband.'

Eleanor Laing also feels her worst moment was when the press wrote about her divorce and private life: 'If I'm being honest about it, the worst that's happened to me since being a Member of Parliament, and one of the worst things that has ever happened to me, is when I was going through my divorce, the *Sunday Mirror* put it on the front page, and that was just excruciatingly horrible. And do you know the worst bit about it? The worst bit was that the photograph that they put of me on the front page of this paper, which was then copied in other newspapers, was of me, eight-months pregnant, on the night of the general election. Now, can you imagine how tired and big I looked at eight months pregnant at 3 a.m., standing up on the platform hearing my election result? And they said that I was fat and frumpy! Now that annoyed me more than anything.'

Fiona Mactaggart says that when she was a Home Office minister she felt saddened by one incident above all: 'The death of the Chinese cockle pickers, where I had signed a letter very shortly after I'd been appointed as a minister, which put me into the middle of the debate which was very difficult. That was the worst thing that has happened to me.'

Despite the 'knockabout' nature of politics, it is clear that women MPs enjoy doing the job. Many are discerning enough to concentrate on the aspects they most enjoy. Some may see themselves on a career path that takes them to ministerial positions and as secretaries of state members of the Cabinet, but others are happy to be backbenchers, campaigners or select committee members. A large number across all parties are simply happy to be known as the constituency MP and focus largely on this work from which they evidently draw huge job satisfaction.

NINE

Reform of the House

The history

When the 120 women MPs of 1997 took up their parliamentary seats in
Westminster, it was not just the miles of seemingly endless corridors, the
lack of office space or modern computers and support equipment that they
had to come to terms with; they were also entering an institution that, at that
time, had no fixed term-dates. MPs would not know when the House would
sit or rise, and there was no time limit on the all-night sittings, so debates
would frequently run into the night or early hours of the morning. It was not
just 'the biggest boys' drinking club in the West' as some have referred to it,
but the House was also conducting its business when MPs were exhausted
and struggling through tiredness to summon up coherent thoughts. This
was the climate in which many important debates were conducted and votes
were taken. It was a culture shock to many of the women who thought the
waiting round in the Lobby pointless, the sleeping under a coat in the
corridors unprofessional, and the whips' office initially unfriendly and
unsympathetic to those who had families, although that did subsequently
change.

They found the patterns of work and working practices obscure. Claire
Curtis-Thomas says: 'We don't have a job description, we don't have a
personnel function, we don't have a care function as such, so I mean I was
very concerned that if people dropped dead on the job, who writes the 'in
sympathy' letter? Who sends the flowers? Who sends the cards? It's a very ad
hoc world for that. So if you're popular, yes you get loads of cards, if you're
truly unpopular, you get bugger-all, and that really isn't how you should be

handling a significant workforce, which is what the Labour Party are here in government.'

Ruth Kelly agrees: 'When I came in in 1997, what I found, and I think this is in common with nearly all new MPs, was a real vacuum, that there wasn't an automatic way of finding support and help, that people were working very much on their own initiative. I was lucky in 1997 because there was such a large new intake of MPs, which meant there were lots of people in the same boat together, and that meant we clearly had each other. But really, there is no personnel function; there is no help and support – or very little. There is some, but there's not much, actually, and really it's up to people to take the initiative and get on with it.'

Linda Perham read a book by another MP to find out what she was and wasn't supposed to do as a new MP: 'People ask you, "What is a typical day?" Well, there isn't one, and there are not many jobs where you can do exactly what you like. You can choose what you get interested in; you don't need to turn up to anything, really. I mean, if you don't turn up to votes – well, you can be reported to your constituency party, you could be deselected next time, but really . . . There's a wonderful book by Paul Flynn called *Commons Knowledge*.[31] Now that was a great help to me.'

Joan Walley was surprised too by the lack of a proper job function: 'There wasn't anybody to give any advice or to go to about anything. We just had one session with the Fees Office saying what money we got for allowances, but, in terms of what went on where, what committee rooms, what we were interested in, what skills we had, what we could contribute, absolutely no human resources management, I think either from within the parliamentary Labour Party as much as in the House of Commons authorities as well.'

Their previous professional careers may have prepared them for government but had not prepared them for this. Maria Eagle: 'I think the lack of support and obvious structures was a bit of a shock to a lot of people. I mean, myself, I was a lawyer, I'm used to having people around me; secretaries, whose job was there to make my job – which was making decisions about cases and running litigation – as easy as possible.'

Soon after 1997, the women MPs across parties began to push at their party whips' doors for change. The changes and reforms they achieved, particularly Parliament finishing earlier in the evenings, are highly significant and symbolic. Parliament's new fixed-term calendar is popular with most women MPs. The House also sits fewer Fridays. However, although Parliament finishes at 7 p.m. on Wednesdays and 6 p.m. on Thursdays, on occasion debates can run on to 10 p.m. It used to also finish at 7 p.m. on Tuesdays; however, on 26 January 2005 opponents of the reforms managed to reverse Tuesday sittings to the old hours again. The voting to restore the old Tuesday hours was 292 to 225.

Since the 2005 general election, MPs' working patterns begin with sittings on Mondays and Tuesdays from 2.30 p.m. to 10 p.m. On Wednesdays, which survived the backlash by traditionalists, they continue to sit from 11.30 a.m. to 7 p.m. They also sit an hour earlier on Thursdays, from 10.30 a.m. to 6 p.m., which allows Scottish and northern MPs to travel back to their constituencies. Robin Cook, who introduced the new hours when he was Leader of the Commons, appealed to MPs in the January 2005 vote to keep the reforms in place saying that debates would be reported less by the media: 'The whole point of carrying out effective scrutiny is to do it when the people outside are listening and noticing.' Peter Hain, the Leader of the Commons and a keen moderniser, said 'that to revert to later hours on Tuesdays would be a significant step backwards.' Many women MPs fought hard to keep the changes that had been made. Joan Ruddock joined with others to argue for earlier sittings.

The House began to change its hours in 1995 when the Jopling Committee reforms were put into practice, but this did not solve the problem of late-night sittings. The first Report published in the 1998–99 session on the modernisation of the House of Commons says: 'Changes in the hours of sitting have not kept pace with the changing role of a Member of Parliament. By about 1990, Members' main concern was to reduce the number of late sittings, and this led to the establishment of the Jopling Committee in 1991. It is often suggested that the Jopling reforms, which were introduced in 1995, ended the practice of sitting after 10 p.m. This is not the case, although the number of such sittings reduced substantially. These reforms made different arrangements for several of the items of business, which were customarily taken after 10 p.m., but they did not affect the government's ability to move to suspend the 10 p.m. rule whenever it judged necessary. The problem of late sittings cannot therefore be regarded as having been solved for ever.'[32]

The Report pointed to other perceived defects in the Commons hours and calendar: 'Uncertainty about the House's pattern of work makes it difficult for Members to plan their working lives effectively and affects their ability to fulfil their obligations to their constituents. Those Members who are ministers find it difficult to plan their official engagements for the same reason. There is particular discontent over the lack of certainty with regard to the start of the summer adjournment when the actual date is often announced only days in advance (and then sometimes changed).'[33]

In reality the symbolism of the changes has been as important as the practical affect. Finishing Commons business at 7 p.m. mainly benefited London MPs, who may then have had time to get home to their families and read bedtime stories to their children. Those living further away would not have been able to do that. Even some London MPs found it less convenient; previously they may have gone home in the late afternoon and early evening to see their children and have dinner with their families, returning to Westminster later on for the 10 p.m. sittings. However, some MPs do mention how much they enjoy just having a normal evening at home. Rosemary McKenna says: 'Even as a Scottish MP it has improved my life tremendously, but more importantly, it makes us look more like the rest of the world.'

Some MPs believe that the 7 p.m. finishes and early starting times destroyed the atmosphere of the Commons and prevented MPs from networking and interacting with one another. They also argue that it makes the Commons less able to scrutinise important bills and legislation and makes it generally harder for MPs to conduct their other work on committees and deal with their constituency correspondence in the mornings.

MPs have often been criticised for their long summer holidays that could stretch from the end of June to the beginning of October when the party Conferences finished. Under the new rules, they now have to return for the first two weeks of September, to the displeasure of some who do not regard this as helpful or progressive.

The journalist and former Conservative MP Matthew Parris remarks in his autobiography how bewildering it used to be for an MP even after many years to find their feet in the House, given that it did resemble a club rather than a modern workplace: 'The impression might be gained that it was all a bit of a romp, but it was not a romp: not for me and not for a great many other MPs then or today, Labour, Liberal or Conservative. Their testimony is seldom heard because they worked hard to get there and are privileged to be there, and don't have to stay there if they don't want to, and I do not wish to sound sour.' He continues: 'They carry on willingly enough and they will stand again at the next election. But their secret story is that even after many years they haven't found their feet or even quite worked out what they are supposed to be for. I sympathize with them. I never found my feet in the House of Commons.'[34]

In his autobiography, Robin Cook talked of how the women MPs of 1997 have 'humanised' the House. He also credited them with having a major influence on the modernisation agenda: 'It was the Labour women MPs who encouraged me to stay ambitious about my programme for reform in the dark moments when I might have been tempted to scale back.'[35]

Jackie Ballard thinks her life now is more civilised as Chief Executive of the RSPCA than when she was an MP: 'It's a more powerful job than being a backbench MP in the third party, actually, and I make decisions here every day that affect both my employees' lives and the lives of the beneficiaries of the charity. But I have a normal life; I have a work/life balance. I don't have to be in the local newspaper spouting my opinions every week. I don't have to go to the local supermarket and have people coming up to me and saying, "What do you think about the dog mess on my pavement, then?" I don't have to stop and think about every opinion that I utter, even if it's at a dinner party, that people will think is representative of the views of my political party. So I think I am in a good position to say that the kind of life Members of Parliament are forced to lead in this country is almost barbaric, it's certainly not conducive to being able to understand their constituents' concerns.'

All-night sittings

The women MPs who came into Westminster in 1997 still recall the barbarity of late-night sittings and the impact they had on their lives. Diana Organ remembers driving up to Westminster one Monday after doing a surgery in her constituency and not being able to shower and change her clothes until the Wednesday: 'It was some Bill that went through the night, and then the next day, which was a Tuesday, I was on a health Bill in committee, and the bill committee was behind and we were told on the Tuesday night that we'd be going late. And finally, at 2.30 a.m. on Wednesday morning, we left this building, and they didn't realise that the Health Committee were sitting on the Bill still, and the lights had been turned off, and we were groping down a corridor trying to find some lights, and I remember thinking, What is this? You know, the last time I had a shower and put on clean clothes was Monday morning 7 a.m., and it's now early hours of Wednesday morning, and this bloody building has turned its lights off.'

Patricia Hewitt remembers how dreadful and old-fashioned she found late-night votes: 'I think the first year or second year I was a minister, we were doing a lot of late-night votes, sometimes through the night. And it was madness, and I remember David Blunkett on one occasion when we'd gone right through the night, and he'd been expected to vote, and he said: "[I have] a really important public spending meeting at 9 a.m. and how [am I] supposed to do a really good job when [I am] brain-dead?"'

Jacqui Lait didn't mind the late-night sittings: 'It's fallacious to say that you can't concentrate at 10 p.m. at night; some people can't, but then some of us can't concentrate at 7 a.m. in the morning. It's how your rhythms and yourself react. I've always been somebody who's worked late at night so it never bothers me, it never fusses me. And I just think that we've made a mistake and hope we go back.'

Others, who support the changes, also admit the late-night sittings were exciting and atmospheric, particularly on important historical votes. Anne McGuire: 'Sometimes it could be a bit fun, to be frank with you, particularly when you were doing good things, like at 4 a.m. in the morning, supporting the national minimum wage. It gave you a real sense of achievement, and you thought, Well, you were up there fighting a good cause at 4 a.m. in the morning when other people were in their bed, and I thought that was okay, but that sort of old-fashioned style of working actually doesn't chime well with modern life.'

Anne Campbell remembers that when helping to organise the change in hours, some of her female colleagues were helpful, but others were not: 'I remember the Prime Minister [Tony Blair], actually, saying: "Yes, we must reform Parliament," you know, "we must reform the hours, make them more family friendly," and so on. Fine. So, I suppose three to four years into the Parliament, some of us sat up and thought, Well, where is this reform? It hasn't actually happened. Life was absolute hell, it really was. The Tories were making it very, very difficult for us, because we never knew what time we were going to get home. It was often two, three in the morning. Sometimes we were there all night, and I just felt like a complete zombie, you know. I mean, I just couldn't function like that.'

Harriet Harman was another of those who pushed for change: 'I remember the miserable faces of my Scottish colleagues when in fact their children would start their summer holidays in June and they would nearly be back to school before the House had risen. And one of the things I argued for was finishing earlier on a Thursday and also bringing forward the recess so that colleagues who were Scottish colleagues could at least have some of their children's summer holidays with them. So it has benefited all members who want to spend more time with their families. It has disproportionately benefited people in London, but just because a benefit that is to everybody benefits disproportionately some doesn't make it a bad thing.'

Dawn Primarolo says the change in hours was important because it was symbolic: 'I think it's the symbolism of changing the hours. My constituency's in Bristol, so I'm away from home, and I divide my time. When I'm in London I pour all my effort into the work I need to do in London and my ministerial work, and you know, we're great controllers of time as Members of Parliament. I certainly am. I want to make sure that I know what I'm doing at different points and that I can fit in my constituency commitments once I'm back in Bristol – my home's in Bristol. So the hours didn't really alter anything for me in terms of being able to get better access to my family and friends . . . I think that the changing of the hours was important in demonstrating that it was a normal place.'

Those who live a long way from Westminster, and have no hope of going home and seeing their families, support the changes. Two Scottish Labour MPs, Sandra Osborne and Anne Begg, are fans. Sandra says: 'I very strongly support them because they are of an advantage to other MPs who have young families, and I do think that's very important, especially for women. You're never going to get women involved in the political process unless you remember that they have family responsibilities, and I know that the younger men now take much more to do with the upbringing of their children, but I still think ultimately women are the main carers over children.' While Anne Begg says: 'Well I voted for the change in hours and we were sent a questionnaire recently as to whether we would keep them, and I did vote to keep the change in hours. But being a Scottish MP and not being able to get home, I'm down here anyway.'

Welsh MPs, who are in the same situation, also support the reforms. Julie Morgan: 'I'm very much in support of the change in hours because although it doesn't affect me directly, I can't go home, I can't go back to Wales in the middle of the week, but I just feel that it's a move to a more normal lifestyle.'

While there were influential women MPs supporting the changes, there were a number of the most senior women in Westminster opposed to them. The then Speaker Baroness Boothroyd was one of them: 'I didn't approve of them, the change in hours, because I didn't feel that it provided the proper scrutiny that I thought was necessary for Bills and for legislation. I also didn't approve of them because, whilst we are trying to open Parliament to the public, you are actually closing it to the public, because by sitting at 11.30 a.m., the public have to be out just after 10 a.m. in order for the sniffer-dogs and security to take place, and therefore people couldn't come. The schools couldn't come unless they came late in the evening, and they can't do that. So it's all right for the Home Counties and for Londoners, but, you know, there is more to this country than the Home Counties and London, and whilst we say that we're trying to open it up, what we've done is we've closed it to people.'

Another opponent was Gwyneth Dunwoody. She believes it has had an adverse impact on the scrutiny of legislation. She does not pull any punches when she says: 'The change in hours has been an unmitigated disaster because, of course, those of us who run select committees, you can never hold select committee sessions without having to get up and run down, and suspend for fifteen minutes while you vote.'

Virginia Bottomley agrees: 'Ken Clarke would always say that, whatever we do, we must remember that one day we will be in opposition, and the ability to annoy the government, to keep the government up all night, to stop the government getting its business is part of what Parliament is. Parliament should be a place of argument, debate, people up late at night, talking, debating, thinking. It should be like a university, and it's now become like a municipal town hall, and it's tragic.'

Others support the reforms and do not think the reforms have gone far enough. Barbara Follett: 'I think there's a great deal of nonsense about [the reforms] being family-friendly. That's not what the hours are, they're not family-friendly, mainly because most people are here without their families. But one of the big factors is that far fewer people have died since we introduced the new hours. The death rate has fallen amongst MPs. There was a unusually high death rate, and mainly because of the stress of working 18-hour days.'

London MPs have been the main beneficiaries of the changes. Julie Kirkbride: 'We all voted on what our own circumstances were. My circumstances are that during the week I have to live here in London with my husband and I want to see my little boy; and having my evenings free to do as I want to do with them, which may include working, I hasten to add, but nevertheless free to do what I want to do with them, just makes my life that bit easier, and so I do like the change in hours.'

Estelle Morris says the changes haven't helped her: 'I've never gone for the argument that we should finish at 7 p.m. to have more family life. That is an argument that has been put forward by London MPs who've got their families here. Full stop. If your family's not in London, it makes no difference. So I think I've never bought the argument that we ought to have what you might call 'family-friendly' hours. I personally don't think it's a job where that can happen.'

After voting in favour of the changes, some MPs now oppose them. Helen Liddell: 'I voted and supported the change of the hours because it was going to make no difference to me. In fact, it was just going to mean that I'd be hanging around in the evening doing nothing, but I thought it would help my female London colleagues. But the reality is they've ended up with the worst of all possible worlds in that they don't see the children in the morning now because we start so early, and now they don't see the children in the evening either because instead of finishing at 7 p.m., we often finish well after that.'

Others think the change in hours has altered the atmosphere in the Commons. Ann Clwyd is doubtful about the reform: 'I'm not sure if it was a good reform because it's certainly taken the atmosphere out of this place now. After 7 p.m. on Tuesdays and Wednesdays, people tend to just vanish into thin air, and I think there are far more lonely people as a result because you haven't got the collectiveness you had before. Because people were eating together, frequently spent long hours together – you did build up a rapport with people, which I think sadly, is lacking now.'

However, whether women MPs support or opposed the changes does not follow party lines. The Conservative Theresa May supports the changes: 'I think that changing the hours has been a good thing . . . There are a number of colleagues that have different views, but I think that in general [it makes] sense, in terms of people seeing Parliament as a body that is making decisions on their behalf and that affect their lives in a sensible and appropriate way.'

Liberal Democrat Sarah Teather supports the reforms: 'I don't want them to return to the old way. During the Health and Social Care Bill, and actually it wasn't just that, there were a couple of Bills before Christmas when we were playing ping-pong with the Lords. And we sat really late, and everybody went to the bar, because there was nothing to do between votes, and I could see that it was all kind of fun and cosy and there was an awful lot of drinking done. But I got into the chamber, and the number of words per minute was less than the average heartbeat. I can't believe that that is a good way of carrying on. The quality of debate was appalling. That's no sensible way to debate laws – 3 a.m. in the morning? No, I don't think so.'

Vera Baird thinks the change of hours sends out a positive message to the public at large and women who want to pursue a career in politics: 'I'm a million per cent in favour of these reforms, and totally opposed to them being reversed. Of course, it helps only a relatively small range of people to see more of their family, the MPs who live and represent a constituency in the greater London area. But it's still quite a whack of people, and beyond that, it's kind of disclosing a sensible face to the public at large.'

What difference has reform of the House made?

Women MPs of all parties allude a lot to how it takes time to gain acceptance for and implement change in Westminster. Margaret Hodge says the new women MPs have been slow to progress change: 'I'll tell you what's interesting is I thought that we did have the critical mass to make all the differences we want. I now understand that it's going to take longer. And it's right across the way we do our business. If you think about those very limited reforms to working hours and how there's been a reaction against that.'

Others think the reforms have destroyed the quality of debates, and that the changes in the hours mean you get to know your colleagues less well. Ann Widdecombe: 'The chamber has been destroyed by television, and I voted in favour of televising Parliament and I remain in favour of it. But we now have live feeds in all our offices. Nobody goes in the chamber any more, they watch the whole proceeding [from their offices]. But the hours have actually clobbered *esprit de corps*. Because when we used to go through to 10 p.m., there comes a point where you stop work, you go to the tearooms, to the dining room, to the bars, just to sit and read newspapers, whatever it might be, and you talk to colleagues, and you know your colleagues, and you form alliances with your colleagues. And for that matter, you talk to some on the other side as well where there's joint interest. It doesn't happen now, this place is dead at 7.30 p.m., absolutely dead. Everybody's gone home.'

Some don't see all the fixed term–date changes as being for the good. The recall of MPs to Westminster in September has not gone down well. Maria Eagle: 'I'm not sure these two weeks in September work tremendously well. I think they were a sop to tabloid journalists, from whom you get no credit whatever you do, so I'm not convinced they work.'

But fixed term–dates have worked according to Caroline Spelman: 'Well, the most helpful thing above all with the modernisation of the way in which the Houses of Parliament work is the fixed term–dates, so that we actually know in advance when the term will start and when the term will end, and therefore when we have recess.'

Some think the past seven years have been highly significant. Jackie Lawrence: 'I think the nature of the establishment was so chauvinistic, so old-boy's school, that the women who did get here, and as you know, there were 120 of us at the time, we just got together for a bit of a rethink, and although we're a small minority still and continuously banging our heads against a brick wall on things which men didn't think were important, I think we have, over the seven-year period, made something of a difference. We've finally got the message home.'

The role of the whips

The role of the whips' office is one of the most contentious in Westminster today. Bullying, intimidation and sometimes fear were words that often became associated with government and party whips on all sides of the House as they cajoled, persuaded and sometimes pressurised MPs to follow their party lines and vote with the government of the day.

There is evidence that whips are now more progressive in supporting Members to have a family life, but even during this government's tenure, MPs have to fly back from foreign countries, are carried in from hospitals on stretchers and prevented from attending important family and social events because their vote is needed to carry through or defeat the government's business. In any other workplace this cajoling or bullying would be an unacceptable way for an employer to behave, but even though Westminster passes our employment laws, it still sticks to what some regard as an antiquated method to control the behaviour of MPs.

Margaret Hodge tells one perplexing story about how she was treated by the whips: 'I remember when we were in opposition I had lunch with a *Sunday Times* journalist, and I suggested we should job-share ministerial jobs . . . it got covered in the *Sunday Times* with a picture, and that Monday, when I came into Parliament – I was still relatively new, I'd only been here a couple of years – the whips called me into the office. They'd stuck the photo up in the whips' office and they were putting darts into it . . . both female and male whips. My own party. And the response I got was, "Margaret, if you don't like it, if you don't like the way we do things, there are hundreds of people who want your job. Stop rocking the boat."'

Barbara Follett has another upsetting tale: 'My mother was very ill and went back to South Africa and I wanted to go and say goodbye to her, and they [the whips] wouldn't let me go because there was some poofling vote – now I would just walk out – which we won by 150. So I never did say goodbye to her, and she died about ten days later.'

Some MPs who wanted to spend more time with their families were not allowed to. Dawn Primarolo explains: 'You couldn't get time off. I couldn't get time off when I wanted to go down to Bristol if my son was playing in rugby matches for the school, or football, or particular things, our hours were much longer and it made it really, really challenging and I thought, I've destroyed my life, what have I done?'

The Chief Whip Hilary Armstrong has been trying to introduce changes: 'He [the Prime Minister] wanted it as a political job, and I do it very much as a political job, where you persuade people through political debate and political argument, and that might be unusual for chief whips historically, but that was what was expected and that's what I seek to do.' Hilary Armstrong herself has been accused of bullying but says sometimes the whips are easy targets for MPs to get at the party: 'It's what goes with the territory. I can't reply, I can't say what I did in discussions. They know they've got an easy hit, so anyone who's got an agenda, we're easy targets, but, you know, that goes with the territory.'

Anne McGuire recalls trying to tell the Whips' Office how women MPs needed to be supported: 'I was a whip. I was a government whip for four years, from 1998 through to 2002. I think in there – which many, looking at it from the outside, would say is a male culture – I think there were issues that I used to try and encourage them to understand, that there were different pressures on women. I'm not saying there are not pressures on men, because there are, but there were slightly different pressures on women . . . sometimes we actually did have to look at the way in which we managed people. I don't take total credit for that, because, I mean, a whip's job is a difficult job at the best of times, but I think part of the conversation, let's put it like that, encouraged some of my colleagues to see things slightly differently.'

Other MPs remember how much they learnt about politics when they worked in the whips' office. Angela Watkinson: 'I arrived very late in my life, much later than most people, after I thought I'd retired from local government, and suddenly I have another career. So I was, if you like, the wrong gender, and the wrong age, and there I was neither wealthy nor connected, it was a bit of a puzzle how I got here. So I was very surprised in my first year to be promoted to the opposition's whips' office, which is an absolutely wonderful place. It's cloaked in mystery and nobody knows what goes on in the whips' office until you get in there. But it has two main functions. One is a sort of personnel function, and the other is a management function – of the daily business of the House. It's a wonderful place to learn how this works.'

One senior Labour woman MP and one senior Conservative woman MP tell remarkably similar stories about negotiating time off with their whips' office to see their children after 1997. Conservative Caroline Spelman remembers negotiating time off to see her daughter perform in a school play. 'Well, I finally sort of screwed up the courage to ask . . . and he stood up, turned round and said, "Of course you can; I said you could, and if it makes you feel any better, I'm going to go and see my daughter in the school play on Thursday, so there you are." And I thought, Wow, it's true! It works.'

Labour's Patricia Hewitt tells a similar story of changing the culture in her whips office: 'They were reluctant, but I got permission to go off and do a parents' evening. So that was fine, I did the parents' evening, probably came back for a 10 p.m. closure or something. And the next morning, I saw this particular whip sitting in the tearoom, and I went up to him, and I said, thank you . . . And I've had a really good relationship with him, almost ever since.'

Regional whips have been singled out for praise for helping new members find their feet. Rosemary McKenna: 'John McFall was the Scottish whip, and he was superb. He was very, very good, he met with us every week and just continued to meet with us until we felt we'd had enough, and he was excellent . . . I think that's a very important role of the whips. I think they have a pastoral role as well as a government role, and they're learning to do that better.'

Vera Baird wants to see a radical reform of the whips office: 'They don't, I think, fully see themselves as managerial, as human resources people. They see their prime function still as discipline. There are some people who far more fit the human resources managerial model in place now than there were even when I came, but still the culture is a long way from anything but, "Why aren't you here? Null excuses."'

Beverley Hughes thinks that the whips behave inappropriately on occasions: 'I think on one of the first few days [after the 1997 election], all of the parliamentary Labour Party convened in Church House for Tony to speak to us, and there was a tremendous air of excitement. It was very early after the start of Parliament, after the election, and I was sitting fairly near the front and I was just talking and people were milling round. And suddenly, this male whip, kind of a gruff person, who's still in the government, just came along and he got hold of my shoulder and kind of pushed me down onto the seat and went all along this line of women and said, "Now, come on, come on, stop talking. Tony's getting ready to come on," and just treated us like school kids. I just couldn't believe it.'

What can be done in the future?

Proponents of further reform would like to see voting online, plenary sessions [fixed concentrated dates of Commons sittings in Westminster attended by all members] as are held in Europe, leaving more time for MPs to see their constituents, a circular chamber like the European, Scottish and Welsh Parliaments or Assemblies have, job-share MPs, the publication of the Speaker's list, and more debates in Westminster Hall. For every proponent of these radical ideas there is an opponent.

Mo Mowlam would like to see extensive changes to various aspects of the parliamentary system: 'Oh, I'd do a whole lot. I'd have a circular chamber; I'd have a second chamber. I'd have people from the regional governments and the European Parliament, so that all three levels were represented. I'd either keep parish or district, but not keep both, because you have too many tiers of government. I'd reform the Civil Service, which desperately needs reform, but no one can reform the hand that feeds it, very difficult to do. What else would I do? I think the party system is getting outdated. I think the way that people view the party system is negative now, and when you look at where people are going to voice their feelings – you see it in the young people in the street, you see it with the fuel protesters that took to the streets . . .'

Some think respect for parliamentary tradition stops further reform. Phyllis Starkey is one: 'The whole notion of modernisation was resisted. There is – in my view – an overblown respect for parliamentary tradition, a feeling that it is sacrosanct, that any tinkering with it is tinkering with the whole nature of our democratic system . . . a very significant section of parliamentary opinion thinks that absolutely no change is necessary at all, and that the only reason for change, the reasons that are being proposed for change by the modernisers are because we don't want to be in Parliament, and we don't really want to spend much time doing parliamentary debate.'

But others would not change the traditions. Angela Watkinson: 'I just love it all. I don't think it's strange at all. I just think it's absolutely wonderful, and I wouldn't change anything, I love all the traditions in the House.'

Glenda Jackson wants a change in electoral methods: 'Absolutely, I would reform it. But the only way you can actually reform it is to change the electoral methods sending people here in the first place. You have to get rid of this antiquated, ancient mode of debate, which sets us two sword-lengths apart.'

Amongst women MPs there is support 'for' and 'against' electronic voting. Anne Campbell: 'I've always been an advocate of electronic voting. I think that the way that we have to file through the lobbies in order to register a vote is absurd and archaic, and also very time-consuming.'

Barbara Follett: 'It's got to be a slow process, but I would certainly do electronic voting, which the first modernisation select committee looked at, and it was rejected by the traditionalists, who are generally older, and who can't conceive of any other way of running their life. This is their life, and the phrase 'get a life' is actually – or 'get another section to your life' – is very necessary here.'

But others oppose electronic voting. Mo Mowlam: 'No, I think that takes away the spirit of the House of Commons. I think they could vote online from their constituencies, but they'd want to go fishing in Scotland. That wouldn't work. Some would just bugger off. So I don't think it's an easy solution.'

Dawn Primarolo: 'I'm worried about the concept of voting online if we don't have some way of making sure that we're in that social melting pot that takes us to vote. So I'm happy to see what comes forward, but I want to make sure that I can still organise my time to make sure that I've got a life apart from being a Member of Parliament, that people still have access to me while I'm a minister.'

Anne McGuire: 'I don't like the idea of voting online. Then I think we just become Big Brother. You see, I think we need to be careful that politics doesn't just become a matter of the process, you can vote online, you can vote by telephone, you can give a proxy to a whip; all of those things could be tried and tested . . . But politics is a bit more than a process. Politics is also about engaging with other people, sharing ideas, sharing views, sharing concerns.'

Many years ago, the first woman MP, the Conservative Lady Astor, was in favour of a circular chamber. Others agree with her today. Valerie Davey: 'Just the physical House of Commons; it's two swords length apart, you know, "toe the line" and all the rest of it. It needs to be less Oxbridge debating, and more seeking a way forward which people will share and understand.'

Estelle Morris: 'I'll tell you what I think is very wrong with chamber: you've actually got nowhere to lean on. Unless you're a minister, or a shadow minister, you never have a desk in front of you, and it's banked. So it's not the fact that it's opposite one another. I still think that if you stand behind a desk, I think it's a more business-like thing, or if you could actually speak from a sitting position, but we never permit that anywhere in the House of Commons. It's always speaking from standing. So if there was a movement of furniture, somewhere to put their papers on, that could change the tone.'

Annette Brooke: 'Well, I'd certainly like a circular seating formation. Perhaps we better be a bit like the EU and be terribly extravagant, and actually change chambers. I would always want to meet here sometimes, because it is so special, and it is good to remember our history, but I can't actually see us making strides in having good debate unless we have a different formation, because it's inevitable that it's confrontational, and it's very frustrating being a third party, with everything split into two viewpoints.'

Taking power away from the Speaker, who can decide who speaks when, leaving many to sit waiting, waiting, waiting, and feeling they are somehow not a chosen one would be favoured by some. Some favour publication of the Speaker's list. Anne Campbell: 'One thing, which sounds a bit silly, but is actually terribly important, is publishing a Speaker's list. At the moment, when you want to speak in a debate, you send a note in to Speaker and you get your name on the list, but nobody knows what it says. And the Speaker, and the Deputy Speaker are very reluctant to divulge the speaking order, so it means you have to go in there and you have to just sit and just wait and hope that you'll be called.'

There is a good deal of support for the debates that are now held in

Westminster Hall. Phyllis Starkey: 'Well, I think as regards modernisation I am proudest of the setting-up of the second chamber in Westminster Hall, and I was very pleased that it was a debate that I initiated that was the very first debate ever in that second chamber, which was a debate on Palestinian refugees.'

Margaret Beckett, an old hand, also approves of the Westminster Hall debates: 'The introduction of the extra chamber at Westminster Hall, gives greater opportunities for backbenchers to have more debates in an atmosphere which is less sort of kickabout than the chamber.'

Some MPs support a move towards plenary sessions so that they work for longer hours when they are in Westminster with those times being much more concentrated into shorter sessions. This would then allow them to be in their constituency more. Hazel Blears: 'I would like to see a really radical reform of Parliament whereby – a bit like the European Parliament – you have a week in your constituency maybe, then you have a week of a plenary session, and then you have a week of committee sittings. I don't know why we have to be in plenary full-time, which is what we are in this country, so that's probably as radical as trying to get rid of the House of Commons. I'll probably get into trouble for that as well!'

Jackie Lawrence: 'When I'm here, what I would prefer to do is concentrate my work in a short period of time, and get back to my constituency, the area that I represent, and my family, for as long as possible. What I've found is that it's now becoming more difficult to do the job, because the hours have been shortened, and I'm isolated here in London. I don't see the purpose. I actually would have preferred, and still would prefer, a model on, say, the Australian lines, where they have maybe three weeks' plenary session, very concentrated, and then they go back and spend three weeks in their constituency.'

They may be ridiculed for it, but some women MPs will still speak up in favour of job-share. Margaret Hodge: 'I think we should have job-share ministers. I see absolutely no reason why I couldn't – I'd love to share my job, because I'm getting my balance right between my work and the rest of my life. It is impossible at the moment.'

Sue Doughty: 'It would be great if we could do job-share. I could see how it would work because we could divide the work that you do in the constituency between different policy areas, but what happened if one of you gets promoted and the other one doesn't? For example, I'm a shadow Environment minister, but what would my job-share partner do, or would we miss out on promotion? It's all these different things that in practical terms, I'm sure it could be worked out . . .'

As Robin Cook admitted, the contribution of women MPs to the modernisation of Westminster has been significant. They have challenged the established working practices to make Westminster a more efficient and professional working environment. The decision in January 2005 to revert back to late night sittings on a Tuesday disappointed many. Some would support an even wider reform agenda. No doubt some of their proposals will be reintroduced at some point, be reversed later and then be reintroduced again when their full impact is felt; and only then, some say, will a parliamentary career become attractive to a broader cross-section of the population.

TEN

Feminising the agenda

The achievements of Women MPs

The contribution Labour's 101 women MPs have made to Labour Party policy since 1997 has been significant. Fiona Mactaggart's assertion is supported by other women MPs, that when one door closes on them, her female colleagues have a tendency to go round and knock on the back door, persistence, persuasion and nagging; in other words, they keep knocking until the door opens. Women MPs use the terms to describe their particular contribution to British political life, and they feel that this has resulted in quantum leaps on behalf of the women and families they represent in their constituencies.

These changes should not be taken for granted. There are those who can recall the days when women only got given certain jobs in government to do. Gwyneth Dunwoody: 'When I first came in here, there was an unwritten rule that said that women only did certain things. They did Education and they did Health. Well, the Health bit I would go along with. But I remember saying that I would not take a job in government that was regarded as, in quotes, a "Women's Subject". Barbara Castle went into child support and I went into trade [and industry]. And it was a bit of a culture shock, and it was a culture shock for the then President of the Board of Trade, who was absolutely stunned at having this working-class woman thrust on him. Not over-delighted, I think, although he once said to somebody in my presence that I was the only "politician" amongst the five of his ministers. But that was a long time afterwards.'

Tessa Jowell believes that the Labour government is the 'most feminist government in history', with six women Members in the Cabinet, 35 women ministers and as many women holding ministerial office since 1997 to May 2005 as held office in the entire period from the end of the Second World War to 1997. Tessa Jowell: 'I think that feminists will always criticise governments for not having done enough because the high level of expectation of a Labour government is the best guarantee that Labour governments will go on delivering, but the fact is, this is the most feminist government in history. If you look at what we've done for women; for example, from the national minimum wage, the New Deal for Lone Parents, to childcare, to Sure Start, to breast screening for women over 55 years old to the more broadly based improvements in the health service or paid maternity leave . . . Margaret Jay and I were heavily involved in negotiating extended maternity leave and extended statutory pay, flexible working for women returning after having their babies, and so on and so on and so on. So much of what we've done has had a disproportionate benefit for women.'

Vera Baird believes women have raised and achieved significant changes on certain issues because they themselves have or might experience them: 'I mean, it's clear that since we've had what you could call something approaching a "critical mass", issues such as domestic violence, rape, childcare, many women's issues across the board, have come onto the government's agenda in a way they never would have done before. Once they've been raised by a powerful group of articulate people, who are on their side in every other way – the government's picked them up – and there are men now who are as strong sisters on these issues as the women themselves. But it never would have occurred to them; the issues about rape, for instance, issues about domestic violence, don't have that imminence in your psyche and your emotions if you're never going to be capable of experiencing them. They have to be told, and then, of course, they understand, and they run with you. Numbers [of women] are important to make sure that happens.'

Some would argue that these issues were of their time and would have been progressed in Westminster without the help of the women MPs working behind the scenes. They would say, for instance, there are now more dual-income families, so therefore paternity leave would have been put on the agenda without the help of the women MPs.

Harriet Harman asserts that whatever the critics say, men did not raise the issues before: 'Left to their own devices, the men would not have brought it forward and they had plenty of time to and they didn't.'

And it is also widely acknowledged by some of their male colleagues that women MPs have given the impetus and provided the momentum for change. It is now standard practice across departments in Westminster for women ministers to ask their civil servants to explain what impact new policies will have on women. Women ministers also pick up the phone, network and talk to one another about the implications of policies on women. As one woman minister pointedly states off the record: 'The women turn up for the meetings'.

But critics say the feminist reforms of the Labour Party and government have not been radical enough. They point out the number of women in Westminster subsequently dipped to 118; that Blair's macho 'football-loving' inner circle refused to embrace feminism despite the fact that the Prime Minister's wife was openly supportive; that Britain has failed to make real progress in childcare, equal pay and the comparatively long hours worked by British employees. Some also believe the Strategy Unit is openly hostile to feminist policies.

Clare Short has said: 'I wrote in my diary at the time that the election campaign was very centrally controlled, media obsessed and very "boysey" – this is an aspect of the Blair leadership style that many women comment on. It is strange because there are more women in senior positions than ever before, and yet there is a feel of a group of boys who have taken over and find it exciting to exercise power over others through their own little gang.'[36]

It was also true that in the first term of the Blair government, 'feminism' remained deeply unpopular. The term was also unpopular in society at large. Research shows that even when women MPs are said to see themselves as 'feminists' the term remains deeply unfashionable.[37]

One initiative for women that stands out in the early years of the new Blair Government was the launch of the policy document called 'Listening to Women'. This ambitious consultation exercise built on the work already begun in opposition by Tessa Jowell, Patricia Hewitt, Margaret Hodge and Harriet Harman, who had worked to get the views of women heard. Some saw this as a new form of politics bringing women's issues such as low pay, childcare, domestic violence, work/life balance into the House. They also began to reform the House itself.

To promote what women had actually achieved in Westminster and to defend Labour women against the charge of being too loyal and not radical enough, the Home Office Minister Fiona Mactaggart wrote a Fabian Society report in 2000 on women's role in Labour's first 1,000 days. She listed 100 achievements and concluded 'you cannot judge effectiveness by propensity to vote against the Government.'[38]

Fiona Mactaggart argues that women MPs were behind the Protection of Children Act, 1999 – the first-ever childcare strategy which offered improvements in maternity pay and provision for paternal leave – have pushed for a better deal for women in the yearly budget; have helped increase child benefit; have tightened up the sale of alcohol to children; have banned age discrimination in job adverts; and pioneered a strategy for teenage pregnancies.[39] She also argues that women MPs have raised questions that were previously unheard of, such as food safety in Agricultural Questions and the welfare of servicemen's families in the Defence Select Committee.

More recently there has been the publication of the first comprehensive legislation on domestic violence; new laws on child protection; new laws protecting rape victims; the launch of the Sure Start programme which promotes health and care for the under-fives; and the call for manufacturers to consider the impact of food advertising on children's health.

Research has shown that women MPs also use Parliamentary Questions and Early Day Motions to good effect.[40] Labour women themselves point to Ruth Kelly's work on paternity leave, Christine McCafferty's campaign to remove VAT on sanitary products, Ann Cryer's work on forced marriages, and Harriet Harman's general concern with women.[41] Some also believe that many women constituents prefer to see a woman MP, rather like the choice of having a man or a woman as their local GP.[42]

Jean Corston thinks women have brought their own experiences into Westminster: 'The Government is being exposed to different types of experience, because we all bring our experiences here. Our own experiences, as well as those of the people we represent, and if you are the most sensitive man in the world it's sometimes – well, it's impossible to represent the experience of growing up as a woman in this country. And I'm not saying that women are better politicians, I'm just saying the female experience has been brought into this place now, in the kind of mass and variety which is more representative of the women in this country, particularly younger women, which is why I think that sometimes across the chamber there's a great bewilderment about how society is now, because they don't really feel they represent it; which I think is the position we were in for a while in the 1980s, looking back.'

Achievements in Westminster

In Westminster, women MPs have championed a diverse range of issues. One of the landmarks of the reforms was when Debra Shipley initiated a private member's bill for the Protection of Children Act. Often they have used their own personal experiences and tragedies to inform and educate others on the issues they care most about.

Dame Marion: 'That one thing I did in 1985 [made law the Prohibition of Female Circumcision Act] has actually created a platform for me to do something on behalf of children internationally, and using my status as a Vice-Chairman of the Inter-Parliamentary Union, British Group, I was able to keep standing up at assemblies and keeping banging, and banging on about children's rights. They keep talking about human rights but they really relate to parliamentarians, democracies and human rights of adults. But children's rights somehow got slipped off the edge.'

Ann Cryer: 'I'm most proud of the work I've done for Asian women and their total lack of human rights frequently. Right from day one, I started off as I meant to go on, and when a large Asian man brought his daughter to see me and said, "Right, Mrs Cryer, I want you to sort out the entry clearance for my son-in-law," I said to him, knowing full well who the sponsor was, "Oh, are you the sponsor?" and he said, "No," and I said, "Well, who's the sponsor?" and he said, "My daughter," and I said, "Well, I'm sorry, it's your daughter I want to talk to, not to you, do you mind leaving the room?" And that was my first advice surgery. It didn't go down well, and the following day I happened to have a small sort of social gathering with a group of Asian men, down at the Labour Party rooms in Keighley, and I told them of this experience, and one of their number, who it turned out, I didn't realise it at the time, was actually a Labour councillor for Bradford, he took great exception to my comments, and he said, "Ann Cryer, you don't understand the Asian community, you wouldn't talk about things like that, you should have talked to that man about his daughter." He said, "You have no understanding of the Asian culture," and I remember my words very clearly, I said, "You're wrong, actually I do understand the Asian culture, I understand it probably too well, and that's why I intend to change things." And I've been working at it ever since. It's a very slow process . . .'

Joan Ruddock has worked alongside women in Afghanistan to achieve change. She explains how initially she was ridiculed by Lobby correspondents in the national media for asking questions about the plight of women in Afghanistan during the war. 'I had to find Afghan women and find out what Afghan women want . . . I've continued to press the Ministries – defence and foreign affairs – constantly on the issue of delivering to women, for women on the constitution issues; every aspect . . . That's something I'm very proud of.'

Ann Clwyd has also won cross-party respect for her work in Iraq: 'I'm very involved in Iraq, and I've particularly championed the position of women in Iraqi society. Every time I go to Iraq, I meet groups of women there. They've got the same problem as we have in Wales, women are always grossly underrepresented in politics, and now there's an opportunity for democracy, and for women to make their voices heard. But they need quite a bit of encouragement. There are some very good women in Iraq.'

Caroline Spelman, who was a former Conservative spokesperson on International Development, helped launch a fund for one high-profile Iraqi boy: 'I'm sure you remember the picture of Ali Ishmael Abbas, the little boy who lost both his arms, his father, and some of his brothers and sisters in the bombing of Baghdad. Like a lot of mothers, I saw that picture and I thought, Well we have to do something to help. And the very next day, I rang up the Limbless Association, here in Britain, with whom I'd worked on the provision of ambulances to Afghanistan, and we launched the Ali Fund here at the House of Commons, a few days later.'

Sylvia Hermon has tried to change the approach of her party towards conflict in Northern Ireland: 'Women do politics very differently from men.

We try to find a way forward. I think that in fact we tend to focus less on what has gone in the past. We are what we are, but we are trying to find a common way forward. We women, I think, are less confrontational, though I have to say that it is because I am a minority of one I find myself arguing frequently with my male colleagues to try and change the agenda and to stop bashing other personalities from other Northern Ireland political parties. And to try and be a little bit more constructive in their attitudes and to look at different policy areas, as well, instead of regularly repeating, "Decommissioning, decommissioning, decommissioning." '

Helen Jackson talks about her work in the Northern Ireland team in the Good Friday Agreement, which brought to an end the systematic killings and deaths in Northern Ireland: 'It was work that I thoroughly enjoyed. I was asked to pay particular attention to what women in Northern Ireland were saying, and not to spend too much time in Parliament, but to get over and do my own thing. A long piece of rope was given to me by Mo Mowlem, Peter Mandelson and John Reid. So I got to know countless people in Northern Ireland, particularly at community and women level . . . So I've enjoyed doing that very much.'

Domestically, Liberal Democrat Jenny Tonge has worked on sexual health issues: 'As soon as I got into Parliament, I started campaigning for the morning-after pill to be available over the counter in local pharmacies, because as a woman doctor and a family-planning doctor too, I found that it was crazy the way women had to see doctors all the time and things. And we eventually got that through. It was a very hard struggle, it went on for years actually, because there were rear-guard actions from Baroness Black, Baroness Thatcher, and Ann Winterton, and all sorts of people coming up with reasons to try and stop it all the time, though we actually succeeded and it's there in place. And I know that not just women in my own constituency, but also women all over the country are benefiting from that. So I'm very pleased about that.'

Claire Curtis-Thomas took on another tough sexual issue: 'Well, I suppose the achievement I'm most proud of is that I didn't duck issues when I could have done. I'm a chairman for the All-Party Group for Abuse Investigations and I started to talk a number of years ago about the fact that we might have wrongly judged or sentenced and convicted people of sex offences when they

179

were innocent. Even talking about it today makes me feel a bit weary because people have a view about people who try and rally individuals to a plight of sex offenders, but I believed that there was a great issue about miscarriages of justice, and people who have been accused of hideous crimes have a legitimate right to have their grievances heard just as much as anybody else.'

Anne Begg: '[Of] the things I've done individually I suppose the one area where I took the biggest, the most prominent part, was in suspending parliament to change the regulations on stem-cell research.'

Virginia Bottomley says she is proud of the work she has done on bereavement: 'I've grown used to the idea that you can use your role as a parliamentarian to fly kites, so I have another passion, which is that I'm very interested in death and dying and bereavement. So I opened the first ever National Funeral Services exhibition in Birmingham, but the real taboo is about death and bereavement.'

Dari Taylor has pursued a personal issue: '[An] achievement I look to with great affection, with sheer pride from involvement and from achievement, was the Adoption and Fostering Bill. When David [my partner] and I started, we were told after a year by the Social Services that we were too old [to adopt], and they took a year to tell us, they knew our ages at the start. It was monstrously hurtful and so undermining.'

A high point for Jane Griffiths was: 'Introducing under the ten-minute rule my own Bill, Civil Partnerships Bill, which is effectively just about to become law. It's a government Bill now, and it came through a consultation, which immediately followed the introduction of my Bill, so justice for partners is something that I've been part of achieving, and I know it will become law before I leave Parliament, so that's great.'

The Liberal Democrat Patsy Calton worked on an issue she herself was concerned about as a parent. She explains: 'I'm a parent myself and I was horrified when schools suddenly had all these food machines and drinks machines at a time when we know that more and more children are becoming obese. More and more children are behaving badly in school, I believe – I was a teacher – as a result of excess sugar, excess caffeine, excess all sort of things.'

Vera Baird considers one of her achievements: '. . . now the position is that it's 36 weeks that a person keeps their [pension] book before having to surrender it, and that's something like 95 per cent of people who go into hospital is well out by then. So I thought that was a major, quick achievement that was going to have a lot of benefit for a lot of people. Not a dramatic thing, but a good one.'

Anne McGuire: 'I think on a policy basis, I do have to say that the handguns ban was a really important thing for me. We could have taken the easy route out, which was to say that we should still allow some elements of handguns for sports and the rest of it – but we didn't, and I remember meeting with the Prime Minister and some of the parents from Dunblane just after the election. I felt the Labour Party should be about listening to people.'

Angela Eagle: 'When I look back at my career to date, I think "getting quotas" and allowing those 101 women to be in the House in the first place, which I played a central role in, is one of my proudest achievements. As a minister, there were other things that I did, but to transform the party, that's probably the one I'm most proud of.'

And, as Baroness Boothroyd points out, sometimes MPs achievements relate directly to their careers: 'The achievement I'm most proud of is becoming Speaker, obviously. I mean you can't whack that one, can you?'

It also must not be forgotten how many women MPs list their biggest achievement as getting selected in the first place. Rosie Winterton: 'I'm proudest about becoming an MP in the first place, really, because that was the, you know, that's the biggest battle that you face.'

Achievements in the constituency

Women MPs undoubtedly find their constituency achievements equally or more rewarding than their time in Westminster, and these achievements often reflect the diversity of the people they represent.

Gillian Shephard: 'I had a constituent of six who was battered to death by abuse from her stepmother, who is, as I speak, in jail. This child died. She was in school for eighteen months before she died, she was age six and she lost four stone in weight, and as far as I know, the teachers did not report their concern to anyone. Had they done so, of course her life would have been saved. When I took this up with the authorities locally, the Director of Education said, "Well, you better change the law then, hadn't you." I was, of course, a backbench opposition MP by this time – this was a couple of years ago – so I thought, Right, I will. So I got a change in the law to make it a disciplinary offence for teachers, or governors, or indeed people in FE Colleges not to report concerns about possible child abuse to the local authorities. And the law is now changed, and that is now in the law, but it was of course the government that agreed it. Nevertheless, we got it done.'

Ann Widdecombe went to Morocco to help one of her constituents who was in trouble: 'One of my biggest achievements was not in any front-bench capacity at all, it was as a backbencher, when I got one of my constituents released from a Moroccan jail. By the time his wife came to see me, he'd been sentenced, convicted, and he'd lost his appeal and he was facing nine years in a Moroccan jail, for a crime that frankly not even Moroccans were really convinced he'd committed.'

Glenda Jackson: 'The one area where Parliament was valuable was when I had a constituent who had been taken prisoner by an African government, and they were denying that they had this child, and I made a speech on the floor of the House on a Wednesday morning, we had Adjournment Debates and the kid was out of prison on the Thursday. Now that wasn't because of my speech. It was because it was raised on the floor of the House, it was picked up by the press, and that was an example of the power of Parliament.'

Helen Clark: 'It's great if you have successes, like I have done, on forcing a public enquiry into the death of David Bennett, who was actually an Afro-Caribbean constituent of mine who died under control and restraint methods in the Norfolk clinic. That was five and a half years of work. We got the public enquiry, we got the recommendations, and perhaps if I'd not been there, well, I mean, I was the person who took it up.'

Patricia Hewitt: 'The first, almost the first thing I did in the constituency after I was elected, we had in my most disadvantaged estate – I mean it's in the bottom ten wards in the country for educational disadvantages, it's really poor, this is a white, working-class council estate – there was a tiny little crèche attached to a very small adult education centre. Tiny little place, struggling away, and they'd run out of money. I mean, it's a bit emotional, and Camelot had made themselves deeply unpopular, because they'd awarded themselves, do you remember, a very big pay-rise, or bonus or something. And I thought, A-ha. So I sent them a letter, didn't mention their bonuses, but I said, "Desperately poor community, crèche, blah-di-blah, would Camelot, not the lottery, Camelot like to make a donation?" and there it came. I thought, Yup, absolutely, and I think I got £5,000 from them, and £5,000 from BT.'

Sue Doughty took up the concerns of her constituents over gambling: 'With the recent draft Gambling Bill, I tabled a raft of questions, as I realised it was a constituency concern about gambling amongst children, about whether the government had actually taken this into account, whether they'd taken into account the addictive nature of fruit machines in chip shops, for example, which is something they were proposing. And to see that when the Bill came out in its next form, a lot of the points that I'd raised through questions about whether the government had done its research, the government had withdrawn all those clauses that I was very unhappy about. So I was really pleased about that.'

Anne Campbell: 'What I really like is being able to sit above things. I mean, as I did in 1993 when I started Opportunity Links, to be able to bring people together from different parts of the city and to sort of bang heads together, I suppose, and get solutions that one of them by themselves wouldn't be able to do, so it's that sort of coordinating role I think I find most interesting.'

Baroness Boothroyd sums up the feelings of the majority of women MPs across all three parties: 'I enjoyed my constituency work most of all. I think I enjoyed being responsible for a huge area, a lot of people: the quality of their life in that area, of industry, of education, of cultural development of the area, and I just felt very proud, and I think they would be, and to be a representative and to help improve – I could just generalise by saying the quality of life of the people in that area and being responsible for them. I felt responsible for them.'

Putting issues on the map

Women MPs believe they have pushed for reform and changes in legislation, both in the Chamber and from behind the scenes. As evidence, they frequently cite new legislation on domestic violence, child protection, and rape. Working behind the scenes, they have often achieved all-party support for their reforms not only from other women MPs, but they have brought the men along too.

Many Labour women MPs have now been in ministerial positions, or even better, in charge of departments; there are currently six women secretaries of state. They have been championing issues and have also been in a position where they can actually do something about them. But it is also true that some women do not like to take up traditional campaigning issues on behalf of other women.

Examples, as we have seen, include Labour's Sure Start programme for children which extended the welfare state to the under-fives. It is one of the successful family policies that has become mainstreamed and the Conservative Party also now says it would retain the policy.

Tessa Jowell remembers working with her colleagues to gain acceptance for the policy: 'I was very clear what Sure Start should achieve, and it was to me very much inspired by the wonderful health-visitor that I'd had when my children were born, and because my mother did not live near me, what it reminded me of was the importance of that kind of validation, that kind of support when you have a new baby . . . Sure Start was designed as a programme that was about developing and improving the quality of relationships that young mothers have with their babies. It's a nurture programme, plain and simple. It's now developed, and developed I think in very good ways and is set to become a universal programme. But what's important is that it always maintains, at its core, that focus on nurture, and that focus on enriching what for tiny babies is the most important relationship.'

It is not only family issues, but also tough legal issues that are being addressed. Harriet Harman used her former position in the Solicitor General's office to campaign for women's rights in the law courts: 'They've got what they call the justice gap, and I think that a lot of people who are raped just think that they can't face the extra ordeal of the justice system, it was bad enough the offence, they just can't face it. So I think a lot of extra work has to go into supporting the victim, reassuring the people that the criminal justice system has changed, it will take rape seriously, it won't just say, "Oh well, she'd had sex with him before, so what's the fuss about?" or "She was drunk, so therefore it's fair game" or "She was wearing a short skirt, so she was asking for it." Those kinds of prejudices, which are still around –

to some extent – in the public's mind. They are very much being challenged in the criminal justice system.'

Harriet is also seen by many to be a champion over many years of a whole host of women's issues generally: 'I would say that I've been most proud of identifying issues that are of huge concern to women, but which have not had a proper place on the political agenda, and speaking up for those issues, and making sure that they get embedded into the heart of the political agenda. I would say women's representation is one of those . . . Childcare and nursery provision, that was not a political issue, it was regarded as absolutely nothing to do with politics. Now it's recognised as being an important issue. Concerns about the work/family balance. They used to be regarded as not a proper political issue, now they are. Domestic violence, we've got a Domestic Violence Bill.'

The economic concerns surrounding childcare is an issue where women MPs feel they have mainstreamed their concerns into concrete policies, Yvette Cooper explains: 'Another good example is children's tax credits. There was a lot of debate when they were first introduced about making sure women got the money. That was something that women MPs were particularly sensitive about . . . The Treasury did a lot of work on ensuring that this money would actually go to the carer, the main carer, which was predominantly women, and that was only because women MPs raised it, discussed it, Dawn Primarolo was obviously critical in making sure that was sorted. But that was only because women MPs arranged it.'

Minister Margaret Hodge: 'I am really, really absolutely thrilled and proud of a lot of what I've achieved. For example, I mean, I'm a granny now – I've always cared about nursery education, childcare, the position of women in society. The fact that we have been able to create nursery education for all three- and four-year-olds as a right, a generation after my children, but nevertheless we've done it, I'm really proud of it . . . I also had responsibility as a junior minister for disabled issues, and I was able to steer through legislation and establish the first Disability Rights Commission, and I'm really proud of that.'

Ruth Kelly: 'Well, I think the parental leave example is probably the most obvious one, where I achieved full-front-page coverage on the day that the pamphlet was launched. And I actually do think it influenced the opinion in the party . . . I suppose my single personal achievement of bringing the Child Trust Fund through to delivery stage and delivering that in Parliament is probably the thing I'm proudest of.'

Estelle Morris is proudest of: 'My achievements in education because I think – without sounding boastful – some of them have changed the education system for ever and I think that's what every politician wants, irreversible change . . . The thing that I think will have the biggest long-term impact if it goes right is the teacher-workforce reform.'

Maria Eagle: 'As a minister – I'm an under-secretary, so you can't think that you can turn round the whole welfare state or anything like that, but there have been a few small things as Minister for Disabled People that I have been proud of, that I have taken up and done: recognising British sign language, for example.'

Sandra Gidley thinks that the numbers of new Labour women supporting and promoting better policies for women and families has been very influential: 'I think – this is an impartial view – that such a bulk of Labour women MPs get together, they talk about how from a woman's perspective they want to have an impact on legislation, and then they decide which of them is going to do it. And they can do that and still take up the mainstream issues.'

Hazel Blears says she does feel a responsibility to help other women: 'Because I'm a woman minister, I feel an extra responsibility in my portfolio area to promote the cause of women. I support Sure Start, I'll do things around childcare issues, but I like to think that a male MP would do that too, because these are issues that are important to families as a whole. But I am very much a woman. I don't want to be a man, I want to be a woman MP.'

Some women do not feel any empathy in the slightest for feminising the political agenda. Ann Widdecombe says there are no such things as 'woman's issues': 'I deny that there is such a thing as a woman's agenda. I can remember one of the things that got me very, very angry early on in this place. The Conservative government was introducing its health service reforms and we were creating NHS trusts and I was on the standing committee of the Bill that was examining the detail. And Harriet Harman . . . said, "Well it was very important to have women on the boards of these trusts, because," and I quote, "They know what it's like to get a double buggy through a door." And I stood up – and it's all there in Hansard – and I said, So, the reason we have men on the trusts, then, is because they understand hernias, and prostrate operations and things, is that why we have men on the boards of these trusts?" And that is the sort of nonsense I hate.'

However, others take great pride in having provided the push that put women's issues on the map across a number of different government departments. Joan Ruddock: 'We did an enormous amount, I can't believe how much we actually did, albeit that people on the outside thought we did absolutely nothing – but the greatest challenge was actually creating government machinery that could deliver any kind of programmes that tried to advance women's agendas.'

Domestic violence is a key policy area where women have worked across their parties to achieve changes that benefit women resulting in the first comprehensive legislation on domestic violence. Since 1997 an all-party parliamentary group chaired by Margaret Moran has been very effective in its lobbying of ministers for better legislation. It also conducted an on-line consultation called 'Womenspeak' with women survivors of domestic violence through Women's Aid and the Hansard Society, where survivors talked online to members of the committee who were MPs. The views of these women survivors have helped shape and form policies. The project has become a world first in terms of parliamentary consultations.

Rosie Winterton sums up the feelings of other Labour women: 'One achievement that I was proud of was when I was in the Lord Chancellor's Department actually having . . . amended the Children Act, and I worked with Margaret Moran on doing that. There had been quite a lot of resistance to it, but we amended the Children Act . . . and worked with judges. There were some very good women judges who worked to help [and we ensured that] seeing or hearing domestic violence would be taken into account when looking at contact issues. That was something that was, you know, a small change, but was quite significant and one that did require a lot of persuading, actually, to bring about.'

Yvette Cooper says the number of women has been important: 'I think the impact on women has been very significant . . . I think it's certainly the case that we would not have seen a lot of things, whether it's the domestic violence work that Harriet [Harman] and Margaret [Moran] had done, whether it's the details of the tax credit, whether it's the pace of expansion of Sure Start and childcare.'

However, Cheryl Gillan, a former shadow Women's Minister for the Conservative Party, says domestic violence is an issue that crosses party lines but you don't necessarily promote it just because you are a woman: 'I think it's been long overdue. It's a taboo area of our life. People don't want to admit that domestic violence exists . . . We are working cross-party, yes, just because it's a sensible thing to do, and I would do so irrespective of my sex. This is not about gender politics as far as I'm concerned, it's about common sense.'

Eleanor Laing: 'I think what we have managed to do on Conservative Party policy – and what I hope I'm instrumental in doing at the moment – is to bring these issues that affect women's everyday lives to the top of the political agenda.'

Some important policy areas that critics would say should have been mainstreamed have not yet become so. The pay gap is one issue that women MPs mention as needing further impetus. Judy Mallaber: 'There are areas that I'm involved with where we haven't made the progress that we should. I mentioned equal pay, and there's a whole issue there, particularly about occupational segregation and people going into particular jobs, and whether the opportunities are open to them . . . there should be more opportunities available.'

Christine McCafferty's campaign to remove VAT on sanitary-ware also had an element of sensitivity for some male colleagues. Judy Mallaber explains how she asked a question about the removal of VAT on sanitary-ware after she noticed by chance that it was mentioned in a speech the Chancellor was making: 'I thought that I'd get up and see if I could raise it in Prime Minister's Questions, because it hadn't been mentioned in the budget at all. But my local paper, the *Derby Evening Telegraph*, the woman journalist there said she'd had problems getting it in the papers, because the boys in the newsroom didn't think it was important, and she eventually got it in under "The tax that dare not say its name". So you get these little victories sometimes.'

The increased representation of women in Parliament since 1997 was also felt when a group of Labour women MPs fought battles to introduce the system of 'twinning' in Wales, whereby parliamentary seats are paired up so that one man and one woman candidate is selected for each. Julie Morgan: 'It was a huge campaign, and it was raised in the House of Commons as well, and we won, and we went in 50–50 Labour candidates, and ended up, I think, with 40 per cent women on the Welsh Assembly and then at these last selections, it's actually now the only gender-balanced legislator in the world.'

However, Ann Taylor says that 'women's' issues like modernisation and domestic violence were talked about before the influx of women MPs in 1997, and that women and men have worked together to progress them: 'Well, reform and modernisation of the House was something we were talking about before the 1997 election, so it might have been extra impetus by the number of women, or it might have been given extra publicity because of the number of women it [was] being linked to, but actually it was an issue we were talking about for a couple of years previously. In terms of the issues and domestic violence, you know, I think it's wrong to suggest that these issues have only been raised since 1997 . . . There are very few [issues that] no male MPs have taken an interest in, they've taken an interest in a range of issues, which might, on occasion, have been considered women's issues.'

But some of her colleagues do not agree with her. Judy Mallabar explains: 'I do think the fact we have a large number of women has made it easier to get priority given to some of the issues that a number of us have campaigned on over many years. Therefore there's a head of steam behind it, and that's probably easier as a result of the fact that you've got a force here'

There may be more women in Westminster now, but there are also now a good number of younger MPs, both men and women. Frequently, women MPs remark on how much difference the new demographics have made to policy-making and the work of the House. Rosemary McKenna recalls: 'It wasn't just the presence of young women in 1997 that changed this place, it was the fact that the young men with families had the support of the women . . .'

Anne Begg thinks men now have as strong an interest in family issues as women: 'Because I'm a woman, people assume that I must have an interest in women's issues. But I'm not a typical woman; I'm single, I have no family, I don't know what it's like to get your work/life balance – my work is my life, and always has been. I'm a typical spinster in that respect; whereas I think a young man whose family, who's struggling to get that balance between home and life . . . has more insight into these aspects, these issues, which are more often regarded as women's issues, than I do, and he's got that kind of personal knowledge of it.'

Marie Eagle points to influential women who have been working together to achieve change across government departments, with the help of men too: 'Certainly my experience as a minister is that Whitehall is not as female-oriented as the parliamentary Labour Party . . . It's remarkable how many things come across your desk that have not got a female perspective attached; something like pensions, for example. And I will often write things on papers that say, "What about women?" '

Women argue that they have given a new impetus to women's issues, but they also say how many men in their parties have championed these issues too, and that they have needed their support to push the issues through. Diana Organ explains: 'I think the men were glad that we said, "Oh, we can't have this," and they thought, Thank God, that gives us the let out, because they didn't want to break ranks with the other boys. I think a lot of them are really happy about it, which is why some of the things have gone to the vote in the House we've won, because you wouldn't have won it on just the women, the men have had to vote for it as well.'

Others have managed to make a mark for women by putting down questions in entrenched male areas such as Defence. Phyllis Starkey: 'I was on the Foreign Affairs Select Committee for some time. For a long time there were only two women on the committee, that it was only I and the other woman member who ever raised issues about women specifically in the countries that we visited. But once we did raise them, then the male members of the committee sort of backed us up. They didn't resist it, they simply didn't think of it, and didn't initiate women's issues in relation to those countries.'

Teamwork versus the queen bee

Women MPs clearly value working as part of a team, because they mention it often. However, it is also evident that they believe the geography of

Westminster isolates them and this can lead to a feeling of loneliness and alienation.

Hilary Armstrong says being Chief Whip is a team job but other MPs are often on their own: 'I think that's one of the problems for MPs, that they come and they can flounder because they're not part of a team. I think that some of the women can find that particularly difficult . . . I've always worked in ways where I build a team around me, and here I've got a very good team. I've got fourteen whips who work with me, I work closely with people in Number 10, special advisers, so I certainly never feel lonely.'

Jean Corston thinks women MPs of the past were by nature 'queen bees' rather than team players: 'It was a tough world and they made it on the basis of competence, personal charm and all the rest of it. Now, I think that with my generation, because I was born just before the baby boomers, it was somewhat different; our attitudes were different. For us, it was about, "If someone else can do it, perhaps I can," and a lot of that was to do with class.'

Charlotte Atkins enjoys it when she can assimilate the views of her colleagues, through team meetings, into her work: 'A number of ministers do come to the Women's Committee, you know, if they've got time, and it will just be women together, whatever position they might be in . . . It's a good opportunity to raise a whole range of issues that women want to raise.'

Maria Eagle agrees that the women of 1997 work as part of a team: 'I think women do tend to value things like loyalty. They do see us, and I think this is true of the 1997 intake of women, they see themselves as part of a team, so their first instinct is not to go and start fighting, it's to try and conciliate if there's some problem, let's deal with it inside the Party, let's not just go straight out to the media and start complaining.'

Others mention how an MP is on their own and that the team element is not always as emphasised as they would like it to be. Theresa May explains: 'One of the things that I still feel about this place is that it is an odd mixture, in that the emphasis is still very much on the . . . MP as an individual rather than as a team-player. That is strange because in a sense we are here in big teams, and obviously, there's the whipping system and so forth which brings you together.'

Ruth Kelly agrees with Theresa: 'I suppose the single biggest disappointment, perhaps inevitably, is that MPs operate much more in isolated units than people realise. You have your own office, you have your own little staff, you pursue your own objectives and there's much less atmosphere of being part of a team than I thought would have been the case.'

Diana Organ finds Westminster highly competitive at the expense of team play. She explains: 'I've never worked in a place that is less team-orientated, and maybe that's because of the jobs I had before. You were always part of an organisation that was a team. There is very little teamworking here, we all compete with one another.'

Sally Keeble is saddened to have to agree with her: 'I would say that one of the other really sad things here is that we are terribly individualistic, and we tend to do our own thing, and I think that's a real shame, because if we did collaborate much more, worked jointly, then we could actually achieve a lot more.'

Jackie Lawrence puts the sense of isolation down to the geography of the building: 'I was told that there was no map available, for security reasons. This establishment is almost alien to teamwork. Each MP works on their own in an isolated manner, and that's the biggest obstacle I've found here to actually finding your way about, to finding the mechanisms and procedures of the place.'

Rosemary McKenna emphasises the importance of friends in Westminster: 'You find people build up a group of friends in here, because if you don't do that, you die. You can be so completely on your own; it can be very, very difficult in such a lonely job . . . You can come in here and, unless you're an outgoing person, not speak to anyone all day.'

Changing the mind of your party

There are a number of devices an MP can use in Westminster to help persuade and cajole their own party round to their way of thinking. Prime Minister's Questions, Parliamentary Questions, Early Day Motions and Adjournment Debates are the most frequently used ways they can get their own party to change its mind.

If they are exceptionally lucky, and it is the exception rather than the rule, they may get the chance to push through a private member's bill, but this is very rare. Any MP can put down any question they like to the government of the day in Parliamentary Questions and the government, or in fact, their civil servants must answer it. MPs also get like-minded colleagues to sign Early Day Motions which draw the government's attention to an issue. Likewise they can put in for and often are given the chance to speak in Friday Adjournment Debates on issues of their choosing, when cynics would say the chamber is empty because most MPs by then have left for their constituencies. They also use the scrutiny of Bills and legislation and membership of select committees to achieve the changes they are after.

There are those who agree that lobbying behind the scenes in meetings and committees is by far the most effective way to influence your party. Constituency meetings and the annual party conference also afford an opportunity for an MP to change the minds of their party. Motions are passed, defeated, amalgamated, forgotten or adjourned. A more modern way that some MPs now choose to influence their parties is to talk on or off the record to the media – that way they can assure that the issue is immediately raised in the public's imagination and that a minister or even the Prime Minister in No. 10 might read about it over breakfast. Others are critical of what the 'briefers' say to the media. There are some who think that working behind the scenes is the best way to effect change:

Ann Taylor: 'By the time you get to a public confrontation, you've almost certainly lost, and therefore I think you've got to use the mechanisms that we have better than most people do. That can include backbench committees, that can include NEC committees, that can include our representatives on the policy forum, it can include talking to ministers informally, talking to parliamentary private secretaries. There are lots of mechanisms open to people, and one of the things that I certainly noticed as Chief Whip was that some of the people who opposed the government on certain policies just do not take advantage of those mechanisms, because they're not necessarily that keen on changing the party's views.'

One Conservative woman used her party conference to make her views known. Theresa May recalls: 'I'm often asked if I regret making my first party conference speech as Party Chairman where I said, "This party is perceived as a nasty party." I don't regret it. I actually think it was important for that speech to be made, and I was pleased that I had done that, and I think that it did come out well, that it kick-started the change of thinking in the party which was very important.'

Theresa May also used her chairmanship of the party to introduce the first primary selection process in the UK: 'What's important is that we have got – this time, rather than in 2001 – we have actually got some Conservative women, some women standing in Conservative-held seats, which we didn't have in 2001, and we have got women, more women in winnable seats, which is important . . . When I was Chairman, I was pleased to say the party selected the first ethnic-minority candidate – well, the first black man – to stand in a Conservative-held seat in Windsor. Something that people would have thought was not what the Conservative Party would have done some years ago. The first openly gay man was selected, we selected an Asian mother and business woman in Enoch Powell's old seat. These are signs of how the party was changing.'

There are others who think you should talk to the press. Glenda Jackson: 'I think if you're talking about changes in policy, setting aside the Iraq war, then what you would do here is you would ask questions . . . But you're not going to change government policy when you have a majority the size that we have. Because there will always be a sufficient majority . . . to get those bills through . . . I think the best way of exerting pressure on the government in that sense for someone like me – who is completely discountable as far as the government is concerned because of my vocal opinions – is to go via the external officers, who are the press.'

There are those who think you shouldn't talk to the press first. Dame Marion Roe would see ministers first: 'I have gone to see the minister or the secretary of state and explained why I disagreed with a particular policy or an angle of a policy and pleaded that it should be reviewed or tweaked or whatever. I have also encouraged others who might feel the same to join me, so there were a group of people saying we are not quite sure if you got it right, very politely, I have never gone to the press, I have never been seen on the green with a TV and microphone up my nose, undermining any of my colleagues ever, and I think because of that I have more influence.'

There are those who appeal to the party at large. Jenny Tonge: 'It's just trying to persuade the party to be stronger and to raise the issue [the Middle East] more often. You see, when you just get particular individuals, and there's about a dozen of us in the House of Commons that raise this issue time and time and time again, and if you do that, you tend to be seen as a sort of "one-issue wonk", and I don't want that, so you really have got to get your party behind you.'

There is no doubt that if you are an MP in one of the smaller parties in Westminster the chance to meet and influence your leader at meetings is that much greater. Annette Brooke is a Liberal Democrat: 'We're lucky, again, being a small party. We're meeting this afternoon, for example, and of course, we fit into one room quite reasonably, and everybody can speak and have their say, and we are very democratic on lots of issues which are contentious, so I'm not sure that I've ever really changed people's mind, but we do have the opportunity to do that.'

Ulster Unionist Sylvia Hermon: 'Fortunately, my party leader has his office just across the way from my office and he often, actually, strays into my office, thinking that it's just going to be a quick chat, but there's just one soft armchair and I always guide my leader into the soft chair so that, in fact, I have the advantage of sitting in the rather high, harder chair . . . I then berate him in uncompromising terms as to what he must do, what must be said and how he must manage his women members.'

Tessa Jowell concludes that working alongside men in her party, women have provided the impetus for changes in policies on behalf of other women: 'I think that being designed as they have been by women politicians, they take account much more of the psychological and emotional dimensions, the relationship dimensions than would have been the case had they been designed by men.'

It is clear that by thinking strategically and working together, women politicians across all parties have achieved significant policy shifts on behalf of others. However, the increased representation of women in the Cabinet and other ministerial posts who are in a position to discuss, cajole and argue for change on behalf of other women has been highly significant. There are now tougher laws to protect women and children, women MPs are campaigning for women internationally, and the gender analysis of the budget was a first for women.

ELEVEN

The future

Selecting women

The 1997 general election victory was a turning point for women, whatever one's view of the policy of all-women shortlists, whatever the carping personal vilification women MPs have been subjected to and whatever remains to be achieved. It was one of the most significant events for women in the twentieth century.

Women in the Scottish Parliament and the Welsh Assembly have made more progress than their colleagues in Westminster, because of the Labour Party's quota policies. The Welsh Assembly adopted positive selection procedures based on a system of 'twinning', leading to an equal number of women and men being elected to it. The Welsh Assembly First Minister Rhodri Morgan openly boasts of a 'Cabinet with a female majority.'[43] In the Scottish Parliament, that has also adopted twinning, women represent 39.5 per cent of the MSPs, while in Northern Ireland, where there are no positive measures, women make up just 14 per cent of Assembly members.[44]

In Westminster, neither the Conservative Party nor the Liberal Democrats have opted for effective positive discrimination policies. However electoral laws have now been reformed to allow positive discrimination after the Jepson case in 1996 led to a successful challenge to Labour's all-women shortlist system. The Sex Discrimination (Election Candidates) Act of 2002 allowed Labour to target safe seats for women at the 2005 election. In the 2001 general election, when all-women shortlists were not allowed, the Labour Party's 'gender balanced shortlists' led to fewer women standing than in the 1997 election and only 95 Labour women became MPs compared to 101 in the

1997 election. In 2005 that number increased to 98.[45] However, even in 2005, all-women shortlists were still controversial, with one Welsh Independent Labour man winning over his female rival who was Labour's all-woman shortlist candidate.[46]

Research on 2001 selections shows that all the party selection processes are still riddled with injustice and inequality towards women and that they are all 'institutionally sexist'.[47] The Conservatives come out worst; with their current systems, it may take them until 2301 to reach equal numbers of male and female MPs. It is likely to take Labour until 2033, and for the Liberal Democrats it could be until 2101.[48] In short, some believe 1997 was a one-off hollow victory that will be short-lived and the automatic progress of women's representation in Westminster should not be taken for granted.[49]

Women going through the Conservative Party's selection procedures have encountered deep-rooted hostility. 'The male members of the party tend to run a very fine line, 80 per cent of them don't want you as their MP and 20 per cent of them are actually really nice and really try to help you and 100 per cent of them want to shag you,' said one candidate.[50] The Conservative Party believes new systems will now help to remedy this.

It seems paradoxical that the Conservative Party should find itself in this position, when the first woman MP was a Conservative (Lady Astor) and the first woman Prime Minister was a Conservative (Margaret Thatcher). Even as far back as 1921, local associations were obliged to elect delegations to party conference comprising one third women, resulting in far better representation of women than Labour, who had no policy.[51] However, Margaret Thatcher herself observed how difficult the selection procedures are for a woman in the Conservative Party: 'I would be shortlisted for the seat, would make what was generally acknowledged to be a good speech – and then the questions, most of them having the same purpose, would begin. With my family commitments, would I have time enough for the constituency?' She then goes on to say, 'What I resented, however, was that beneath some of the criticism, I detected a feeling that the House of Commons was not really the right place for a woman anyway' and she believed it was women who expressed this prejudice openly.[52]

The Liberal Democrats considered all-women shortlists at their 2001 conference. This met with fierce opposition and the party settled for imposing a target of 40 per cent of women in the seats requiring a swing of less than 7.5 per cent to win. The party insists that neither sex should be allowed to take more than two thirds of the places on a shortlist. This has led to some women candidates complaining about being asked to stand as token women in seats. The party also set up the Gender Balance Task Force to provide training, monitoring and advocacy, and has invested money in helping women candidates, with some improvement on the 2001 position.

Other political parties may not want to admit it but 1997 was a turning point for women not just in the House but in the political parties and their constituencies as well. The Conservative Party began to look white, male and ageing, and there was an open admission that the party needed to appeal to modern families. They realised that women were an electoral asset, and they needed to reform to appeal to those voters, a viewpoint some male Tory MPs endorse: 'We'll be living off a depleted gene pool,' Andrew Lansley MP is quoted as saying.[54]

Barbara Castle herself was able to join in and see the sexual revolution through. Aged 90 and looking immaculate, she walked up to the rostrum to speak at the Equal Opportunities Commission's celebration of 25 years of the Sex Discrimination Act in January 2001: 'My own first launching into political life was due to the women members of my local party insisting on having a woman on the shortlist for the selection of their new candidate. They won because they threatened to down tools over the humbler jobs, which they had always done. Again, it was the threatened revolt of women MPs in the House of Commons in 1969 which enabled me to persuade the Cabinet in 1969 that the demand for equal pay had become irresistible.' Greater equality in the future will also depend on women's absolute belief in, 'their right to it', she told the conference.[55]

Feminist academics have no doubt how Westminster's large number of women MPs has been achieved. In the 2002 Fawcett publication *Women and Candidate Selection in British Political Parties* the authors argue: 'Where women's representation is at its highest in the UK – in the Labour Party in Westminster following the 1997 general election and in the Scottish Parliament, National Assembly for Wales and Greater London Assembly – this has largely been the result of positive discrimination measures that have been adopted by one or more parties. Positive discrimination is used throughout the world as the most effective means of securing fair representation for women.'[56]

Another study concludes that in Europe, 'at least one major party in all nine Parliaments which achieve 25 per cent women or more use quotas. Without this mechanism, the number of women represented never rises to acceptable levels.'[57]

There has often been the perception that the all-women shortlist candidates were somehow inexperienced. In fact many had come up through local councils, had been council leaders and had many years' experience in local politics before they got selected for their seats. Many of the men who were initially not in favour of all-women shortlists later came to the conclusion that the shortlist candidates that they did see were of infinitely higher calibre than they had ever seen in previous elections. Constituency parties will often now say that they have benefited considerably by having a woman. That shows up in the polls as well – they achieved a higher than average share of the vote for Labour.[58]

Even today it is clear that all-women shortlists remain controversial, not least among some of the Labour women who were selected through them. Conservative women MPs do not, in the main, support them. But women in the Liberal Democrat Party regret that their party did not opt for an all-women shortlist system when it had the chance.

All-women shortlists and reservations

Among Labour women, Candy Atherton was the first woman to be selected using the all-women shortlist system: 'I was the first all-women shortlist. I was the first candidate selected under any procedure before 1997, and that was partly because some of the local men were in absolute uproar that the party had gone for an all-women list. In fact, once I was on the scene, I think I ended up with something like 97 per cent of the final ballot and it was settled very quickly when I came on the scene. I don't for a second think that I would have been selected if there hadn't been an all-women list.'

In Scotland Anne McGuire supported them: 'The reality is that, no matter how often women took the chance and thought they were good, or thought they were not good, thought they were as good, or thought they were as bad as our male colleagues, they still couldn't get through. They still couldn't get through the glass ceiling . . . sometimes, you actually had to take a hammer to break the ceiling, and I think that's what we did with the all-women shortlist.'

In Wales Jackie Lawrence was an all-women shortlist candidate: 'My constituency actually volunteered to be an all-women shortlist. And I remember the constituency treasurer at the time saying, "Jackie, we've volunteered to be an all-woman shortlist, because we're going to select you anyway, so we're going to sort of fly the flag."'

Harriet Harman explains how all-women shortlists were a last resort for the Labour Party after all other attempts to get more women into Westminster had failed: 'I do [support all-women shortlists] on the basis of experience because what we did was we tried everything before we tried the brutal remedy of excluding men from the shortlists and having all-women shortlists. We tried having a woman on every shortlist because we used to have all-male shortlists; that would be the standard position, men-only shortlists, women weren't officially excluded, they just weren't on the shortlist. So then we had a rule that you can't have a shortlist unless there's a woman on it, and then what would happen is they'd have a woman on the shortlist and they'd always select the man. So we still never got women selected.'

Strangely, within the Conservative Party one former Tory MP agrees with Harriet Harman. Teresa Gorman remembers: 'I once did a Ten-Minute Rule Bill calling for the doubling-up of constituencies, and then each constituency elects two individuals, one from a list of women, and one from a list of men . . . Well, that's the only way in which we actually would have made this a *fait accompli*, I did a Ten-Minute Rule Bill to propose that. But of course, Ten-Minute Rule Bills are the equivalent of Chinese newspapers, you know, you paste them on the wall and they're blown away the next day.'

The former Conservative Party Chairman, Theresa May, is not totally opposed to all-women shortlists: 'I don't believe women-only shortlists should be imposed on anybody, but if a constituency chooses to have a women-only shortlist, then yes, by all means. Funnily enough, as it happens, certainly for the final selection there have been a number of Conservative selections that have women-only shortlists.'

In the Liberal Democrat Party, Sandra Gidley wishes her party would adopt a system of all-women shortlists: 'It's not my party policy, I must stress that, and people think it's an odd thing, and say, "Well you've made it without positive discrimination, so what's the problem? If women like you can make it, anybody can." And I said, "No that isn't the point, you don't understand. We need to address this balance very quickly."'

Jenny Tonge reluctantly supports all-women shortlists: 'I do feel that we have a problem within the Liberal Democrats about women. We've got lots of women at local level, in local government. We haven't got so many in Parliament, and we [tried] very, very hard to get our party . . . to do what the Labour Party did . . . The way they got a whole lot of women elected was to have all-women shortlists. Now I don't particularly approve of that, but I think you've got to sort of break the deadlock on this, and you've got to somehow do something really radical like that to get more women in post. The trouble with the Lib Dems is that it's rather more difficult than for the Labour Party because we all fight very, very hard to win our seats.'

Helen Jackson says it was tough getting the Labour Party to change: 'I've put a lot of effort in, because that effort that we put in during the years I was in opposition led to the establishment of all-women shortlists in the run up to the 1997 election. I felt, along with Jean Corston, Ann Clwyd, Harriet [Harman], Joan Ruddock, those of us who had really been pushing that within the shadow Cabinet, and saying, "We've got to do this, we've got to do this"; and so I felt very much a part of that, and was immensely proud of the 101 women that we ended up with.'

Angela Eagle: 'I massively supported [all-women shortlists] and was instrumental in getting the Parliamentary Candidates Act 2002 onto the statute book as quickly as possible to at least overturn the Jepson judgment for twenty more years. People in the party knew that it would be difficult, but couldn't see any other way of making any progress . . . That whole wave of new women simply would not have happened without those rule changes.'

Although a number of Labour women MPs have reservations about all-women shortlists, they often support them, but with caution. Mo Mowlam says: 'I had some doubts about making it all-women before it was put through, because I don't think that's the way that you change male attitudes to work with them, because I think you've got to get women on, but at the same time, you've got to take men with you and change their attitudes, otherwise you'll never break through. The male club will continue and it'll get worse. So I had some doubts about an all-women shortlist, but after the results came through, I could tell it was worthwhile, because there were so many women that it made a big difference.'

Louise Ellman: 'I've always felt a bit uneasy with it. However, having been selected by one, I feel I shouldn't talk like that, and I do recognise that was in fact the only action that did result in more women coming into Parliament, and I think that is a good thing, more representative of society, so despite the unease I felt, I think it has been a positive move.'

Estelle Morris: 'I must admit that I'm not a great lover of it, but I think it was essential to get over the hump, it was essential to get that move forward, and without it, we would not be where we are today. But I think we've made it when we don't need it. And I think the Labour Party, given the importance of the trade union movement, in enabling you to get selected in safe seats, we need it.'

Ann Clwyd: 'I still think it's difficult for women to get selected. I have got certain criticisms of the all-women shortlist, but when I look at some of the men who are here – some of the men really shouldn't be here. And so it's not fair to say, you know, "some of the women who came in on those lists shouldn't be here," because we always used to be told, you know, "Ah, well, women will get there on merit." Well if it were just merit, there'd be a number of men who wouldn't be here.'

Some Labour women still firmly oppose the all-women shortlist system. Baroness Boothroyd: 'I just don't believe in positive discrimination to get in here, that's all. I don't feel that that is the way. I think that women can be competitive. Why haven't they got the confidence to compete with men, is that what you're saying? Because that's how I read positive discrimination: "I can only compete with my own sex, I can't compete with another sex."'

Ann Taylor: 'No, I wasn't in favour of all-women shortlists. I suppose in retrospect, it has helped to make a breakthrough. I've always felt that the problem was there weren't enough women coming forward. I'm not sure whether there are more women coming forward now. I'm not standing at the next election. Mine was an open shortlist, and I'm amazed that more women didn't put their names forward. Hardly any women put their names forward, because there was another all-women shortlist next door.'

Helen Liddell: 'No [I don't support all-women shortlists] because I think this is a tough business. If you are helped in and you don't realise just how rough and vicious and nasty it can be, once you get in here it can destroy you. And I've seen people come in here; I've seen them go off the rails because they've not been prepared for how rough it is. You've got to know from day one, this is a rough business. And I think putting a sort of barrier around women and saying, "This particular selection has got to be protective," it could be very, very destructive to me personally if I get selected.'

Helen Clark: 'I think the whole business of all-women shortlists . . . gives your enemies a rod to hit you with, really. It's "Oh well, second class MPs", etc, etc, and I also think it puts you at a disadvantage in terms of your party, in the constituency. You know, it's almost, "Oh well, we fought to get you in, we fought to have an all-women shortlist and you owe us one, Miss," that sort of thing, whereas I think if you've got mixed sex, no one can say, "I'm not here on my own merit, etc."'

Hostility to all-women shortlists is greatest amongst Conservative MPs. Caroline Spelman: 'We supported the change in the law so that we could use positive discrimination in our selection process as well, and we do. We don't use women-only shortlists: that's true. That's one end of a spectrum of measures that you would describe as positive discrimination and it's our female candidates themselves who don't want that. They feel that the effect of that would be to undermine their standing with their male colleagues, who would therefore think that they had got in on a false premise, and it creates resentment.'

Ann Widdecombe: 'Positive discrimination is first of all profoundly demeaning to women. I believe that any woman in this place has got the right to look any man, from the Prime Minister downwards, in the eye and know that she got there on exactly the same basis as he got there. If she can't do that, she's a second-class citizen. And that is what positive discrimination produces. It produces second-class citizens. Secondly, I think it's profoundly undemocratic.'

Gillian Shephard: 'I cannot think of anything that would more reinforce these attitudes that I've described; you know, "Poor things, they're so useless and can't get in unless you fix it for them." Well, you know, you can't have that.'

Eleanor Laing: 'I really, really don't believe in positive discrimination. I think it undermines a woman's position. I'm afraid that, although many of the women on the Labour benches are, if not quite friends of mine, they're acquaintances . . . I feel that I'm aware of those who were elected in 1997 because of there being a huge, unexpectedly enormous Labour victory and because of all-women shortlists, and I distinguish those women from the other women who would have been elected anyway.'

Virginia Bottomley: 'I'm viscerally opposed to all-women shortlists. The person who most influenced me, or one of the people who most influenced me, was a wonderful woman, Nancy Sear, who was the leader of the Liberals in the Lords, and she said, "If you have all-women shortlists, soon you'll be having all-over-65 shortlists, or all-disabled shortlists, or all-black shortlists and this is insufferable. When you are a Member of Parliament, you represent everyone, regardless of their gender or their race and their age'. What I believe in is energetic and enthusiastic positive action, so I believe in recruitment, development, coaching . . .'

The new suffragettes?

Women MPs across all parties appreciate the struggles the suffragettes made to gain the vote on behalf of women. Some think the suffragettes might look at them today and think, What wimps! but others think they would stand back and be proud of their achievements, if a little surprised that it had taken so long to get a significant number of women into Westminster.

Caroline Spelman: 'Well, I think they would be disappointed with two things. One, they would be disappointed that there are still so few women in politics. I think they would have thought that by now, if not achieving sort of parity with men in politics, they would have expected to see a few more of us here. I say probably not parity because the job is difficult to combine with family life, I'm not suggesting that it's easy, so women don't need to apply in equal numbers. But we're still well short of what I think is critical mass. And I think the second thing is that they would be terribly disappointed with today's young women that when we door-knock, those women who come to the door and say "Oh, you know, I don't vote" and I say to them, "What do you mean, you don't vote? Haven't you heard of Emily Pankhurst?" And they haven't.'

Eleanor Laing: 'I hope they'd be proud of us. You know, one of the early inspirations of my life was, when I was a little girl, the lady who lived next door to us, Miss Hamilton – I never knew her first name, she was Miss Hamilton – was born in 1900 and she was at Glasgow School of Art at the time of the suffragettes and so she was with that fashionable student movement at that time, and when I was little – she was an artist; she was a lovely, lovely, intelligent lady – and she used to tell me when I was little, "You must always use your vote, because we fought for women to have the vote, and you must, as a woman, take that responsibility when you become a woman, you must take that responsibility seriously," and boy, would she be proud to see what I'm doing now.'

Ann Widdecombe: 'I think, had I been around at that time, I would have certainly been a campaigner for women's votes. I doubt very much that I would have flung myself under the King's horse, seems very counter-productive to me. I mean, what's the point of not being there any more, you know? Can't carry on the fight if you do that.'

Glenda Jackson: 'I'm sure Mrs Pankhurst would be appalled. I think Sylvia would be delighted. What the great unnamed number of women, the unknown number of women who worked for the suffragettes would think . . . In the main I think they'd probably be pleased. There would still be issues that they would be appalled by that we haven't managed to crack. No, I think, in the main, they would be pleased with there being more women in Parliament.'

Candy Atherton: 'Well I collect suffragette memorabilia and I started about six or seven years ago, and I've got I suppose about 40 original suffragette postcards and some figurines and some things like that . . . One thing that comes across is that they came from different positions and they had different views and they had different politics, but they were all committed to ensuring that women had the opportunity to vote, and I suppose they might say to me, "What are you doing to ensure women are using that vote?" And they might be very disappointed at voter participation.'

Anne Begg: 'I suppose the fact that somebody like me has been able to make it will be a vindication of all that they did. I suspect that they had no conceptions that 80 years after they were fighting, that somebody from a very ordinary background, who happened to have a fairly major disability, would be able to get elected to Parliament. We had to wait 80 years, mind you.'

Ann Cryer: 'Oh, my grandma, I hope she would be very pleased with me. I'm sure she'd have criticisms because she was like that. And she would always have something flattering to say when I was little, but she'd always say, "Well don't you think you could do such a thing?", you know, and I think probably if she was alive today, although she'd be about 100-odd, you know, I think if she'd been here today, she would agree with most of the things I'm doing, and I think she would be amazed at how many women are in [generally], not just in Parliament for the Labour Party.'

Women MPs' advice to younger women

Women MPs enjoy their political careers and would encourage other women to go into politics. Mo Mowlam sums up her advice to younger women: 'I'd say to her, "Go for it. It's worth women doing it and you should try, but you must be sure that you want to do it." First you have to choose a party, join a party as early as you can, then get a life, get a job. If you're going to get married and have kids, do it, get it out of the way quickly, because otherwise it gets very difficult later in life when you want to go back, because you're an old mum who doesn't work, because you've got so many other pressures on your days. So do that early, get it done, and then start working for it, but don't kill yourself, because it's worthwhile doing, but it's not worthwhile wasting ten years of your life for, because luck is an incredible part of it.'

Gisela Stuart: 'It is an awkward job, it is a 24-hour commitment, that is the nature of the job. There are quite a few women who say, "That is not what I want life to be about," and I actually think that it's a very legitimate answer to that, and what was significant to me about this now infamous picture of the 101 women MPs, yes, there were 101 which was important, but much more important was the tremendous diversity of these women on those pictures, which were from Claire Ward, the youngest in her 20s, to Ann Cryer, who came in with her son, who was a widow in her 60s.'

Estelle Morris: 'I think my message to women is, it's not a nine-to-five job, and it's not a normal hours sort of job, but it's a job that can work for women.'

Barbara Follett: 'Yes, the first message is that it is worth doing. There are things you can do and you can change. Don't be put off by the prevailing message in Britain today, "why should I bother?" . . . You should bother because this is about your life. And you should get in there and do something about it.'

Hazel Blears: 'Think really hard about why you want to do it. It isn't a job, it's a vocation. It isn't like any other job in the world. It'll take over your life, but it is the most satisfying thing that you'll ever do, because you'll be achieving real change in the country, and we need you. So, "Please do it," would be my sentiments.'

Sally Keeble: 'I think it's worth doing, and I think that you have to have women MPs, and you must have women with children because before I had my children, my work experience and my attitude was exactly like my male colleagues, and I used to poo-poo women who fussed about childcare, and I thought they were just being a bit soft and soppy. And it wasn't until I had my own children that it kind of hit me like an express train. But I think what I'd say to this place, is that actually politics needs women more than women need politics.'

Oona King: 'I think the message given out to young women in particular and young people in general, and especially "normal" people, who value a family life or any sort of life, the message going to those sort of people is completely wrong. It's that a) you have to enjoy Punch and Judy shows, and be able to scream and shout and score cheap points against everyone; b) you have to be willing to give up seeing your family, given a lot of the working hours, despite the changes; and c) you have to be happy with procedures that were formulated in the eighteenth century because that's how a lot of Westminster works.'

Hilary Armstrong: 'The first thing is they've got to be confident about themselves and know themselves, because what you've got to be able to do here is handle yourself. But they shouldn't come here expecting it's going to be a normal nine-to-five job. It can never be. Politics is not nine-to-five, so you're going to be engaged in political discussion and so on, and your constituents will have expectations of you, so you've got to know yourself, you've got to be able to organise yourself, and you've got to be able to manage more than one thing at a time. And the other thing I would say is you've got to know how you relax and build that into the job, but that might not be on a daily basis. For me, it's about a six-weekly basis.'

Patricia Hewitt: 'I think what I would also say to young women as well as young men is, "Get yourself some real expertise and experience before you get elected." I mean, for some people, they get elected in their twenties, and they're brilliant. But I think people who say, "I want a career in politics," that raises questions for me. I don't think people should want careers in politics. I think they should have a burning desire to change the world, really.'

Helen Liddell: 'Be absolutely sure it's what you want to do. Don't do it because it looks like an exciting or glamorous job. You've actually got to have a driving ambition to change the world, and you've also got to be prepared to acknowledge that there are sacrifices, and those sacrifices could be pretty acute.'

Sandra Gidley: 'We can always think of reasons not to do something, actually, and I think there's a tendency in lots of people to think that, I can't do it because . . ., and actually you should turn that around and think, I can do that. I mean for years I thought, Oh, it would be very interesting to be in politics, but I thought, I can never do that because I don't do public speaking. I mean, I was a pharmacist, you speak one to one. I don't do this and I don't do that . . . And I met some of the male MPs, and I watched it and watched some of the turgid speeches, and I thought, Well, I'm not brilliant, but I could do better than that.'

Theresa May: 'Well, I would hope that a message could be given that Westminster does matter, it does affect people's lives, it does make a difference. That's why I think that women should get involved, get involved in politics in terms of voting, but also look on it as somewhere where they have a role to play.'

Julie Kirkbride: 'If, on my tombstone, it was, "Julie Kirkbride, MP for Bromsgrove" and nothing else, I would say, "She lived a very rewarding life".'

Virginia Bottomley: 'It's a brilliant career for a woman! I think it's a very good career for a woman, so long as she can find a way of living . . . either she's got to be accessible to Westminster, or she's got to have a good domestic arrangement where she lives, if she wants to combine it with children.'

Ann Widdecombe: 'I would say, "Make the most of what you can do, what you can be, what you can have, you only get one chance. And you've got to decide where your priorities are. And that is why I think it's a huge waste of time, for example, only going for what you can have. Because what use is it to you at the end? But if you go for what you can do, you leave a lasting legacy. It's not one that anyone would recognise and attribute to you, but what you have done goes on having an effect. And so I think it's very, very important that you concentrate on "doing". But whatever you concentrate on, you only get one go.'

Need they say more? There may be as many differing strands of advice as there are women in political parties but the enthusiasm, optimism and spirit with which they convey their 'do come here', 'do it too' message is a sign of how much, despite the knocks, setbacks, personal attacks and criticisms, they actually enjoy the job of being an MP and making a difference to the lives of others. Their words are an inspiration to other women MPs in the making.

APPENDIX

METHODS OF RESEARCH, CONDUCTED IN MAY 2005

1. Since 1997 there have been 135 women MPs elected to the Commons across all the parties, including Labour, Conservative, Liberal Democrat, SNP, UU, DU, SF.
2. 83 Women MPs across all parties were interviewed for the study. 63 out of a possible 106 Labour women; 12 Conservative out of a possible 15; 7 Liberal Democrat out of a possible 8; and 1 UU, as representative of the other 6 from fringe parties.
3. 15 of the 135 women MPs had left Westminster and five of these were interviewed.
4. Boni Sones visited the three spokeswomen for Labour, Conservative and Liberal Democrats in the Commons to secure permission for the interviews to go ahead. All three parties were keen to cooperate.
5. The interviews lasted between 30 minutes and 3.5 hours each. Most were around 50 minutes. In some cases return visits were made to continue the interviews.
6. All five members of the Cabinet in the Commons were interviewed, including Patricia Hewitt, Tessa Jowell, Hilary Armstrong, Margaret Beckett. Ruth Kelly was also interviewed before her recent appointment to the Cabinet.
7. Emails were sent to all the Westminster MPs in January 2004 and again in March and April 2004 setting out the purpose of the book. In addition to those who replied positively to emails, phone calls were made to those who it was thought had a significant contribution to make, including all women in the Cabinet.
8. All of the interviewees were sent beforehand a list of the 23 questions they would be asked, and the names of the five female journalists

carrying out the interviews. In addition to the scripted questions, the journalists asked their own intuitive questions as well. 99.9 per cent of the interviews are on the record with a few sentences here and there that were off the record only. The interviewees were not allowed to see transcripts of their interviews.

9. All of the material has been captured on mini–disk to broadcast standards and will be lodged in the British Library with a time-bar on it where MPs have granted their permission to do this.

10. The interviewers were: Linda Fairbrother, Senior Broadcast Journalist Anglia TV; Angela Lawrence, former political correspondent BBC TV and Senior Broadcast Journalist, BBC Radio Suffolk; Deborah McGurran, Political Editor, BBC TV East; Dr Eva Simmons, Senior Broadcast Journalist, BBC Radio Cambridgeshire; Boni Sones, former Political Editor, BBC TV East, correspondent and senior broadcast journalist.

11. The transcripts of the interviews were read by Professor Joni Lovenduski who identified themes from them. Information was then sorted from the transcripts into the chapter headings and themes. This was done objectively by a manuscripts adviser, Natalya Cernecka.

12. The MPs were asked:

   1. How did you learn the ropes as a new MP and learn how the House of Commons works? How long did it take? Who helped you and who hindered?

   2. Did you feel welcome when you first went to the House of Commons? Were you welcomed by women, by men? In your party? In other parties?

   3. What were your first impressions of the House?

   4. What are your impressions now?

   5. What achievements as an MP are you most proud of and why? Have you personally changed policy on an issue?

   6. What would you still like to achieve in the future?

   7. Which aspects of the job of MP do you most enjoy? Why?

   8. What is the most effective way to influence your party when you disagree with something it wants to do?

   9. Have you ever tried to change your party's policy on an issue that you

thought was of special concern to women?

10. Have you worked with men in your party (or in other parties) on an issue that you thought was of special concern to women?

11. How do you organise your work and family life during a typical week when Parliament is sitting?

12. What reforms of Parliament have been most useful to you and why?

13. What message should young women be given about Westminster?

14. How could Parliament be improved to make it easier to be an MP? A woman MP?

15. What do you think men need to learn about women's approach?

16. Why do you think the media perceived women MPs badly; and if you are a Labour MP, what approach did you have to the cut in Lone Parent Benefit?

17. How do you think you are perceived by the media and do you agree with that impression?

18. What are your views of the reporting of Westminster?

19. What do you think the suffragettes would have thought of you?

20. Who do you most admire in Westminster today?

21. Have you a story of Westminster that sticks in your mind?

22. What is the worst thing that has happened since you have been an MP?

23. Do you agree with positive selection criteria?

WOMEN IN WESTMINSTER ACROSS ALL PARTIES FROM 1997 TO JUNE 2005 ELECTION

In total the 1997 Parliament had 120 women MPs including 101 Labour, 13 Conservative, 3 Liberal Democrat, 2 SNP, and the speaker Betty Boothroyd. The women are listed with the titles by which they choose to be addressed in the House.

The 101 1997-elected Labour women are:

Ms Candy Atherton	Ms Beverley Hughes
Ms Charlotte Atkins	Mrs Joan Humble
Miss Anne Begg	Miss Melanie Johnson
Mrs Liz Blackman	Mrs Fiona Jones
Ms Hazel Blears	Helen Jones
Mrs Helen Clark	Ms Jenny Jones
Ms Karen Buck	Ms Sally Keeble
Mrs Christine Butler	Ann Keen
Dr Lynda Clark, QC	Ms Ruth Kelly
Yvette Cooper	Ms Oona King
Mrs Ann Cryer	Ms Tess Kingham
Ms Claire Curtis-Thomas	Ms Jackie Lawrence
Valerie Davey	Fiona Mactaggart
Mrs Janet Dean	Judy Mallaber
Julia Drown	Ms Chris McCafferty
Maria Eagle	Ms Siobhain McDonagh
Mrs Louise Ellman	Mrs Anne McGuire
Ms Lorna Fitzsimons	Shona McIsaac
Caroline Flint	Mrs Rosemary McKenna, CBE
Ms Barbara Follett	Ms Gillian Merron
Mrs Linda Gilroy	Laura Moffatt
Eileen Gordon	Ms Margaret Moran
Jane Griffiths	Ms Julie Morgan
Mrs Sylvia Heal	Ms Kali Mountford
Rt Hon. Patricia Hewitt	Mrs Diana Organ

Ms Sandra Osborne
Ms Linda Perham
Joyce Quin
Christine Russell
Joan Ryan
Ms Debra Shipley
Angela Smith
Miss Geraldine Smith

Ms Jacqui Smith
Ms Helen Southworth
Dr Phyllis Starkey
Ms Gisela Stuart
Ms Dari Taylor
Ms Claire Ward
Mrs Betty Williams
Ms Rosie Winterton

Others (Labour) from previous elections:

Miss Diane Abbott – 1987
Irene Adams – 1990
Janet Anderson – 1992
Rt Hon. Hilary Armstrong – 1987
Rt Hon. Margaret Beckett – 1983
Rt Hon. Betty Boothroyd – 1973
(Speaker)
Mrs Anne Campbell – 1992
MsJudith Church – 1994
Ann Clwyd – 1984
Ms Ann Coffey – 1992
Rt Hon. Jean Corston – 1992
Rt Hon. Gwyneth Dunwoody –
1983
Angela Eagle – 1992
Mrs Maria Fyfe – 1987
Mrs Llin Golding – 1986
Rt Hon. Harriet Harman – 1982
Rt Hon. Margaret Hodge – 1994

Miss Kate Hoey – 1989
Ms Glenda Jackson – 1992
Helen Jackson – 1992
Dr Lynne Jones – 1992
Rt Hon. Tessa Jowell – 1992
Jane Kennedy – 1992
Mrs Helen Liddell – 1994
Mrs Alice Mahon – 1987
Rt Hon. Estelle Morris – 1992
Rt Hon. Majorie Mowlam – 1987
Ms Bridget Prentice – 1992
Ms Dawn Primarolo – 1987
Mrs Barbara Roche – 1992
Joan Ruddock – 1987
Rt Hon. Clare Short – 1983
Ms Rachel Squire – 1992
Rt Hon. Ann Taylor – 1974
Audrey Wise – 1974
Ms Joan Walley – 1987

The 13 Conservative MPs after the 1997 election were:

Rt Hon. Virginia Bottomley – 1984   Anne McIntosh – 1997
Mrs Angela Browning – 1992   Mrs Marion Roe – 1983
Mrs Cheryl Gillan – 1992   Rt Hon. Gillian Shephard – 1987
Mrs Teresa Gorman – 1987   Mrs Caroline Spelman – 1997
Miss Julie Kirkbride – 1997   Rt Hon. Ann Widdecombe – 1987
Mrs Eleanor Laing – 1997   Mrs Ann Winterton – 1983
Mrs Theresa May – 1997

The three Liberal Democrat MPs after the 1997 election were:
Mrs Jackie Ballard – 1997
Dr Jenny Tonge – 1997
Mrs Ray Michie – 1987

The two others were:
Mrs Margaret Ewing – SNP – 1974
Ms Roseanna Cunningham, SNP – 1995

The Speaker was:
Rt Hon. Betty Boothroyd, 1974

At two by-elections Mrs Jacqui Lait (1997 Cons) and Sandra Gidley (2000 LD) were elected as MPs. Audrey Wise died and Betty Boothroyd retired bringing the total back down to 120 women MPs.

In 2001 twelve new women were elected, and fourteen lost their seat or did not stand, bringing the total number of women in the House to 118.

Vera Baird – Lab   Lady Hermon – UU
Annette Brooke – LD   Ann Mckechin – Lab
Patsy Calton – LD   Meg Munn – Lab
Sue Doughty – LD   Anne Picking – Lab
Annabelle Ewing – SNP   Iris Robinson – DU
Michelle Gildernew – SF   Angela Watkinson – Con

That total rose to 119 when the LD Sarah Teather won a by-election in 2002.

In May 2005, 38 new women were elected, and 29 women MPs either stood down or lost their seat, bringing the total of women in the House to a record 128 across six parties: Labour, Conservatives, Liberal Democrats, Ulster Unionists, Democratic Unionists and Sinn Fein.

There were 26 new Labour women (although Labour lost seats overall, it was able to still increase its numbers of women MPs by using all-women shortlists to select candidates for most of its retirement seats), six new Conservatives and six new Liberal Democrats.

The 26 new Labour MPs are:

Celia Barlow
Roberta Blackman-Woods
Lyn Brown
Dawn Butler
Katy Clark
Rosie Cooper
Mary Creagh
Natascha Engel
Helen Goodman
Nia Griffith
Sharon Hodgson
Meg Hillier
Sian James
Diana Johnson
Barbara Keeley
Madeleine Moon
Jessica Morden
Kerry McCarthy
Sarah McCarthy-Fry
Linda Riordan
Alison Seabeck
Angela Smith

Anne Snelgrove
Emily Thornberry
Kitty Ussher
Lynda Waltho

The new Conservative MPs are:

Nadine Dorries
Justine Greening
Anne Main
Maria Miller
Anne Milton
Theresa Villiers

The new LD MPs are:

Lorely Burt –
Lynne Featherstone
Julia Goldsworthy
Susan Kramer
Jo Swinson
Jennifer Willott

WOMEN MPS WHO HAVE BEEN INTERVIEWED FOR THIS BOOK:

(* indicates stood down at 2005 general election. ** indicates lost seat in 2005 general election.)

Labour MPs:
From 97 election:

Ms Candy Atherton**	May 1997 – Falmouth and Camborne (21.9.55)
Ms Charlotte Atkins	May 1997 – Staffordshire Moorlands (24.9.50)
Miss Anne Begg	May 1997 – Aberdeen South (6.12.55)
Ms Hazel Blears	May 1997 – Salford (14.5.56)
Ms Karen Buck	May 1997 – Regent's Park and Kensington North (30.8.58)
Mrs Helen Clark **	May 1997 – Peterborough (23.9.54)
Yvette Cooper	May 1997 – Pontefract and Castleford (20.3.69)
Mrs Ann Cryer	May 1997 – Keighley (14.12.39)
Ms Claire Curtis-Thomas	May 1997 – Crosby (30.4.55)
Valerie Davey **	May 1997 – Bristol West (16.4.40)
Julia Drown *	May 1997 – South Swindon (23.8.62)
Maria Eagle (September)	May 1997 – Liverpool Garston (17.2.61)
Mrs Louise Ellman	May 1997 – Liverpool Riverside (14.11.45)
Ms Lorna Fitzsimons **	May 1997 – Rochdale (6.8.67)
Ms Barbara Follett	May 1997 – Stevenage (25.12.42)
Ms Linda Gilroy	May 1997 – Plymouth Sutton (19.7.49)
Jane Griffiths	May 1997 – Reading East (17.4.54)
Rt Hon. Patricia Hewitt	May 1997 – Leicester West (2. 12.48)
Ms Beverley Hughes	May 1997 – Stretford and Urmston (30.3.50)
Miss Melanie Johnson**	May 1997 – Welwyn Hatfield (5.2.55)
Ms Sally Keeble	May 1997 – Northampton North (13.10.51)
Ms Ruth Kelly	May 1997 – Bolton West (9.5.68)
Ms Oona King**	May 1997 – Bethnal Green and Bow (22.10.67)
Ms Jackie Lawrence*	May 1997 – Preseli Pembrokeshire (9.8.48)
Mrs Anne McGuire	May 1997 – Stirling (26.5.49)
Mrs Rosemary Mckenna	May 1997 – Cumbernauld and Kilsyth (8.5.41)
Fiona Mactaggart	May 1997 – Slough (12.9.51)

Judy Mallaber	May 1997 – Amber Valley (10.7.51)
Ms Margaret Moran	May 1997 – Luton South (24.4.55)
Ms Julie Morgan	May 1997 – Cardiff North (2.11.44)
Mrs Diana Organ*	May 1997 – Forest of Dean (21.2.52)
Mrs Sandra Osborne	May 1997 – Ayr (23.2.56)
Ms Linda Perham**	May 1997 – Ilford North (29.6.47)
Christine Russell	May 1997 – City of Chester (25.3.45)
Dr Phyllis Starkey	May 1997 – Milton Keynes South West (4.1.47)
Ms Gisela Stuart	May 1997 – Birmingham Edgbaston (26.11.53)
Ms Dari Taylor	May 1997 – Stockton South (13.12.44)
Mrs Betty Williams	May 1997 – Conwy (31.7.44)
Ms Rosie Winterton	May 1997 – Doncaster Central (6.3.41)

From previous elections:

Rt Hon. Hilary Armstrong	June 1987 – North West Durham (30.11.45)
Rt Hon. Margaret Beckett	June 1983– Derby South (15.1.43)
Mrs Anne Campbell**	Apr 1992 – Cambridge (6.4.40)
Ann Clwyd	May 1984 – Cynon Valley (21.3.37)
Rt Hon. Jean Corston *	Apr 1992 – Bristol East (5.5.42)
Mrs Gwyneth Dunwoody	1974 – Crewe and Nantwich (12.12.30)
Angela Eagle	Apr 1992 – Wallasey (17.2.61)
Rt Hon. Harriet Harman, QC	1982 – Camberwell and Peckham (30.7.50)
Rt Hon. Margaret Hodge, MBE	June 1994 (by-election) – Barking (8.9.44)
Glenda Jackson	Apr 1992 – Hampstead and Highgate (9.5.36)
Helen Jackson*	Apr 1992 – Sheffield Hillsborough (19.5.39)
Rt Hon. Tessa Jowell	1992 – Dulwich and West Norwood (17.9.47)
Mrs Helen Liddell*	June 1994 (by-election) – Airdrie and Shotts since May 1997 (6.12.50)
Rt Hon. Estelle Morris*	Apr 1992 – Birmingham Yardley (17.06.52)
Bridget Prentice	Apr 1992 – Lewisham East (28.12.52)
Rt Hon. Dawn Primarolo	June 1987 – Bristol South (2.5.54)
Joan Ruddock	June 1987 – Lewisham Deptford (28.12.43)
Rt Hon. Ann Taylor*	June 1987 – Dewsbury (2.7.47)
Joan Walley	June 1987 – Stoke-on-Trent North (23.1.49)

From 2001 election:

Vera Baird	June 2001 – Redcar (13.2.51)
Meg Munn	June 2001 – Sheffield Heeley (24.8.59)

Conservatives:

Rt Hon. Virginia Bottomley,*	May 1984 (by-election) – South West Surrey (12.3.48)
Mrs Cheryl Gillan,	Apr 1992 – Chesham and Amersham (4.4.52)
Miss Julie Kirkbride	May 1997 – Bromsgrove (5.6.60)
Mrs Eleanor Laing	May 1997 – Epping Forest (1.2.58)
Mrs Jacqui Lait	Nov 1997 – Beckenham (16.12.47)
Mrs Theresa May	May 1997 – Maidenhead (1.10.56)
Dame Marion Roe, DBE*	June 1983 – Broxbourne (15.7.36)
Mrs Caroline Spelman	May 1997 – Meriden (4.5.58)
Rt Hon. Gillian Shephard*	June 1987 – South West Norfolk (22.1.40)
Rt Hon. Ann Widdecombe	1987 – Maidstone and The Weald (4.10.47)

In 2001:

Angela Watkinson	Jun 2001 – Upminster (18.11.41)

Liberal Democrat MPs:

Annette Brooke	Jun 2001 – Mid Dorset and Poole North (7.6.47)
Patsy Calton	Jun 2001 – Cheadle (19.9.48)
Sue Doughty**	Jun 2001 – Guildford (13.4.48)
Sandra Gidley	May 2000 – Romsey (26.3.57)
Sarah Teather	June 2001 – Finchley and Golders Green (1.6.74)
Dr Jenny Tonge*	May 2097 – Richmond Park (19.2.41)

Others:

Lady Hermon (Sylvia) from UU   June 2001 – North Down (11.8.55)

Of the 16 who have left:
Jackie Ballard (Lib Dem) (4.1.53)
Rt Hon. Betty Boothroyd. (Lab) (8.10.29).
Baroness Golding (Lab) (21.3.33)
Mrs Teresa Gorman (Con) (9.31)
Rt Hon. Mo Mowlam. (Lab) (18.9.49)

WOMEN MPS IN PARLIAMENT IN OR SINCE 1997 WHO HAVE NOT BEEN INTERVIEWED

Labour: Current
Miss Diane Abbott
Irene Adams
Janet Anderson
Mrs Liz Blackman
Dr Lynda Clark
Ann Coffey
Mrs Janet Dean
Caroline Flint
Mrs Sylvia Heal
Kate Hoey
Mrs Joan Humble
Helen Jones
Dr Lynne Jones
Ann Keen
Jane Kennedy
Ms Chris McCafferty
Ms Siobhain McDonagh
Shona McIssac
Ann McKechin
Mrs Alice Mahon
Ms Gillian Merron
Laura Moffatt
Ms Kali Mountford
Anne Picking
Rt Hon Joyce Quin
Mrs Barbara Roche
Joan Ryan
Ms Debra Shipley
Rt Hon Clare Short
Angela Smith
Miss Geraldine Smith

Ms Jacqui Smith
Ms Helen Southworth
Mrs Rachel Squire
Claire Ward

Previous:
Christine Butler (previous)
Judith Church (previous)
Eileen Gordon (previous)
Maria Fyfe (previous)
Mrs Fiona Jones (previous)
Jenny Jones (previous)
Ms Tess Kingham (previous)
Audrey Wise (died)

Conservative:
Anne McIntosh
Angela Browning
Ann Winterton

Liberal Democrat:
Ray Michie (previous)

Other: Current
Annabelle Ewing (SNP)
Michelle Gildernew (SF)
Iris Robinson (DUP)

Previous
Roseanna Cunningham (SNP)
Margaret Ewing (SNP)

BIBLIOGRAPHY

Aaron's, *Famous Quotes and Stories of Winston Churchill.*

Benn, T. (2002), *Free at Last! Diaries 1991–2001*, Arrow Books.

Campbell, B. (2003), 'The revolution betrayed', *Guardian*, 11 October.

Cook, R. (2004), *The Point of Departure*, Pocket Books.

Childs, S. (2004), *New Labour's Women MPs*, Routledge.

Childs, S. and Withey, J. (2003a), 'Signing for Women? Sex and Early Day Motions in the 1997 Parliament', paper presented at the PSA Annual Conference, Leicester, April.

Eagle, Mactaggart, Jayatilaks, Nirwal (2002), 'Positive Action: A Fair Deal for Women', Communication Workers Union.

Hollis, P. (1998), *Jennie Lee – a Life*, Oxford University Press.

Jones, W. (1985), *Political Issues in Britain Today*, Manchester University Press.

Kochan, Nicholas (2000), *Ann Widdecombe, Right from the Beginning*, Politicos.

Lovenduski, R. (1993), *Contemporary Feminist Politics*, Oxford University Press.

Mackay, F. (2003), 'Gender and British Politics: the state of the "discipline"', article prepared for *British Journal of Politics and International Relations.*

Mactaggart, F. MP (2000), 'Women in Parliament: Their Contribution to Labour's First 1000 Days', paper prepared for the Fabian Society.

Maddox, B. (2003), *Maggie, the First Lady*, Hodder and Stoughton.

Mowlam, M (2003), *Momentum, her autobiography*, Hodder and Stoughton.

Parris, M (2003), *Chance Witness*, Penguin.

Perkins, A (2003), *Red Queen, The Authorized Biography of Barbara Castle*, Macmillan.

Rogers, R. and Walters, R. (2004), *How Parliament Works*, Pearson.

Shepherd-Robinsion, L. and Lovenduski, J. (2002), *Women and Candidate Selection in British Political Parties*, Fawcett publication.

Short, C. (2004), *An Honourable Deception*, Free Press.

Thatcher, M. (1995), *The Path to Power*, HarperCollins.

NOTES

Chapter 1
1 'Commons Club', Michael Portillo, *Sunday Times*, 10 April 2005
2 Perkins, 2003, p. 253
3 Hollis, 1997, p. 243
4 Hollis, 1997, p. 140
5 Aaron's Famous Quotes and Stories of Winston Churchill

Chapter 2
6 Rogers & Walters, 2004, p. 69
7 Jones, 1999, p. 29
8 Perkins, 2003, p. 326
9 Thatcher, 1995, p. 284
10 'Commons Club', by Michael Portillo, *Sunday Times*, 10 April 2005

Chapter 2
11 Hollis, 1997, p. 373
12 Perkins, 2003, p. 455
13 Perkins, 2001, p. 216

Chapter 4
14 Shepherd-Robinson, Lovenduski, 2002, p. 3
15 Perkins, 2003, p. 253

Chapter 6
16 Childs, 2004, p.160
17 Kochan, 2000, p. 208
18 Maddox, 2003, p. 88
19 Perkins, 2003, p. 233
20 Perkins, 2003, p. 259
21 Mackay, 2003, p. 25
22 Mackay, 2003, p. 25
23 Tony Benn, *Diaries* 1991, p. 5

Chapter 7
24 Perkins, 2003, p. 261
25 Hollis, 1997, p. 173

26 Mowlam, 2003 p. 21
27 Kochan, 2000, p. 196
28 Maddox, 2003 p. 72
29 Maddox, 2003 p. 71

Chapter 8
30 (Sixteen as at March 29, 2005: Lab 12, Cons 3, Lib Dem 1. Lab: Dr Lynda Clark, Jean
   Corston, Julia Drown, Helen Jackson, Jackie Lawrence, Helen Liddell, Alice Mahon,
   Estelle Morris, Diana Organ, Joyce Quin, Debra Shipley, Ann Taylor. Cons: Virginia
   Bottomley, Marion Roe, Gillian Shephard. LD: Jenny Tonge)

Chapter 9
31 Flynn, 1997, *Commons Knowledge*
32 'The Modernisation of the House of Commons' – first Report published in the 1998–99
   session, paragraph 20
33 Ibid, paragraph 24
34 Parris, 2002, p. 239
35 Cook, 2003/4, pp. 234–5

Chapter 10
36 Short, 2004, p. 102
37 Childs, 2004, p. 96
38 Mactaggart, 2000
39 Mactaggart, 2000
40 Mactaggart, 2000
41 Ibid
42 Ibid

Chapter 11
43 Campbell, 2003
44 Mackay, 2003, p. 15
45 This represents 28 per cent of the party. Although Labour lost seats overall, it was able to
   still increase its numbers of women MPs by using all-women shortlists to select candidates
   for most of its retirement seats.
46 Peter Law is MP for Blaenau Gwent. He defeated Maggie Jones, the Labour candidate.
47 Shepherd-Robinson, Lovenduski, 2002, p. 3
48 Shepherd-Robinson, Lovenduski, 2002, p. 4
49 After the 2005 Election, the Fawcett Society estimated: 'At the current rate of change, it
   will take the Conservatives 400 years to achieve equal representation. While the Lib Dems
   have nearly doubled their number of women MPs, the rate of change is still well behind the
   Labour Party's, meaning it will take them more than 40 years to achieve equal
   representation. At the current rate of change it will take Labour around 20 years to achieve

equal representation.'
50 Shepherd-Robinson, Lovenduski, 2002, p. 25
51 Campbell, 2003
52 Thatcher, 1995, p. 94
53 Shepherd-Robinson, Lovenduski, 2002, pp. 38–40
54 Campbell, 2003
55 EOC press release, January 2001
56 Shepherd-Robinson, Lovenduski, Fawcett, 2002
57 Eagle, Mactaggart, Jayatilaka, Nirwal, 2002, p. 7
58 Eagle, Mactaggart, Jayatilaka, Nirwal, 2002, p. 11

INDEX